MAKING RENT IN BED-STUY

MAKING RENT IN
BED-STUY

A MEMOIR OF TRYING TO MAKE IT
IN NEW YORK CITY

BRANDON HARRIS

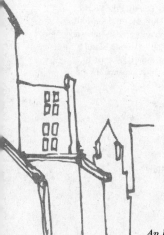

Amistad

An Imprint of HarperCollins*Publishers*

This is a work of nonfiction. The events, experiences, and perspectives I have detailed herein have been faithfully rendered as I remembered them and as they have been told to me. In some places, I've changed the names, identities, and other specifics of individuals who have played a role in my life in order to protect their privacy.

HarperCollins books may be purchased for educational, business, or sales promotional use. For information, please email the Special Markets Department at SPsales@harpercollins.com.

Acknowledgment is made to the following publications in whose pages, both paper and electronic, these essays first appeared: *n+1* for "2500 Rhode Island Avenue," "227–241 Taaffe Place," "551 Kosciuszko Street," parts of each appeared in the essay "On Bed-Stuy" (*n+1* #18, Winter 2014); *newyorker.com* for "158 Buffalo Avenue," expanded from "Recovering Weeksville" (November 7, 2014); *The Brooklyn Rail* for "730 DeKalb Avenue," parts of which appeared in the essay "Change You Can Believe In" (October 3, 2013); *n+1* for "75 South Elliott Place," parts of which appeared in the essay "Blood Couple" (*n+1* #22, Spring 2015); *The Brooklyn Rail* for "75 South Elliott Place," parts of which appeared in the essay "The Black Liberation Kool-Aid Acid Test" (March 4, 2016); *n+1* for "200 Gholson Avenue," parts of which appeared in the essay "Dwight and Paul Have Left the Building" (June 1, 2015); *vice.com* for "5920 Rhode Island Avenue," parts of which appeared in the essay "Ta-Nehisi Coates 'Between the World and Me' Is as Important and Necessary as Everyone Says It Is" (July 24, 2015); *Film-maker* magazine for "5920 Rhode Island Avenue," parts of which appeared in the essay "Microcinema Blues" (September 3, 2015); *newyorker.com* for "5920 Rhode Island Avenue," parts of which appeared in the essay "One Week in Cincinnati" (August 10, 2015); *The New Republic* for "485 Lexington Avenue," parts of which appeared in the essay "The Life and Loves of a Young Obama" (September 21, 2016).

FIRST EDITION

Title page illustration courtesy of Shutterstock/Marharyta Kuzminova

Designed by Renata De Oliveira

Library of Congress Cataloging-in-Publication Data has been applied for.

ISBN 978-0-06-241564-6

17 18 19 20 21 LSC 10 9 8 7 6 5 4 3 2 1

For CUK

" *There are more and more things black people thought they had a handle on that they have seen slowly slip away from them, and they be saying, 'Damn, what happened to that? Dot dot dit dit dot dot dash, son, I'm damned if I know.'*

—GIL SCOTT-HERON "

CONTENTS

MAKING RENT IN BED-STUY

2500 RED BANK ROAD

Early on the morning of July 4, 2006, I was walking south on Taaffe Place, in Brooklyn. It was just after midnight and I was wearing camp-counselor clothes—a blue polo, cheap white sneakers, and tight green shorts—on a nearly deserted block leading to my building's front door. A phone conversation with a friend in California was ongoing, radiation-spewing Motorola Razr glued to my left ear, tucked right next to my brain.

Half a block from home, a man in a white T-shirt offered me a cigarette, his voice escaping his mouth in a low, dreadful mumble. I didn't notice it at first, but as I passed him, shaking off the invitation to smoke, I glimpsed what appeared to be a sawed-off bike handle in his right hand. As I continued walking up the block, I gleaned that he was following me from the play of his shadow on a brick wall to my right.

I'm a high yellow Negro who weighs over two hundred pounds. I used to play offensive guard on a half-decent high school football team. But I was dressed like a buffoon, almost never got in fights, and had a man-purse with a brand-new black MacBook in it. Mark. When I realized the man was following me, I was saddened by the prospect of having to smack a motherfucker in the face with my new laptop. So I ran.

Across the street, up the block. The man pursued me to my building's front door, but I was able to open it quickly and pivot into the building before he could strike me with his peculiar improvised weapon. He lashed the sawed-off end of the bike handle at me, but I ducked out of the way and proceeded to smash his arm, several times, as hard as I could, with the very heavy glass-and-metal door that led to 227–241 Taaffe Place.

Another man, pale and older, stood aghast near the elevator, looking on in horror as my attacker removed his now surely injured limb from the door. I slammed it shut, my assailant cursing loudly from the other side of the glass, his slender body shuddering. He was in great pain. I hadn't hung up the phone, so my friend in California, hearing the commotion, was loudly asking me if I was "all right" as I held the phone near my chest, breathing hard, staring at this man who had meant me harm.

He was clearly much worse off than I was, for reasons no doubt of his (and our) own making, long before the possibility of stealing from me was something he had conjured in his spiteful mind. "Fuck you, fuck you, yella-ass nigga, I gonna get y'all mothafuckin shit, this is Bed-Stuy, bitch," he said from the

2

other side of the glass door, tears in his eyes. Then he sauntered off. I went upstairs, to the seventh-story loft I lived in, smoked a spliff, and got ready to face the phony celebration of national independence that the day to come promised to offer.

"THIS IS BED-STUY, BITCH." THAT'S NOT WHAT EVERY-one else was saying.

In the summer of 2006 I thought, and Tony, my childhood friend, thought that we were moving to Clinton Hill, in Brooklyn. Early in our apartment search, Tony rebuffed the idea of living in Bed-Stuy. He didn't want to do it. I blinked twice as he said this, unsure how to respond as he spun out his logic. Without saying so, it became clear that he preferred somewhere already gentrified, and if not in the ragingly hip precincts to our north (Williamsburg!) or the increasingly refined enclave to our west (Fort Greene!), then at least somewhere that wasn't Bedford-Stuyvesant. He grimaced and shook his head when I mentioned Bed-Stuy again, further into our search. It wasn't for him. I neglected to ask why.

We were soon to exit college, Tony and I, and as April became May and May became June, options that would suit him seemed plentiful, but options that I would find affordable, whatever my post-film-school job prospects, did not. Eventually, he suggested his parents would foot the bill for a nicer place than we would reasonably be able to afford on our own. "It's not my money, it's theirs," he would say, absolving himself of the privilege he would temporarily and conditionally share with me. I'm an agreeable person, perhaps to a fault, so after some time, as it began to look like we might end up staying at our parents' Ohio homes if we didn't say yes to an apartment, I relented and agreed to live above my means on the seventh floor of 227–241 Taaffe Place.

It was a huge and impressively airy space, all high ceilings, and polished wood floors—four tall windows lined the western side of the building, which faced onto Taaffe Place, the elevation providing us with a panoramic view of Fort Greene and a portion of downtown Brooklyn to the west. The bedrooms were located behind the first two doors on the left side as you entered. They were too close together, the flimsy walls and strange window between the rooms providing neither of us with much in the way of privacy. When walking into the office to sign the lease agreement, which required us to pay $2,400 a month in rent collectively, neither of us could have anticipated how much of a problem our choice of dwelling would become.

It was far nicer than my first Brooklyn apartment, a two-bedroom affair that had gone for $1,200 two summers before. The Craigslist ad said that apartment was in East Williamsburg. I rode the elevated train there, miles of lonely track, through neighborhoods I didn't know, to see it one early summer afternoon. I had been squatting at the Harlem apartment of Ray, Tony's and my friend from Ohio, a recent transplant like us, and was halfway through the State University of New York at Purchase's undergraduate film school. I had only recently left my dorm and had never found my own apartment before. There are better phrases than "ripe for exploitation," but none come to mind right now.

It was the summer of 2004 and I was going to live with a club-promoting, tech-utopianist hacker from Serbia and a hard-drinking, backwoods New Hampshire rube—M&M—I knew from film school, during what we hoped in futility would be the final summer of George W. Bush's presidential term. A Hasid, tall and skinny, stoic and prematurely aged—a Jewish Abraham Lincoln of sorts—awaited me at the door of 166 Throop Avenue, the best lead we had acquired so far. I climbed up a recently renovated wooden staircase with this strange man and came to a maroon door, also recently painted. Once we reached the flat, the air smelled of wood chips and the recent use of electric saws. Unassuming light fixtures and dull white walls in the main room, a tight bathroom down a short hallway. When one turned around, there was a kitchenette, just off the "living room," that could hardly fit two people. A fire escape, accessible from one of the two bedrooms, allowed for rooftop access; a Catholic church that no one went to anymore stood just a few blocks away, the elevated train that had brought me to this foreign land, this "East Williamsburg," a bit beyond it.

My mother, a cashew-colored lower midwestern Negro who owns guns, drives trucks, and used to destroy buildings for a living, agreed to be the guarantor; nearing the end of her fourth marriage but at the peak of her career as a home construction executive, she had the means and willingness my friends' parents seemingly did not. I, nor my roommates-to-be, had no credit history to speak of. The apartment was a three-block walk to the J, M, and Z trains, the line from which the famous rapper fetched his name, and across the street from Woodhull Medical Center, a hulking modernist hospital that wouldn't be out of place in the city skyline from *Blade Runner*.

The circumstances in which I lived with Tony couldn't be more different. Whereas my mother was the most well-to-do parent in the previous housing situation, it was assumed from the jump that Tony's family would foot the bill for our housing deposit, for the most expensive pieces of furniture; my mother provided us with a truck, and a driver named Gus, an ignorant, good-humored, diabetes-riddled cat who kept catcalling girls once we reached Brooklyn. He was a great help and a mild embarrassment. But these sorts of things were where the buck stopped.

I remember saying to my old friend, "I'm going to really have to hustle to make this rent." My mother had made it very clear that, beyond my share of the deposit, moving expenses, and the first month of rent, she would not subsidize me. I had hardly ever made $800 a month at my various jobs—bookstore clerk, art-house movie theater popcorn sweeper, work-study equipment-room flack—let alone paid that much to live anywhere. He nodded past me, as if a passerby had said something vaguely interesting that he hadn't quite heard.

I HAD MET TONY AT THE SEVEN HILLS SCHOOL, A PRI-
vate K–12 at 2500 Red Bank Road that educated the children
of the city's wealthiest families, just a five-minute drive from my
mother's Kennedy Heights home, a two-story, three-bedroom
brick house on a hilly street in a mostly integrated part of our
segregated hometown, Cincinnati. My mother, a demolition
executive trying her hand at construction in the mid-'90s for
the first time, had carved a street out of a thick, undeveloped
tract of forest and named it after me: Brandonburg Lane. Ours
was the first of nine houses on the row, a tangible departure
from the low-slung bungalows and four-family apartments
that line the working-class Cincinnati suburbs of Kennedy
Heights and Silverton, which surround Brandonburg. I had
grown up on those streets, in a house my grandfather had built
as his demolition firm began to grow in the 1960s.

The spring before sixth grade, tired of the unruliness and
intellectual stultification of the elementary school I went to
in Silverton, I asked my mother to send me to the Seven Hills
School, which I would pass as we rode along Red Bank Road
toward I-71. The gray wood buildings of 2500 Red Bank would
float past as I sat shotgun in her gas-guzzling GMC Suburban,
gazing at the well-manicured baseball fields, connected by
walkways and ringed with neat, inviting landscaping, and the
Olympic-sized track and field of rubber and grass. The one I ran
and leaped on at the Silverton elementary was made of black-
top, the baseball fields pockmarked with weeds.

As you entered the I-71 on-ramp near the school, you had

a dynamic view of the shrubbery lining the hillside, cut in such a way that "SEVEN HILLS SCHOOL" was spelled out in green foliage to those descending from the freeway. I recall my mother being somewhat astonished by the request. The $9,000 per year tuition was the largest educational investment our family had ever made in one of its children at that time—my mother and her sisters went to college in an era, the 1970s, when schooling cost considerably less, even if, like my mother, you began your college career in the Ivy League.

Class was a slippery thing in our family; my mother's mother had come from a distinctly middle-class household that had sent their entire prewar brood to historically black colleges; my grandfather, a tall and charming light-skinned Negro from the hills of northern Kentucky, never finished high school. It's a pairing that seems more imaginable then than it would be now, in our time of alleged social mobility; black women with college degrees, even amid the complaints of "not enough available black men," no longer marry Negroes from the Bluegrass State who have only passed through elementary school.

Eventually he made enough money in the demolition business to purchase, through his white lawyer, a plot of land in Walnut Hills, an exclusive east side community that was normally protected from Negroes by restrictive covenants. With his second wife, whom I've always known as my grandmother, he built a handsome house, one he designed himself. By 2002 they were respected enough in society to be the subjects of a glowing *Cincinnati Enquirer* profile that referred to them as "generous philanthropists, willing to write a check when needed, willing to chair a gala, willing to roll up their sleeves when necessary to make something happen."

Yet behind closed doors, they complained of the same corruption and racial graft that common Negroes did. Even in the loom of success, discontent among "our class" of Negroes seemed high. The white folks with whom my grandparents share their social calendar, be it at their country club or a benefit to induct them into the Ohio Civil Rights Hall of Fame, see them as pillars of the community and probably wouldn't recognize the deeply distrustful version of their neighbors that springs forth in the privacy of black company. Their dissatisfaction, through which I first learned that America allegedly had a race problem, was not restricted to the behavior of whites.

Skepticism about our ability to forge a commonwealth within our ranks became a form of received wisdom in this period of my life. The complaints my family members launched at the ineffectiveness of black collective action made me so. "If only we were like the Jews" was a common refrain. Jews reminded one another of their history, their oppression, while collectivizing in ways that provided their ranks protection and wealth, so went the legend. You would hear it at kitchen tables littered with Little Caesars pizza or at a barbershop in Evanston while awaiting a fade, but not out in public, among whites. These conversations were kept at bay there.

In these days, I watched elderly black fingers wag at the sagging pants and billowing white T-shirts and fat girls with expensive weaves and too many kids. To replenish the spring of self-loathing from which so many well-to-do blacks draw was to lack a vision of transcendence and, like so much of America, to remain deaf to the sounds of justice. My grandfather is a man who, like so many of his generation, did his best to assimilate and segregate at once, to upend and uphold an old order. He grew up in a Kentucky where you didn't look at white women for fear of your Negro life.

So perhaps ours is an uneasy truce with the future; I've never taken my white girlfriends home to meet him and I know he prefers it that way.

AT MY NEW SCHOOL, TONY AND I BECAME FRIENDLY AL-most immediately—we sat next to each other in sixth-grade science class—but we didn't become very close until high school. Tony was, in his early youth, gangly and awkward, bookish and intense, a child of silver spoons that he kept mostly private. His parents had done well in the world of plasma centers and lived in an elegant three-story white frame house on the top of a hill that lined one of Cincinnati's most exclusive east side neighborhoods, but he carried himself with an unassuming air in his flannel shirts and Chuck Taylors. Like many a young rich person I've known, he liked to brag about how his father was a self-made man; it's often an easy way to signal that they haven't been terminally spoiled, that the successful people who've spawned them imparted a knowledge of struggle and belief in a work ethic. Still, in the middle '90s, it was somewhat iconoclastic of him to befriend the nerdy, overweight, *Star Trek*–obsessed child of black Cincinnati strivers whom he sat next to in sixth-grade science.

He had a reserve, an aloofness, that I envied and had tried, mostly with little success, to cultivate in myself. I thought the dispassionate way his class of whites went about their business was what you had to emulate to get ahead. There were two other black boys along with me in our sixth-grade class that first fall, but I was the only new one; they were already acclimated to our surroundings, where we were given "fruit breaks" and the assumption of our innocence and burgeoning intellect was never in question, so I thought. But when, in that same science class in which we sat together every day, I was accused, the only black child in the section, of stealing a hissing Madagascar cockroach, I recall no one coming to my aid. No one leaped forward to speak for my character. I was the new kid, and black. Suspicion naturally gravitated toward me.

Our teacher, Mr. Barker, had prized his cockroach, which he dubbed Seymour, ordering it all the way from the island off the southeast African coast for which this particularly rare species of cockroach is named. It mysteriously ended up in my bag, likely as a prank by a classmate who didn't approve of my presence or what I wore. After arriving home that afternoon, I placed my bag down near the doorway and retreated to the living room so my father, who had picked me up from school, could make me a sandwich.

When I returned to the office to start my homework, my right hand instinctively went for the light switch. When I brought it back toward my body, a hissing Madagascar cockroach was staring at me from just below my knuckles. They really do hiss. I screamed and threw it across the room. My father and I trapped it and, a few days later, I took pleasure in gassing it to death in a mason jar.

Via Encarta for Windows 95 I discovered that the bug I had found was quite a rare coup, and I included it with pride in my insect classification assignment for Mr. Barker's class. He recognized Seymour immediately and hauled my mother in for a meeting. Suspicion remained, but no proof emerged, so no punishment was meted out, just a lurking sense that the standard upon which I would be judged was always to be different than my peers. The look on my mother's face as we left our meeting with Mr. Barker let me know she had been putting up with bullshit like this her whole life.

Although one of the other black students became a lifelong friend, I gravitated, in my three years there, first toward a cadre of short, swarthy nerds, people who would take an interest in *Star Trek* cards and nascent attempts at fantasy baseball, before turning to the jocks, among whom I was a natural leader and far from the only black, and then steadily toward the kids that experimented with drugs and liked edgy movies, almost all of whom were white.

Cincinnati was the eighth most segregated city in America as Tony and I grew up. My mother managed to persevere in the midwestern demolition industry, an almost exclusively white domain, but nonetheless as an adult never acquired close friends who were white. She surely knew my path would be different, acquiescing to my conscious request to go to an almost uniformly Caucasian school full of entitled rich kids while fretting, to her friends over cocktails, about making sure I had enough exposure to "my own" culture. I saw less and less of my friends from my elementary school days and spent more time, slowly but steadily, in the parlor rooms and upstairs attics of those same east side families my mother had no real interest in getting to know. She was trying to build her own slice of modern middle-class housing for black families in generally black neighborhoods, residential projects that would increase property values for everyone in the surrounding community, she posited. This was in stark contrast to forging alliances with those who had the real money and heading for the hills, as the black professionals she would meet up with for top-of-the-weekend Happy Hour at T.G.I. Friday's had done.

This kind of spirit informed the frustrated, defiant tone in my mother's voice when driving through nearby Madisonville, a mostly depressed black enclave with pockets of both black and white prosperity tucked away from its fast-food-joint, hair-product-and-discount-sneaker-outlet-dominated main drag of Madison Road. "Our community doesn't have to look like this," she would intone, but then, even as a child, I would ask, "Well then, if that's the case, *why does it?*"

They never covered this in American History at the Seven

Hills School. Why are so many Negroes so broke? Why can't they have nice things too? Of course, many of those I knew did—in Silverton, we were thought of as rich Negroes. While my grandfather and his wife fully entered a strata of east side, Hyde Park society, hosting parties where many of the city's power brokers hunkered down for bourbon, my mother generally shunned such social climbing. But in the prosperous '90s even she, who drives a pickup truck and is in perfect harmony with the world when she encounters a sack of chicken wings and an episode of *Martin*, indulged in the clubs of the city's black elite *and* played bid whist with hairdressers and McDonald's staffers.

I went to daytime house parties and Kings Island Amusement Park field trips with a chapter of the black children's club Jack and Jill as a preteen. We didn't seem quite as well off as most of the black professional families that made up this awkward, self-selected assortment of the talented tenth and their offspring, those who had fled to the white suburbs or the old, moneyed east side neighborhoods, but that's not why I never completely fit in—I just liked hanging out with the working-class black kids from my extended family and the rich white kids from my school more. I was especially alienated from the girls—I was fat and didn't take on a particularly hard, ghetto mode of speech or demeanor, something those rich black girls loved at the time, reminding them as it did of the macho cousin or uncle they knew who hadn't made it to the other side of Clinton-era prosperity, the risk-taking hothead kids who went to Withrow or Hughes High School, the hip-hop stars they could watch every afternoon on MTV's *Total Request Live with Carson Daly*. While consorting with the children of other classy Negroes was something I was never much good at doing back then, my growing intimacy with Cincinnati's diverse and self-enclosed tribes, its posturing ascendant Negroes and its relatively poor blacks, its working-class Catholics and its wealthy east side WASPs and Jews, left me with an ability to code-switch, to find ways to speak a common language, grasp a set of common values, among people in almost every part of the city's class hierarchy. Yet it also left me with a cognitive dissonance about the value of modern black American symbols.

Despite the kente cloth I wore to eighth-grade graduation and my penchant for accosting white girls over their inability to "confront their guilt" following my first reading of *The Autobiography of Malcolm X*, I too had been conditioned by an America where black institutions and neighborhoods and vernacular were things the culture told you were inferior, regardless of the two-bit nationalism a young Negro child like myself encountered when seeing the Nation of Islam guys on the corner near Swifton Commons Mall or outside the diner they ran on the strip of Reading Road, near where my mother lives now, that has given way to open-air drug markets. Was hardly a bulwark against these sentiments.

Our collectivism manifested itself in ways I found strange sometimes. Watching the O. J. Simpson verdict with my classmates at Seven Hills, I was the only black student in the room as "Not Guilty" passed through the speakers of the TV in the central atrium. I couldn't help but feel alienated as pale faces reddened and tears, along the edges of the room among the adults, were shed. You could sense the righteous indignation spread among some of the teachers, most of whom quickly stifled it. Not in front of the children; American innocence had to be protected for them, for now. I thought O. J. was guilty, and so did my mother, but in our home I had heard the voices of black people who would be happy to see him walk anyway, if just to get back at the white man. "What did we win?" Chris Rock joked a year later in *Bring the Pain*, the HBO comedy special that truly made him a star. Not a damn thing, but schadenfreude is a powerful animating force in many black minds toward many a white person for reasons that are older than all of us.

Tony didn't know the first thing about those anxieties then, and not what they actually meant to me, but for some reason, like so many white people I've befriended in my life, I sort of assumed he did. He certainly seemed to have insight into blacks that extended beyond stereotype; he was immersed in black forms. As the years went by, I admired not just his thinly concealed melancholy (I had my own), but his knowledge of black literature and boxing and soul music. These cultural signals kept me thinking he probably empathized more than he did. I was still too young, too gullible myself to have gleaned that whites who loved black culture didn't necessarily understand black people.

Eventually, toward the end of middle school and beginning

of high school, Tony and I ran in a coherent circle of friends. Even though I no longer went to Seven Hills, having gone to a less expensive, less diverse, more conservative Catholic high school that had attracted me with dreams of football glory, most of my closest friends remained at the prep school for the city's elite. Seven Hills was barely a mile down a steep hill along Daniel Drake Park from Brandonburg, where we lived both before and during my mother's fourth marriage, this time to an arrogant and foolish preacher whom she had known most of her life.

In my early high school years, the second floor of our handsome home played host to the rampant misbehavior of our posse; dropping mushrooms and ecstasy after seeing *Magnolia* in the cinema or during a long night of *The Late Late Show with Craig Kilborn* followed by a VHS of Aronofsky's *Pi*, I became someone my mother wouldn't have recognized had she the guile to climb the stairs and discover what we were up to. She caught my friends and me stealing her booze after one raid had proven too brazen for her not to notice; ever the entrepreneur, she extorted money out of each of my friends in order to replenish her stock, threatening to expose them to their parents if they didn't come through. We stopped partying at my house.

My friends and I prided ourselves on being edgy intellectuals, dabbling in drinking and drugs, punk shows and Ralph Nader, García Márquez novels and David Fincher movies. Long evenings on the Ludlow strip, a series of hip businesses near the University of Cincinnati in the city's Clifton district, we would drift from coffee and chess at the old underground location of Sitwell's Café to an inevitable house party or a night logging around, smoking weed, and watching specialty movies that weren't quite art, like, say, Guy Ritchie's *Snatch*, over and over and over. Eventually, as seniors, we rounded up enough people to invest in our own apartment, which we dubbed Party House. Despite earning the highest grade point average I ever did in high school, I spent most of my senior year in front of a television at Party House, playing Grand Theft Auto and watching Tom Tykwer movies. We grew weed in the closet of the sole bedroom, often smoking it out of a six-foot bong to better take years off our lives, and hung an American flag upside down with an anarchy sign written on it. It was a slice of gutter paradise.

Across many years class meant little to us—we were just boys having an adolescence together—even as its portent grew more obvious. Tony attended private and pricey Sarah Lawrence for his Westchester County college education, while I opted for the nearby film conservatory at SUNY Purchase, to which I still tithe my wages while teaching a new generation of future Purchase debtors how to dream in cinematic terms. Tony grew into the type of rich midwestern white man on the coast who, despite his station in life, would vote for liberals with some ounce of self-pride, "loyalties to his class," as he would have it, be damned; he lionized his father—a ranching and hunting enthusiast from the South—for bucking the trend of the wealthy and southern to support Democrats as well.

This difference in relative economic and social advantage

didn't weigh on us sitting through Hype Williams's *Belly* and Keenen Ivory Wayans's *Don't Be a Menace to South Central While Drinking Your Juice in the Hood* three times each, listening to John Coltrane or Motown albums all day while mutually slacking. These were activities Tony would participate in happily, without irony, by himself. Beneath his cool patrician vibe was a genuinely searching and tortured and open person with whom I shared a lot of laughs and from whom I learned multitudes. I miss him.

But the gaps between us, cracks of misunderstanding in which the entire relationship would become mired, began to overwhelm the thing before I ever had the life experience or self-awareness to bring language to how unnerved I was often made to feel. His parents, generous and hospitable upon every visit I've ever made to their home, were the type of white liberals who might bemoan the presence of young, unrefined-looking black boys walking through their tony part of Cincinnati's east side. Tony's brother, who took to dealing dope in high school and college like the rap stars he idolized, lived largely without fear of life-altering repercussions while doing so, despite several run-ins with the law. Tony confided his parents' behavior to me with a look that asked, "Can you really blame them?" That these same people could visit me, a Negro child, while I was sick and potentially dying with liver illness, never failing to drive me home or feed me or make me welcome in their home as a high schooler, speaks to just how deep is this mess that we're all in together.

I spent the better part of my time in high school perfecting how to use drugs on the third floor of their hilltop white frame house, taking shelter from the state-sponsored danger that awaits the black drug user in the streets of the city's west and central districts. I felt perfectly at home with privilege. I realized mine was more precarious than most, but not here. There was safety in those walls, on that champagne-colored carpet of the study and game room where I watched so many championship fights over the years, blunt smoke wafting in the air.

In college, Tony and I grew closer still, seeing each other as somehow more reliable than the other people in our circle from back home, many of whom were fleeing Cincinnati for the coasts, but with what we saw as less aplomb. Our Westchester County campuses were only twenty minutes from each other by car or forty-five by public transport, so early in our sophomore year we began to hang out on weekends, swapping party invites and shoot-the-shit sessions. He was not a prankster and neither was I, but a good laugh was our backbone and we shared them frequently, while he crashed on my dorm room couch during Purchase's music festival, Culture Shock, or during a sojourn to Madison Square Garden to watch our first title fight together. Planning trips to see a film in the city or mutually crash at Ray's Lower Manhattan New School dorm was easy, but talking about sex, as opposed to mere attraction and desire, was not; I was far too inexperienced, having just lost my virginity the year before, not to feel threatened by him.

During Christmas break that year, he slept with a girl I

had a crush on. Although the feelings of betrayal that I had toward him persisted for years, by the time we moved in together I thought I was past it. I had met Rolanda, a guest in those tony environs who would become my first serious girlfriend, during one of those Sarah Lawrence visits, and the summer before Tony and I began living together, I had a monthlong fling with his most serious ex-girlfriend, a working-class Irish girl from Cincinnati's west side who was the child of Jehovah's Witnesses and whom Tony's parents had briefly considered putting through Sarah Lawrence so they could remain together. It was a comeuppance that he accepted with what I took for maturity when I told him, later that year, what had happened. We were even.

Yet for all his wonderful qualities, ones that made me love him, such as his modesty—he liked to remark how he hadn't bought a new shirt in years—this was a person for whom entitlement was the air he breathed so naturally that he seemed to hardly notice it. He proceeded through life with the awareness that no financial calamity was likely to threaten his ability to eat and lie down somewhere comfortable, and seemed, because of this, in no great hurry to make his own way. He knew where entitlement ended, though. This lover of jazz and boxing and '60s soul could passively assume in conversation over dinner with a mutual friend that of course black celebrity X or Y "would squander all his money, they always do." No one seems to call this "double consciousness," but someone should.

166 THROOP AVENUE

When I discovered that 166 Throop, despite what the realtors and the Caucasian people had told us, was in *Bedford-Stuyvesant*, 2004 was long over and I didn't live there anymore. I remember thinking it could be worse for the three months that I did, grateful to have my first nonparental or university dwelling regardless of its location or condition. Two bedrooms for three of us—the Serbian and I would take the rooms while my classmate M&M would camp out on an airbed in the unventilated, windowless "living" room, drinking himself to sleep with PBRs in between best boy electric jobs, often while I watched blaxploitation movies on the TV next to his bed or fucked Rolanda, my girlfriend at the time, in the adjacent room. Our rent was $1,200 a month, and for the largest room in the joint, I paid $450 of it.

It was often an oppressive place, 166 Throop, but it proved liberating in ways I couldn't have imagined at the time; the summer I lived there was the last I ever spent without Internet service. I had resolved to pass the summer reading serious black literature, watching blaxploitation movies, and being as off the grid as possible. Despite this desire to live simply and contain myself to my thoughts, it was the first summer I had a cell phone; Don DeLillo novels and inconclusive brain cancer studies had taught me they were bad news, but my mother insisted. I split time between our crib and Rolanda's, a third-floor walk-up on South Second Street in Williamsburg. When we met the previous winter, she had been living on the waterfront in Manhattan, just off the sleepy eastern edge of the Financial District, in a gargantuan rent-controlled loft. It belonged to a university professor who was traveling on a sabbatical that, much to her chagrin, didn't last forever. Her new crib was in a somewhat dingy Williamsburg two-bedroom for which she and her gay actor roommate, pale and fresh from Interlochen, paid $1,400; at the time, I thought that was a fortune for two people.

Multiple generations of a Puerto Rican family inhabited the various floors of Rolanda's building. The woman to whom she paid her rent was always welcoming when we'd glimpse her in the stairwell, her husband the same, although I could see in the occasional sideways glance that she was unsure of our presence there. This woman and her family, remnants of Los Sures, the community that had begun moving into these brick walk-ups in the 1940s, had no reason to doubt that we came as friends. At least as long as she owned the building there was comfort in the fact that Southside wouldn't be completely ceded to hipsters, although if she rented exclusively to them, a potential windfall awaited. The solemnity on her face, how it would return after sharing a wooden smile on the landing or near the gate out front, spoke of a community that wasn't as lucky, one that would simply disperse, regardless of which home owners won and which renters were cast aside.

Rolanda was tall and pretty, blue-eyed and openfaced, her hair dyed a pale pumpkin shade that summer. We'd go see Michael Haneke movies and hold hands, and there was none of the awkwardness I had come to expect with some white girls who were always looking at me and thinking of how to couch it to their daddy. The most honest of them would foreground their ignorance and/or fear of Negroes plainly, such as a blonde coworker from my hometown who'd touched my hair during our shifts selling tickets at an art-house movie theater in the Cincinnati suburbs the summer previous, marveling at the coarse texture of my hair. She only stopped when I scolded her, angrily. In front of a child who was about to see an Eddie Murphy kids' movie with his spectacles-wearing, ruddy-faced grandmother, I asked her, "What am I, your Negro petting zoo?"

A decade later, after intermittent bad sex and a few tears, the same coworker said flatly, "My parents will never accept you," as if reading the news, a difficult truth undergirded with nonchalance.

BACK THEN I DIDN'T GIVE TWO SHITS ABOUT BED-STUY, the community where I was actually living; I did not care to know that Bed-Stuy contained one of the nation's first free Negro communities in the first half of the nineteenth century, that parts of it had been Harlem before Harlem. What I did care to know, due to concern for my physical safety heightened by exposure to a million television news segments, newspaper stories, rap songs, commonly used epithets, and, most significantly, the painful indoctrination into Negro American fear, handed down to me by my loving and forever concerned mother, was that the New York City Housing Authority (NYCHA) projects to the west and east and south of my apartment were foreboding, overwhelmingly filled with the dangerous and needy. This is what America tells you.

The place Shawn "Jay-Z" Carter speaks of when he says "Bed-Stuy was my country, Brooklyn my planet" in the second paragraph of his autobiography, *Decoded,* may well have passed into history by the time I knowingly set foot in the neighborhood, but in the early aughts its specter had not completely passed through history—Myrtle Avenue was no longer Murder Avenue in 2004, but it also wasn't a place to buy million-dollar apartments, as it has now become. The violent, crack-riddled streets and project corridors, the ones conservative journals such as *The Weekly Standard* foolishly claimed were full of "Super-Predators" during Carter's youth, had become, if not universally prosperous, much less riven by shootings and robberies as crime, all over the city and the industrialized Western world, dropped.

But at 452 Marcy, on roughly thirty acres that were once the site of an old Dutch windmill, just two blocks west of where I lived at 166 Throop that summer, the projects where Carter grew up remain. Whenever I would walk by them then, unaware of their significance in the narrative of America's most famous rapper at the time, they would serve as a reminder of the clichés that bind the national imagination when it comes to how the urban black poor get on and get over. Carter calls the twenty-seven six-story buildings that make up the majority of the property "huge islands built mostly in the middle of nowhere, designed to warehouse lives," spaces that kept the struggles of the urban poor "invisible to the larger country." So much of Carter's career, and those of other rappers who came to prominence in the era of the genre's global ascendance, has hinged upon building an audience for stories of the black urban poor in the conscience of the mainstream, which is usually another way of saying among middle-class whites.

In his own testimony, the Bed-Stuy of Carter's preteen years consisted mostly of the inner workings of the Marcy Houses and the streets surrounding the complex. Constructed in 1949, the Marcy Houses are named after former New York governor, U.S. senator, and secretary of state William Marcy. Despite presiding over the Empire State during its first full decade of abolition in the 1830s, he was a Jacksonian Democrat, one who sympathized with southern slavery, a "doughface" in the parlance of the times. The projects bearing his name are a fitting tribute to his sentiments.

The intentional, state-mandated segregation that greeted the construction of New York's public housing stock, enacted a century after Marcy's time, has borne many strange fruit. Surely no system has arisen since the end of the "peculiar institution" to ensure black bondage with more effectiveness than the low-income, exclusively black urban housing project. *Decoded* recounts the bildungsroman of the rapper-entrepreneur who escaped those streets and what they still mean to him. Carter recalls having to dodge the glass shards that lined the "grassy patches that passed for a park" while playing touch football, and tipping a benched, unresponsive heroin addict as you would a cow sleeping in a pasture. He discovered rapping as a preteen, walking those same corridors after coming upon a circle of young ashy kids spitting rhymes in a cipher. He began writing his own verses that very night.

As the '80s wore on, hip-hop, an invention of the Bronx, was transforming the youth culture of the country Carter lived in. Speakers and subwoofers eight feet in height would be set up in the courtyards of the Marcy Houses for epic MC battles that would "rattle" the windows of the families, new and old, desperately poor or solidly working class yet unable to get out, that lived in the projects above. Yet hip-hop wasn't the most profound thing altering the landscape of the Marcy Houses and the surrounding area in the 1980s. When the crack epidemic reached Bed-Stuy, or at least the clutch of buildings that dominated Carter's vision of it, "what had been was gone, and in its place was a new way of life that was suddenly everywhere and seemed like it had been there forever."

Unlike cocaine users, crackheads would use publicly, in those very Marcy corridors and playgrounds, inside apartment hallways and on the stairs leading to the Myrtle-Willoughby G train stop perched on the southeastern end of the complex. People whom Carter had known as authority figures were suddenly part of a new zombie class, "worse than prostitutes and almost as bad as snitches." Aunts and uncles, neighbors and older relatives, members of his parents' generation, many of whom had come of age during the heyday of the civil rights movement, were lost to addiction. It wasn't long until a teenage Carter began to sell crack himself.

"Fuck waiting for the city to pass out summer jobs. I wasn't even a teenager yet and suddenly everyone I knew had pocket money," he explains in the first of many rationalizations for the allure of being a drug-pushing hustler, a life he claims not to have given up until the eve of the release of his debut album, *Reasonable Doubt* (1996). "Guys my age, fed up with watching their moms struggle on a single income, were paying utility bills with money from hustling," Carter continues, before acknowledging that, as the money from the crack game exploded with the epidemic itself, the courtyards of Marcy were soon populated by kids his age who "wore automatic weapons like they were sneakers." Carter claims to have been on the streets hustling over half the time during his thirteenth year.

There is a political element to this recollection; Carter, a major Obama supporter, comes across as a reformed criminal who has grown into a doctrinaire Obama-era liberal, a thoughtful elder statesman of the genre's dangerous years who has earned the right to be the hero of his own wide-ranging tale; he can inhabit the boardroom while maintaining his street cred. He can absolve Bill Clinton—who greatly expanded the carceral state and drove hundreds of Marcy residents further into poverty due to welfare reform while Carter was still slingin' rocks—for his Sister Souljah reprimand during the '92 campaign, largely seen as a way to assure white swing voters he would put a core Democratic constituency in its place. Acknowledging that Clinton, with whom Carter now dines in West Village restaurants the rapper owns, "knew that demonizing young black people, their politics, and their art was always a winning move in American politics," Carter still shrugs it off. "Everyone needs a chance to evolve," he suggests. In a country where self-invention is supposed to be a birthright, he would know better than most of us.

Having become famous well enough into adulthood to recall a time when a lifestyle that included feeding presidents in a restaurant you owned would have seemed absurd, Carter admits to frequently not believing his own good fortune. "Inside, there's a part of me that expects to wake up tomorrow in my bedroom in apartment 5C in Marcy, slide on my gear, run down the pissy stairway, and hit the block, one eye over my shoulder." Like many kids who grow up in dense concentrations of poverty, Carter didn't know he had little. It wasn't until a sixth-grade field trip to a Caucasian teacher's Manhattan brownstone, one that provided a view of nearby Central Park, that he realized he came from humble beginnings. For this kid reared in what he describes as a modern killing field, trappings of success became doubly powerful once the realization of his own unfortunate circumstances took hold. "We talked about how rich we were going to be and made moves to get the lifestyle we aspired to by any means we could," Carter recalls of himself and his school peers. "And as soon as we had a little money, we were eager to show it."

I WOULD GO TO PARTIES ON ROOFTOPS THAT SUMMER of color-coded terror alerts, endless ones, in large expansive, forbidden places, fireworks going off on top of a gargantuan Bushwick factory at close range that sounded like the terrorist bombs I was told would cut the Manhattan Bridge in two at any minute. The men who ran the country told us this was a certainty unless we kept Dick Cheney in charge. I sensed this was as big a lie as when people would say we lived in "East" Williamsburg on those rooftops, as we looked out at "East" Williamsburg, which existed, sort of, farther west than where we were. These people on the rooftops were always Caucasians, and always new to the area. Even in this predominantly Latin and Negro part of town, I'd be the only person of color on most of these rooftops; Caucasians, who were only 1 percent of the neighborhood's population just four years previous as the new millennium dawned, were moving here in drips and drabs in those years, and I lived among them.

They were disturbing times, and it seemed as if I wouldn't have the privilege of living in any other way, that the world, in the few years during which I ascended to the personal and societal responsibilities of adulthood, was going through a great unwinding, one that left global order and the promise of American virtue in tatters. Not that I had ever really believed in that virtue anyway. Just look at the way we were indulging a color-coded class war of our own. For most of the Caucasians on its rooftops, Brooklyn was vast and new, a foreign geography easy to mythologize, to understand as a place to be changed, to be "settled" and "colonized." These terms fall uneasily on the ears of liberal progress, but out there, in high-rises and on corners, black bodies were very much available to project one's white fears and fantasies on. That wouldn't change anytime soon, but the affordability of their apartments would.

White people on rooftops that summer told me I wouldn't want to visit Woodhull Medical Center, which towers over the elevated train for four city blocks along Broadway's southern side, and in whose mammoth parking lot, across the street from our apartment at 166 Throop, one of my roommates would park production trucks overnight. Bedford-Stuyvesant's northernmost hospital had been described by *The New York Times* as "a rust-colored machine of steel and glass that rises out of the urban jumble of Flushing Avenue with immense self-assurance and power." The hulking, ten-story, four-block modernist structure opened in the fall of 1982, billed as a state-of-the-art public hospital for many of the city's poorest residents. It had been a troubled project from the start. Planned in 1968 at a cost of $85 million, when it opened fourteen years later its construction budget had ballooned to $308 million. Despite its ambitions to quickly service the needy, the space wasn't really designed to be a community hospital. Less than a year and a half after it opened, the *Times* reported that "unlike any other public hospital in the city, it was built to give every patient a private room. But the hospital staff soon discovered that there was virtually no space for nurses' stations, doctors' conference rooms or medicine storage cabinets."

In short order, Woodhull became something of a carnival of mismanagement and desperation. Theft was common. Carlos Loran, who ran the hospital from its inception until being forced out in the mid-'90s as the city was considering selling the decaying structure, told the *Times* in the same story that "microscopes, typewriters, and up to 20 percent of the hospital's sheets had disappeared." What one sees in the reporting about the space over time is how the can-do technocratic optimism with which it was planned in the late '60s gave way to the malaise-ridden, anti-commons ethos of the early '80s in which it opened and floundered. Surrounded by blight, by the mid-'90s it was a hangout for prostitutes, who would hunt for johns in its football-field-length corridors. Junkies, and the dealers that exploited them, haunted the place. Its security chief Gene D'Arpe would be forced to resign in September

1994 amid allegations that the hospital's employees were running a drug sideline in heroin and cocaine.

By the time I arrived in these environs, a great fear of Woodhull was taken as an article of faith among the small coterie of mostly white people I knew in this historic black neighborhood that I didn't know. Long waits for admittance, for sterilized medical instruments, for your phone call to get picked up: these were common according to legend, as were contracting infections that turned your hand gray. These were the prevailing sentiments, urban lore passed down over cheap Mexican beer as the J train rattled by outside. Someone always knew someone who knew someone. Ride a bike down Broadway, sideswiped, broken hip, botched Woodhull ER surgery, crippled for life.

And how else would it be? The unspoken logic of those conversations I would have on rooftops, a logic I, the token Negro, would solemnly accede to in my frailty and ignorance, was that it couldn't be any other way; this is a "black" ghetto, hurry up and expect the worst. "Until they make it better," I recall one Caucasian friend telling me, "as the neighborhood changes." Which begs the question, for whom?

My fears were not immune to projection. Walking to the G train stop at Flushing Avenue, I kept my head down so as not to draw eye contact with any young Negroes my age, darker and poorer than I, who seemed agitated or baleful, standing alongside the Marcy Houses next to crying babies and fat women bursting out of brassieres too small for their girth, screaming profanities into the night over spilled fried chicken containers. Was I to assume, given the cumulative force of the American news media, the disillusionment in my mother's eye and the insidiously dismissive attitudes of so many whites, that we were naturally that way, broken and shamed, bound to subjugation, unable to shake the tremors of bondage and systematic ruin? America is so strange that way. It'll try to convince you that it's you who's lost your mind, not Mitt Romney or Paul Ryan.

My friends who made their way to the rooftop of 166 Throop during the first summer of my Brooklyn semi-adulthood lived all over the city; I knew no one who had grown up in my neighborhood, in the massive projects to the south and west of my third-floor walk-up. I had no reason, so I thought, to seek them out, to learn what the place meant to them. In fact, I didn't know that we shared a neighborhood, because I didn't know where I was. Of course, where I was *was* Bed-Stuy, where I didn't live.

THE PROLIFERATION OF GUNS AND GUN VIOLENCE IN the inner cities during the '80s, a trend Carter describes firsthand in *Decoded*'s most salient passages ("Kids were as well armed as a paramilitary outfit in a small country"), is no accident of history. "There are no white people in Marcy Projects," Carter acknowledges, before pointing fingers at a government he calls "almost genocidally hostile" for the "crack explosion" and the increased presence of lethal weaponry that sullied the environment of his childhood and adolescence. But the antecedents of the great rearming of America, and the disastrous consequences this bore for black urban spaces, contain many strange bedfellows, reverberations of failed attempts at black economic sovereignty and political dignity a generation before.

Decoded is littered with photographs of prominent late-twentieth-century political and cultural figures, rappers and singers mostly, but also basketball players and statesmen, filmmakers and the occasional rock star, most, if not all, African Americans. Carter, an epitome of capitalist promise, both illicit and aboveboard, includes images of left-wing revolutionaries: Che Guevara, Malcolm X, and members of the Black Panther Party for Self-Defense are all pictured. The Black Panthers, an organization made up at its inception largely of young black men, barely of legal drinking age, who had promoted the public display of weaponry as a means of liberating themselves from the threat of police intimidation and violence, are "heroes" in Carter's eyes, even if he clearly doesn't jive with their socialism. A dozen years after the party's federally orchestrated demise, a new generation of black men, of which Jay-Z was once part, came of age with the misguided intention—fed at the trough of an American nightmare—to arm and kill *themselves* just as fast as they could, often over what scraps of a poorly paying illicit drug market they could dominate. Despite their free breakfasts and laudable ten-point program, the legacy of the Panthers could be felt in the era of Jay-Z's adolescence in this way most of all. The political arguments of the Panthers were more effectively used by the reactionary forces of the American gun lobby than on behalf of the following generation of imperiled black men, a third of whom would wind up in prison or worse.

The Mulford Act, signed by Ronald Reagan, then California governor, in 1967, disarmed the Panthers, an organization that, despite their guns and revolutionary rhetoric, was doing identifiable good within various black communities in the areas of health care, food service, and political organizing. No such gun restriction was ever imposed on disillusioned black criminals, whose actions in economically disenfranchised black urban spaces from Oakland to Bed-Stuy had organizations across the spectrum of black advocacy groups, from the NAACP to the Nation of Islam, denouncing "black-on-black crime." Carrying guns was a "ridiculous way to solve problems that have to be solved among people of goodwill," Reagan said upon passage of the Mulford Act. Implicit in that comment is that the "problems" the Panthers were confronting by being publicly armed were with antagonists who were acting with goodwill. In cooperation with local police departments around the country, FBI Director J. Edgar Hoover's COINTELPRO program surveilled, harassed, and in some instances, such as that of the Illinois chapter president Fred Hampton, killed Black Panther members. Goodwill was clearly in short supply.

A resurgent and increasingly belligerent NRA of the late 1970s, once an organization that had spearheaded sensible gun-control efforts, was inspired in its lobbying to combat new gun-control laws by the Panthers' argument for firearms as a means of personal, and public, self-defense in an era of increasing crime and untrustworthy law enforcement. In 1980, the NRA endorsed a presidential candidate for the first time in the organization's hundred years of existence. That candidate was Ronald Reagan. His ideas about guns since signing Don Mulford's anti–Black Panther gun legislation had changed considerably. The Second Amendment "leaves little, if any, leeway for the gun-control advocate," Reagan suggested after becoming president. "The right of the citizen to keep and bear arms must not be infringed if liberty in America is to survive." Unless you agitated for the end of military service and the beginning of reparations for African-American bondage, at least.

Meanwhile, a lucrative drug market thrived in spaces where little other economic opportunity was being encouraged, not by the state, not by private individuals of means. The "nunchucks, clackers, and kitchen knives" that young men engaging in street disputes once relied on, the strife-ridden black street kids you find in the early '60s Harlem of Shirley Clarke's *The Cool World* (1963) or the Cabrini Green of Michael Schultz's cult classic *Cooley High* (1975), were replaced by tools of the utmost lethality all over the country in the deregulation-crazed '80s. The stakes were high and most careers ended unsuccessfully. Dee Dee, the dealer who had initially put a young Carter on as a dope pusher, was murdered, shot in the back of the head before or after having his balls cut off and stuffed in his mouth.

Such grisly violence wasn't enough to keep Carter's fifteen-year-old self out of "the Game." Crack led him as far south as

Virginia and as far west as Trenton, New Jersey. Even while still just a boy, untapped new markets—in front of grocery stores and nightclubs, on dead-end streets and within tattered urban parks—were there for the taking, all in pursuit of the glory that comes with a fly ride and some new Patrick Ewing sneakers.

In the first of a series of close calls, Carter was arrested for trespassing at a local high school with crack on him, but it was his first arrest and, being a minor, he was released with a record that was sealed until his eighteenth birthday. Around this time, Carter's musical interest was simultaneously intensifying. He recalls writing rap lyrics on the backs of brown paper bags and occasionally appearing on a friend's mixtape, but he wouldn't see hip-hop as a potentially lucrative career until later. Carter was still too busy getting into turf wars in Trenton with other crack dealers who felt he and an associate were crowding in on their sales by undercutting their price. In his story of the criminal mainline that became a sideline and then fodder for his continuing street cred as a wildly popular rap artist and global brand, guns were often drawn but rarely fired, near misses piling upon one another.

Whenever Jigga returned to Marcy to score more dope for his Trenton exploits, he would link up with Jaz, another MC from Marcy who had first begun to push a young Carter to explore his musical proclivities. They would while away afternoons working on tracks, an activity that began to take up all of Carter's spare time as he'd cut rhymes while subsisting on little more than sugary breakfast cereals and ice cream. Jaz got a record deal before Carter did, with EMI, and invited his protégé to London with him to record. That album tanked after a poorly chosen first single and, given how his mentor had been treated, Carter temporarily gave up his dreams of rap superstardom and rededicated himself to hustling, expanding his crack game farther south, to new territories in Maryland. But his first big break wasn't far.

The future Jay-Z got the chance to tour with Big Daddy Kane in the early '90s after Kane heard Carter's rhymes on a mixtape he had completed with Jaz. A few years later, "J.Z.," as he was then known, had become a full-blown protégé of Kane's and appeared on the single "Show & Prove" from Kane's 1994 album *Daddy's Home*. The only ex–Marcy resident to dine with multiple presidents was, simultaneously, still dealing crack and still living in Marcy.

Crack made it a lot harder to get by in a place where all the weak and poor had to prey on were, for the most part, other weak and poor people. "No one's going to help us," Carter suggests his generation of black people felt, "so we went for self, for family, for block, for crew," before suggesting that the criticism of rappers as "hyper-capitalists" conceals a "rational response" by most imperiled young men who went into hip-hop to the culture within which they were being bred. "People who looked just like us were gunning for us," Carter writes. "Weakness and dependence made you a mark, like a dope fiend. Success could only mean self-sufficiency, being a boss, not a dependent. The competition wasn't about greed—or not just about greed. It was about survival."

Here you see how hip-hop's prevailing ethos is in line with the perverse economic conservatism of the Reagan years, how the underlying dog-eat-dog mentality of the "me generation" was adopted by society's most vulnerable citizens. The myth of intrinsic black criminality didn't begin here, having been provided as the empty, bigoted excuse for white intransigence toward blacks since time immemorial, but it gained a television-fueled currency in the '80s, one whose ramifications we're all still struggling with. There is an irony to unlock here, about how imperiled inner-city black men in spaces with few job prospects, ones that capital investment was largely averse to, created their own bustling, illicit underground economy around a product (crack) that had a growing market and loyal customers at the same time that they were pilloried by pro-business conservatives as lazy, the product of a handout culture. The aspirational, materialist iconography of the good life, from Cristal to fur coats, is the currency upon which so much of Jay-Z's catalog, and the music videos, album covers, and public personas of a million imitators, trades. Capitalism, the only faith America seems to have a fealty toward anymore, is hip-hop's reigning shibboleth. In contemporary hip-hop, there is no such thing as selling out.

AT THE BARNES & NOBLE IN CHELSEA, WHERE I WORKED during that first Bed-Stuy summer of dread, it was hard not to spot the glamorous and the destitute, often right on top of each

other—it was people-watching heaven! Just after you might
have to shoo away one of the homeless people who would consistently come in from the street to camp out in the bathroom
for two hours, Tim Robbins would saunter by, towering and
hard-faced, looking around morosely before asking vaguely
about a Tom LeClair novel we obviously didn't have, Susan Sa-
randon walking around apologetically in his wake. I once sold
Spike Lee, director of the best film ever shot in the neighborhood I didn't know I was living in at the time, a dozen copies of his wife's first novel, *Gotham Diaries*. Having fielded his
brusque call asking if they were in stock ("Give me fit-teen of
'em," he said) in awe, I set them aside and awaited his arrival
with breathless anticipation, cinematic idol that he was in those
days. When he appeared, in a white New York Yankees polo and
red, black, and green wristbands, eyes like daggers behind his
round glasses, I froze for a second, before wordlessly handing
him the books. "Here you are, Mr. Lee." He didn't say "thank
you."

The election loomed, one that was quickly developing into
farce ("swiftboating" is a term that actually entered the political
lexicon, "ratfucking" having grown too coarse, I suppose), and
amid it I stumbled, among the fiction paperbacks one lazy July
afternoon, upon Joe Klein's Clinton campaign novel *Primary
Colors*. It had been all the rage two presidential election cycles
previous. I was an angry and spurned Howard Dean supporter,
one who had watched in horror as his campaign was torpedoed by the American liberal media establishment following

his rambunctious, allegedly "unpresidential" Iowa concession speech, but I tried to read *Primary Colors* with some distance from my anger. It helped focus it, a bit, but also left me with questions I wasn't prepared to answer at the time.

The protagonist of Klein's book, and the Mike Nichols movie it spawned, is Henry Burton, the scion of good civil rights Negro stock. In the book he's mixed race, but Adrian Lester, the British actor who plays him in the movie, has Sidney Poitier's complexion. Lester plays him as a damn near effeminate cultural mulatto who spends the whole movie trying to prove his mettle and staring with googly eyes at a southern governor no "woke" black man in his right mind would ever think could save America. He begins the narrative as a political "true believer" who wants to "change" this country for the better, although in the book and the film's unimaginative politics it remains unclear just what he and his liberal candidate actually believe in. The movie never gives our Slick Willy the chance to Sister Souljah anyone, or its protagonist anything that resembles a youthful black consciousness circa 1992; this brother seems to be all Kenny G and no Eric B., a *Seinfeld* watcher who somehow never heard of *Martin*, someone who would feel right at home with Fran Ross's *Oreo*.

But the movie doesn't have the wisdom to let him be the tragic mulatto its author was unable to fathom. Sure, he ends up disillusioned by the superficiality and vacuous campaign horse race, and ultimately watches from afar, having rebuffed the novel/film's Bill Clinton surrogate ("You got to be with me,

Henry!" John Travolta's Clinton unsuccessfully intones in the movie's penultimate scene) by not following the campaign all the way to the White House. But you know, deep down, this guy ends up on K Street somewhere, shilling for some other charlatan stiff of the American empire.

Henry's blackness is made unimportant in Klein's book yet is the source of revealing humor in the great Elaine May's script, which takes Klein's cluelessness about how a black man's public identity is often bound up in the falsehoods of white sexual anxiety and makes punch lines out of it. Billy Bob Thorton's character, a thinly veiled James Carville, gets to be the film's ethnic essentialist id, calling out our Negrofied George Stephanopoulos as a silent player who is really a white boy in brown drag. After claiming that Henry works that "voodoo sexual shit on white girls" that is the Negro man's stock and trade, he alludes to Henry's Hotchkiss education and claims, "I'm blacker than you are. I got some slave in me. I can feel it."

One imagines that Henry, coming into his own as a late-twenty-something product of the vineyard-summering, Jack and Jill–reared Negro elite, may indeed have wanted to work that "voodoo sexual shit" on white girls and would have been bold enough to offer a word in his own defense; in the novel he sleeps with both a Clinton aide and Hillary herself. But Klein can't burrow his way into Henry's head. Henry, a veritable Spook Who Sat by the Door, remains a cipher, a maudlin and unimaginative rumination on the modern bourgeois Negro; his journey, as depicted here, runs from the multitudes it could contain, the insights of double consciousness a young, smart Negro man at the beginning of the '90s must have carried, being the sole staffer of his hue on a presidential campaign in the era of Willie Horton and crack babies, a Carlton from *Fresh Prince* suddenly playing in the political big leagues. Klein didn't have the confidence to explore this circumstance, however, this Negro among white elites, with the gusto that writers such as Ishmael Reed or Colson Whitehead would have, or that the subject deserved. He was afraid, or he just didn't know what he didn't know.

Klein fails to imagine what double consciousness sounds like in a Negro's mind, except as a tool to castigate niggas. A political reporter who himself was wearing masks while writing this anonymously published book, Klein can offer only this when he finds his political operative waiting for a plane, observing other black people crossing an airport terminal: Henry sees

> *a group of large black kids—college kids, I could tell, enthusiastic, not sullen, but dressed sort of streety, cutting a wide, noisy swath through the terminal. (Even at our hopeful best, we could still seem awkward, inappropriate, too emotive for these white folks, I feared.)*

The phrase "for these white folks" escapes, unexamined in the next passage or anywhere else. The specter of white supremacy at play in the mind of the protagonist remains outside the writer's conscious grasp. The modifiers "streety," "noisy," and "enthusiastic" could describe a "blackness" Henry Burton would prefer to run from, seeing as he was doing just fine being Carlton. Lacking collectivism was healthy, and staying respectable to white people was a lifelong pursuit, Klein seems to be suggesting, but the novel refuses to probe this cancer in Henry's own life—where is *his* black community? His black family, the great civil rights Negroes with whom the Clintons would ingratiate themselves and whose community they would silently stab in the back, remains behind the curtains; Klein didn't feel the need to give his Hotchkiss Negro a family shibboleth to slay; he didn't know what he didn't know.

In my weaker moments, I felt a turn in the gut on many an ebony night that summer striding past the hopped-up Marcy boys on the northeastern end of the houses, by the Flushing Avenue G, as our youthful glances met, one not unlike Henry's when gazing at the wild boys in the airport; the expectation that they'd pop off and try to provoke me never faded. Their rueful glances, confirming within me some latent sense that ourselves, *Negroes*, were the problem, those without vision or dignity, a doomed and longing people, kept me on edge as I passed stoops and park margins full of boisterous dope boys, cutting their "wide swaths," as Klein would have it. I had, in my young life, encountered many lies; this one proved central, our inherent fallenness, but the backwardness of our national mythos was evident in other ways that summer too.

The Republican National Convention came to town and

the New York City Police Department, at the behest of the feds, made a mess of suppressing the outrage sparked by a president who had needlessly entered us in two wars, one of which was being fought on false pretenses and in extremely bad faith, the other smelling mostly of mirthless resource theft. I had scheduled the day off work from Barnes & Noble weeks in advance, and the following day too, in case I got arrested. Marching north on Sixth Avenue on day one of the convention, as New York's finest did their best to unconstitutionally silence the dissenters, took what felt like an entire afternoon. Herded as we were into bullpens of dissent, the Americans who had taken to the streets in protest of the senseless war and arrogant knownothingism were bound with a miserable sense of hopelessness. This was a war we would not stop.

One march a few days into the convention, initially approved by the NYPD, would go from the World Trade Center to Madison Square Garden on sidewalks only. When the arrests came, as people tried to peaceably remove themselves from the "free speech" zones, they came swiftly and violently. Sometimes they even came preemptively. Members of the War Resisters League planned to stage a "die-in" upon reaching the arena, but that never happened, as two hundred of them were arbitrarily arrested after one officer claimed a banner being held aloft on the sidewalk was taking up too much space.

This didn't surprise me much. For a black man, in the city of Giuliani, in the country of Bush, in a time of war, in the Bed-Stuy of our collective nightmares, safety seemed a silly concept, a quaint thing from the past, a myth as far reaching and hard to touch as the divinity of kings and the sacredness of our Constitution, which, before being amended, had sought to make me property. The city fathers and the men who served them, as they have always done in the New York where I came of age, resorted to the most sickening of tactics to quell the expression of unpopular truths on those Manhattan streets.

Almost a full decade went by before these tactics were found illegal in a court of law. The NYPD detained and fingerprinted people in direct violation of their constitutional rights, disregarding whether individuals were in fact providing probable cause for arrest during those desperate late-summer days. More than 1,800 people were arrested in protests during the convention's four days, passing the notorious 1968 Democratic National Convention in Chicago for the most protesters ever held captive at such an affair. Yet in our time the antiwar effort was ineffective, direct action ultimately fruitless. The war continued apace as "Mission Accomplished" floated above the suited-and-booted president, freshly landed on a carrier of doom.

BEFORE ANYONE CALLED IT "RESPECTABILITY POLItics," I knew how to code-switch. I knew not to act like those boisterous black boys in *Primary Colors*, at least in white company. It was another type of shame entirely, but the experience of code-switching can also be exhilarating and is perhaps, in every essential way, no different than jumping from Portuguese to Gaelic. I talked to Rolanda differently than I did my mother, to whom I spoke differently than my drug buddies from high school, to whom I spoke differently than I did my film professors in college. Cynicism and self-flagellation were easy in those years. It was the season of Bill Cosby's "Pound Cake" speech at the Urban League gala celebrating the fiftieth anniversary of the *Brown v. Board of Education* decision, after all.

Fuck code-switching, Cosby was telling us, even if he didn't know it. The way niggas behave is unacceptable. Good Negroes shouldn't tolerate it. It was a logic popular at the middle-class black dinner tables where I often found myself when I went home to Ohio; Cosby called on his audience to recognize the depth of the civil rights movement's failure to secure enduring prosperity for all but a sliver of the country's black citizens, and to see it as the fault of those who remain impoverished.

I confess, I was somewhat in thrall to self-vilifying blacks like this at the time, afraid as we had been told to be of those who wouldn't pull their pants up, who'd shoot you down on the street for nothing; a friend from film school and I would listen to .wav files of Cosby's speech over and over, giggling at his hysterical paternalism, unaware of the promise of grim hypocrisy. As far as Cosby was concerned, along with much of the respectable black establishment, Allen Iverson may as well have joined Al-Qaeda.

Cosby defended police officers shooting young Negro thieves from behind. "These people, the ones up here in the balcony, fought so hard. Looking at the incarcerated, these are not political criminals," he'd said, just weeks before I moved to Bed-Stuy, unknowingly, for the first time. "These are people going around stealing Coca-Cola. People getting shot in the back of the head over a piece of pound cake! And then we all run out and are outraged. 'The cops shouldn't have shot him.' What the hell was he doing with the pound cake in his hand?"

In *Bring the Pain*, his landmark comedy special from a decade earlier that landed just as crime crested across the nation in black neighborhoods, where women of some means like my mother invested in guns and alarm systems, Chris Rock suggested that the only people who hated niggas more than Caucasians did were Negroes. He'd forgotten that Bill Cosby hated niggas more than Negroes did. Unless they were female and unconscious.

As a child, my sense of what it meant to be part of a people I would have then referred to only as "black," despite the frequent usage within my household of the earlier, more rarified and now shamed term, was informed by the underlying logic I detected within these simple explanations for the ever-enduring sense that black America was awry, unable to right itself after being privy to so much civic ransacking. You could find those sentiments in the books I was picking off the shelves late that summer, the air-conditioning in the corporate bookseller where I was trapped eight hours a day whirring overhead, sneaking time to read the hard stuff whenever I wasn't helping someone find a James Patterson novel. Debra Dickerson's *The*

End of Blackness, which had come out the previous winter, was typical, in some ways, among this set of "what went wrong?" polemics; it sought to point out that while the United States was far from a racial utopia, it had become, long after the primary legislative goals of the civil rights movement had been met, a space where racism was no longer the effective driver of Negro misery or lack of opportunity. Negroes could not be prevented from "playing the game," wrote Dickerson, and that game was American capitalism. "No one can stop the American, black or blind, who is determined to succeed."

Who was stopping Negroes from winning at American capitalism? Dickerson surmised, themselves, of course. Dickerson, and even more conservative black thinkers such as the economists Thomas Sowell and Glenn Loury, toed this line in prose I found startlingly persuasive at the time. The linguist John McWhorter, author of *Losing the Race*, an equally polemical work that gained much more "mainstream" traction than Dickerson's book, made an argument that both the nascent and long-standing Negro middle classes wanted to believe; they could look at their Caucasian friends and coworkers and say, "Naw, it's those *niggas'* fault. We ain't like that." Negroes weren't victims, even if the playing field wasn't completely fair, these books argued.

While Dickerson's book points out the delusion inherent in the white citizenry's general know-nothingism concerning the despoiling of black American life, past and present, in most of these works, especially those by the serious academics, the weight of the past was cherry-picked, and the policies of the present underexamined. When *Losing the Race* connects the black educational and economic achievement gap to black anti-intellectualism in the aftermath of the Black Power movement's cultural ascendency and political failure, McWhorter leaves out school funding, tied to property taxes, that disproportionately keeps droves of black kids in the most ill-equipped schools. Where he upbraids the thought and speech within black cultural life that cordons off some uncomfortable truths about black accountability or deems benign words such as "niggardly" to be off-limits to a D.C. politician in a budget meeting, he also stymies other lines of salient structural critique lodged at the white power structure as empty "rabble-rousing."

Not that any of this was of particular consequence to me that summer. I was just looking for cheap pot and a good time most nights. My upbringing had shown me how to talk like any common ghetto street kid when I had to make someone on the street respect me, but I bottled up that side of myself during most hours, and certainly on the rooftops and at the bookstore or wherever I was the only black person in the room. I had internalized, through careful instruction, that this was the way to proceed in life, learning, somewhere along the line, to be a "cultural mulatto," as Trey Ellis would have it, to swim with niggas and Negroes and mulattos and gringos, of varied classes, at ease.

I navigate American apartheid. It isn't without breaking a sweat.

227–241 TAAFFE PLACE

The lineage of Brooklyn hip-hop Tony and I had grown up
listening to in our Ohio bedrooms had prepared me, in
some small degree, to expect a rough-and-tumble "if you can
make it here, you can make it anywhere" New York. In fact, although I didn't know it at the time, many of the genre's most salient and outlandish voices came from the streets we suddenly
found ourselves living among; beyond Jay-Z, Mos Def and Lil'
Kim, Ol' Dirty Bastard and Foxy Brown are all from Bed-Stuy,
where we unwittingly were. Carter's vision of the space didn't
seem, at first glance, to leave much room for ambiguity. "Cough
up a lung / where I'm from / Marcy son / ain't nothing nice."
But ambiguity was everywhere in the Bed-Stuy of my youth.

My mother had taught me to keep aware of my surroundings, to not trust strangers, to run from trouble, to speak the

king's English to police officers, to feel comfortable saying "nigger" in the company of black folks who carried and transcended the past with me, and, perhaps most important, to distinguish between a Negro who seemed a threat and one who didn't, which is largely the same as making that distinction with everyone else on God's green earth. This is a skill that, however commonsensical, is more difficult than it should be for most of our country's law enforcement apparatus, as illustrated by one risible spectacle after another of black men being jailed or beaten or killed under the flimsiest of pretexts by their sworn public servants on camera, but back then streaming video hadn't really gone viral and Twitter wouldn't exist for a few years to come; white folks mostly just didn't know what they didn't know.

Certainly this was the case for my roommate, who was likely encountering his first majority-black space, a place of great mystery and dread, a place that listening to all the soul records in the world couldn't teach him to navigate comfortably at first. In some recess of his mind, I reckon, my roommate couldn't stomach telling his parents he lived in Bed-Stuy in the first place. He imagined his blonde, Park Slope–dwelling girlfriend, who did social work for brown people all day, not being particularly fond of walking the streets of his imagined Bed-Stuy for a late-night tryst, one I'd inevitably hear through the tiny window that linked our rooms in uncomfortable intimacy, even if it was ten feet off the ground.

Rarely venturing too far east down DeKalb Avenue from a place we didn't live, Clinton Hill, into a place one didn't want to go that we actually did live in, Bedford-Stuyvesant, was just as easy. This is how we both behaved, the treading lightly, the assumption of menace, the casual avoidance of corridors where one felt unwelcome at worst and uneasy at best. Is this the general know-nothingism that guilt-free cultural colonialism requires, or the savvy self-preserving instincts of a sophisticated urbanite in a "transitional" neighborhood? While no longer as dangerous as it was during Carter's coming of age, the streets I inhabited were not without reminders of the past.

The night after I broke my assailant's arm with the door leading into my building, I watched as armed black patriots climbed onto their Bushwick roof and started firing assault weapons in the air as the July 4 fireworks commenced. A pair of white jeans I wore that day were ruined when I dived for cover into a murky puddle one rooftop away. That wasn't as demeaning as getting rear-ended and being called a nigger for my trouble by some drunk Caucasian lady as I drove Ray and another friend back to the subway. Getting into my car later in the summer, I watched a homeless man get savagely beaten by a group of young men in Alphabet City and, for fear of my safety, declined to help him, feeling no small amount of shame in the aftermath. I drove back around the block to see if he was still there and in need of assistance, but he had gone, or had been taken, somewhere else entirely.

We lived in a black Bed-Stuy that, while more peaceful than in the crack era and the years that followed, was still less secure than the black Bed-Stuy of the postwar era, one that oddly offered less opportunity for someone like Tony, a musical savant with a real passion for a variety of forms. Although you wouldn't know it from Carter's work, hip-hop wasn't the first musical genre that had Bed-Stuy gangsters and hustlers out starting musical acts. "The Bedford-Stuyvesant neighborhood is an under-documented anomaly in the history of jazz music," Vincent Ramal Gardner writes in his survey of Brooklyn's jazz scene past and present, "We Were Surrounded by Giants." "It comprises an area of just over $3^1/_2$ square miles, but the amount of concentrated jazz activity within its borders throughout the years is nothing short of extraordinary." In a short time after the form's mass popularization, bars and nightclubs that catered to gangsters and good-time girls were as likely to have jazz as the more genteel social clubs and ballrooms patronized by college-educated, well-to-do blacks occupying the gorgeous Italianate town houses north of the Fulton Street strip.

Tony, a gifted bassist with a great love of and appreciation for jazz, was suspicious of hip-hop as a form of musical artistry. "It's really simple music, man, not that sophisticated at all," Tony would tell me concerning the difficulty of constructing the average hip-hop track, earnest music student that he was. As I would look at him blankly, he'd add a "just saying," an apology of sorts from the part of him that was squarely a white liberal.

Tony surely would have much preferred the Bed-Stuy of Gardner's research to the one we were living in then. It was a time when "even the neighborhood gangs had jazz bands." The previous order of black music had arisen out of a Bedford-

Stuyvesant milieu equally as segregated, and as quick to change, as that in which Shawn Carter came of age. Bed-Stuy during the Depression, at the dawn of jazz's ascendancy to the height of American popular culture, was a neighborhood in the midst of transformation yet again.

The Great Migration wave of southern blacks, seeking opportunity and the rule of law, fled north into its Victorian and Italianate brownstones not knowing the extent to which the forces of polite white society would go to keep them from earning their share of the American plunder. Despite this, idylls of black self-determination were carved out in cities across the North and Midwest. Bed-Stuy was, in many ways, among the most significant of them.

Bedford-Stuyvesant's black character benefited from the overcrowding of Harlem as well as the Great Migration; as the completion of the A train subway line, which connected Harlem to Bed-Stuy, eased travel between the city's two most significant African-American outposts, Bed-Stuy's black population swelled. It became a welcoming place for many journeying south from Harlem or north from Dixie, a place where black lives could flourish amid the economic boundaries that fenced its prospects inward. Large row houses and brownstones were subdivided for renters, often by blockbusting landlords who exploited the fact that many of the transplants couldn't acquire Federal Housing Administration–backed housing loans in non-redlined, whites-only neighborhoods. In Harlem, a significant amount of the housing stock during the twentieth century's first half had passed into black ownership, but Bedford-Stuyvesant's legacy of black home ownership dated to the 1830s.

A century ago, the Weeksville settlement first brought black home ownership and self-determination to Brooklyn. The community of Weeksville, still one of four distinct segments of Bedford-Stuyvesant, was at its height in the 1860s, home to about seven hundred families. They collectively erected enduring and sophisticated institutions, forming schools, a hospital, an orphanage, and several old folks' homes. The Weeksville Unknowns were among the country's earliest black baseball teams (Weeksville's women founded their own team in the 1880s), while the community was also home to one of the country's first black newspapers, *The Freedman's Torchlight*. Several churches, such as Berean Baptist, St. Philip's Protestant Episcopal, and Bethel A.M.E., were founded during Weeksville's heyday, places of worship that exist to this day.

The speculators who sought to create an African-American refuge there in the 1830s had the same goals as the blacks who traveled there to escape southern tyranny in the 1930s. They were, consciously and ambitiously, attempting to create a place that was safe and welcoming for people like themselves, marketing the settlement to potential black home owners all over the country. Through landownership, black men, both those born free and those who had to seize their freedom from others, hoped to gain a foothold on the engine of American prosperity. For $250, a black man could own a piece of land in a place like Weeksville and be enfranchised; for the southern black man of a century later, the hope of securing factory jobs and the ability to avoid discriminatory poll taxes or literacy tests in order to vote were equally alluring motivators. This hope, of a place where they wouldn't have to explain themselves or look over their shoulders or act with cowed deference, united the small coterie of cosmopolitan blacks from across the African diaspora who found themselves drawn to the rural hills and valleys of central Kings County since before the Civil War. Free or slave, northern or southern, American or not, Bed-Stuy has long been a place where blacks, across lines of class and region, could aspire to the same dream of safety and opportunity.

And, even if it weren't, housing options were limited. The FHA mandated that developers receiving its financial support must enact restrictive covenants in the deeds signed by home owners, which frequently prohibited the sale of property to Negroes. According to an Economic Policy Institute study of the three hundred largest private subdivisions built in Queens, Long Island's Nassau County, and the suburbs of Westchester from the height of the Depression until just after the end of World War II, "83 percent had racially restrictive deeds." Preambles like "whereas the Federal Housing Administration requires that the existing mortgages on the said premises be subject and subordinated to the said [racial] restrictions . . . [except for] domestic servants of a different race domiciled with an owner or tenant . . ." were common. Because of this, Bed-Stuy was, and still is, a place of remarkable class dexterity within the black community. Due to the inability of blacks, during those immediate postwar years, to self-segregate along the lines of class, the young Lena Horne, a scion of the upper middle class who grew up on Macon Street in the heart of the neighborhood, got her start in many of the same clubs as her contemporary Billie Holiday, the daughter of a prostitute who had been imprisoned for sex work by the time she turned fourteen. Being black, even as high yellow as Lena, was a class unto itself.

Despite all this discrimination, despite the routine experience of having had the rights of citizenry tarnished and the most humble decencies denied being near universal, a pervasive nihilistic hopelessness of the type that colors the accounts of urban Negro life in Carter's generation of mass incarceration and deindustrialization did not take hold. The people who were moving to Bed-Stuy were hopeful, bent on improving their lot. The inevitable consequences of widespread disenfranchisement, nonexistent employment opportunities, cheap drugs, and a surplus of guns were in an unimaginable near future. Deadly street violence would seem as foreign to the members of the more than 115 social clubs that existed in Bed-Stuy from the 1930s to the 1960s as to freckled girls born to Exeter Academy and the General Society of Mayflower Descendants. Competing over who could put together the most impressive big band for a dance until the wee hours, in one of the neighborhood's many ornate theaters or ballrooms, wasn't routinely lethal.

Bed-Stuy's youth culture in this era was, as in Carter's time, centered on music. Dance-oriented big bands were crucial to the fabric of the community, performing for "social clubs," organizations of young blacks that existed primarily, despite the roots many of the groups had in the influential black churches, to throw raucous dance parties. Venues such as Fulton Street's Brooklyn Palace and Atlantic Avenue's Bedford Ballroom held more than 2,500 people for dances, while others such as the Sonia Ballroom, which once took up the entire block of Bedford Avenue between Madison and Putnam, housed 1,500 revelers at a time and was thought of as intimate. Black fraternal orders, such as the police union the Centurions, would meet there, while the Order of the Elks had their own local lodge, the Elks Ballroom. When the Elks first began renting it out for public use in 1932, it was the largest public hall owned by Brooklyn Negroes.

Legends of the big band and swing format, from Count Basie to Duke Ellington, performed regularly at social-club-sponsored dances. Charlie Parker, the great pioneer of bebop, had early bands made up largely of central Brooklynites, either recent transplants like Miles Davis or natives such as Max Roach. Before becoming acknowledged masters of the form, key figures such as Thelonious Monk, Art Blakey, and Charles Mingus cut their teeth at those Bed-Stuy ballroom dances in the years before bebop pushed aside swing and ushered in a revolution in the development of American music.

This pervasive scene, one that supported at least sixty-five jazz venues in the neighborhood roughly from 1930 to 1970, grew as Bed-Stuy became a predominantly African-American neighborhood. Bars like Farmer John, at Fulton Street and

Bedford Avenue, or dedicated jazz clubs such as the Putnam Central at Putnam and Classon Avenues, employed schools of session musicians and sidemen, promoters and barkeeps, creating a dynamic economy around the performance and recording of jazz music in Bedford-Stuyvesant. The latter club was the headquarters of Debut Records, an independent label started by Mingus and Roach in 1952 that was among many that shot up in the neighborhood during the era. Most crucially, perhaps, the Bed-Stuy clubs allowed some of the great jazz musicians, from Davis to Monk to Blakey, a place to work in an era when a musician's cabaret card, a license to work in a New York City establishment that served alcohol, from Prohibition until 1967, could be taken at the slightest pretense by the police, as was the case with each of them.

Jazz created a community of venues and performers in Bed-Stuy, and an economy all its own; live hip-hop performance and studio recording, on a granular level, hasn't had nearly as much significance in the infrastructural life of the place, on the topography or the economy of Bed-Stuy, in the form's thirty-five-year history. By the time hip-hop began to cross over into the pop-cultural mainstream in the 1980s, much of urban black America had become a place with much larger concentrations of intense poverty, where senseless spasms of violence carried on the winds of desperation were commonplace. Regardless of how many rappers came from those streets, aboveboard venues to showcase the emerging form they helped innovate didn't employ nearly the amount of people as jazz clubs once had—large or moderate-sized bands of instrumentalists are unnecessary in hip-hop.

Tony, a well-schooled, out-of-work Bed-Stuy transplant with dreams of playing in professional bands, had picked the wrong era to be alive. In our era, my jazz-loving roommate was out of luck. Bed-Stuy was no longer a neighborhood where you could make a living as a sideman with a few weekly residencies. Unless, of course, you didn't have to earn money to survive.

IT WAS A LITANY OF MISFORTUNE FROM THE START. Early in the summer Tony and I moved in together, in 2006, my car was struck by a Hasidic school bus as it approached the Williamsburg Bridge on Delancey Street. As I was illegally talking to my Serbian club promoter ex-roommate on my cell phone, my car was sideswiped by the bus, knocking the driver's side mirror. Flushed with fear and rage, I followed the bus as it fled the scene, the remnants of the side mirror dangling in the scalding summer wind, all the way across the bridge. Tailgating the bus aggressively and honking my horn as if my life depended on it, I convinced the driver to pull over in Jewish Williamsburg. It was as I was boarding the bus that I first noticed the Yiddish characters on its side; the curly-haired driver, his brown eyes betraying no emotion as a vast sea of children sat eerily silent in their uniforms of faith and watched on, claimed he hadn't hit me. Berating him wasn't making me feel any better; he seemed impervious to anything I might say, such as "Wait here, I'm calling the cops." As soon as I stepped off the bus, he drove away. I tried to scribble down the license plate, but couldn't find a pen in time. Then the rain started and the cops, predictably, never came.

"You were middle class in college," my godmother said to me after I graduated, "but now you enter the world a poor Negro for the first time in your life." Maybe so; my income and zip code certainly indicated such, even if the amount of West Elm furniture in my apartment suggested my proximity to affluence and ease. In such a place it was easy to look out at "Clinton Hill" from our seventh-floor window and dream. I smelled opportunities in those Brooklyn nights and wanted to believe that they would open themselves effortlessly, that I wouldn't have to struggle too much, that grinding class and status anxieties, ones I could hardly fathom at the time, would not have to define my way of encountering the world. We seemed to be living through a hinge point in human history, and all I had to prepare myself for it was a loosely evangelical upbringing, a bachelor's degree in film and film history, and a desire to make movies, but I believed in my own pluck. Unfortunately, facts kept coming to my attention that complicated this sanguine vision of the future.

I had never watched it while in film school, but shortly after I graduated, some friends from Ohio introduced me to HBO's *Entourage*, an infantilizing wet dream of film industry life if there ever was one. Consuming episodes from the show's first few seasons in the weeks before Tony and I moved to Bed-Stuy, I could pretend that that's what making a little indie movie in Queens, or whatever outer borough I lived in, would lead to: easy girls and drugs, opportunities that proved immune to my own ineptitude. Reality ensued after landing in "Clinton Hill," however. Being too broke to make a little indie movie in Queens, I taught film history and the rudiments of production to preteens at an arts summer camp on Long Island instead.

This involved driving an ailing mid-'90s Ford sedan from my "Clinton Hill" loft—a seventy-two-mile round trip on the Long Island Expressway in rush-hour traffic—to teach suburban kids about movies. It paid $6,000 for six weeks of work, enough to pay my $800-a-month share of our $2,400-a-month rent for the time being. It was fun showing the children movies they had no business viewing; we watched parts of Antonioni's *The Passenger* and Godard's *Pierrot le Fou* and all of Kevin Smith's *Clerks II*. In a way, even while staying up at night wondering which of these rich grade schoolers would one day use their parents' dime to make a mediocre but celebrated first indie feature in Queens, it was worth it. But the fact was that none of it, the indie film world I wanted to enter, the apartment in which I was living, the relationships with roommates and lovers, was sustainable. What would I do after the arts camp ended? The dread it embedded within my daily existence began to get tied up in my visions of Tony that "first" summer, lying about on the white leather love seat my mother had given us upon moving in, drinking Sapporos and watching my DVDs ad infinitum.

My great-aunt and good friend Catherine Daniels passed

away that July, a few weeks after I was attacked. Having received the news from my father while on the Long Island Expressway, I had to pull over to sob. The following week I journeyed to Elizabethtown, Kentucky, to see her buried at a country cemetery on an unbearably hot day in mid-July. She was my maternal grandmother's best friend and had raised me every bit as much as my mother and father had. I remember crying much of the day, listening to Animal Collective's "The Softest Voice" for hours straight as the jet pushed me, if not through my unshakable grief and shame, the 630 miles southwest and back again in one day and evening. I had not seen her, due to a family dispute involving my mother, in many years and now I never would again.

When I returned late that night, Tony was fucking his girlfriend, a blonde from another variant of Cincinnati privilege, on the Danish teak couch that he treated like an actual antique instead of a simulacrum of one. Tony knew not of Catherine's death because of our increasingly uneasy communication. I hadn't told him that I was leaving town and returning home to go to her funeral, and he hadn't asked what was wrong as I sulked around in the days before; we saw and spoke so little to each other, only two months into our new living arrangement, that it hadn't occurred to him I'd left when I returned that night. Even though she cooked steaks and pork chops and apple pie for him on many an afternoon of our youth, even though she concealed our mutual drug use in my mother's house, nefarious activity that would have earned him great censure, I wasn't surprised that, when I finally unveiled her passing, he couldn't muster anything resembling common sorrow.

I began to notice in our new home together, for the first time, the sinews of assumed privilege that he would never be able to let go, and that I'd never, regardless of my proximity, be able to make my own. The way he didn't remove his stringy hair from the shower drain or clean his dishes after he dirtied them, leaving them in the sink, were signs of someone who had always had someone to clean up after him. Something about having to work every day while watching him comfortably lounge around our place smashed the solidarity we had cultivated over many years and despite several setbacks. There was no way to talk about it comfortably without bringing up his inherited advantages, something neither of us wanted to dwell on. So we didn't.

Despite our discord, as the summer wore on, I took to Ta-affe Place, whether it was in Clinton Hill or Bed-Stuy. One could step into Sputnik, the Leninist-themed hip-hop bar across the street from my building, which occasionally hosted some of the late greats from a previous era of central Brooklyn rap culture (DJ Premier, M-1, et cetera), and think that some multiracial, class-diverse utopia had found its way to this tucked-away part of the borough. Those were months, which soon turned into years, of magical thinking.

ALL I WANTED TO DO WAS MAKE FEATURES. HISTORY had taught me, already, at a tender age, to expect less because of my color. Our careers, according to the black cinema texts, the essay collections and memoirs I discovered, were shorter, more fragile, less likely to speak to the thoughtfully lived experiences of our people—that's just how the industry worked. Its power centers, like most other centers of authority and wealth in this country, were in white hands who saw little money in supporting the work of a Haile Gerima or a Julie Dash, a Jamaa Fanaka or Kathleen Collins, a William Greaves or a Charles Burnett. When these filmmakers were in their prime, the most significant institutions of American cinema weren't much interested in helping their work get made. Why would I, a neophyte who had done nothing to suggest I could enter such hallowed company, be any different?

Sure, from Oscar Micheaux to Spike Lee, many a Negro had made multiple features, but Lee was the only one ever to make them in the studio system, on his own terms, in a personal way that reached significant audiences. African-American cinema has never fostered careers with the wide-ranging and prolific nature of African-American literature. Show me black film directors who have had the opportunity to consistently make feature films of the reach and scope one can find in the myriad novels of Toni Morrison and Octavia Butler, James Baldwin and Alice Walker, Colson Whitehead and John Edgar Wideman. Dash's 1991 film *Daughters of the Dust* was the first movie by a black woman ever released in theaters, years after Butler, Walker, and Morrison had delivered multiple books, including their masterpieces, to big audiences and great acclaim. This was simply, then and now, no country for black filmmakers.

Movies cost, generally, a lot more than I had stowed away. In my spare time, I finished a short film that I had shot in Manhattan the previous winter as my BFA thesis. I spent many a night at the Sandbox, a long-defunct, Gramercy-based, hip-hop-centered streaming video company. In the days before YouTube was sold to Google and the dreams of the Sandbox's venture-capital financiers were no more, I loitered around the postproduction rooms editing a vampire film called *Evangeleo* into the wee hours, clandestinely using Final Cut Pro stations that were normally reserved for rap videos. It was a postproduction space vastly superior to the first-generation MacBook in my bedroom, and I used the Sandbox's facilities for all they were worth, especially since all I seemingly had to do in order to work there was smoke out the right person every once in a while. Short films never pay any money, and no one acquires them generally; for most upstarts fresh out of film school these works only aspired to calling-card status, an attention getter that hopefully would screen at a significant film festival, one that would help make your name in the industry if it was seen by the right gatekeepers, at the right time.

I needed a new job at summer's end if I was going to afford the $800 a month, and sniffing around on the Internet in the waning days of August, just as my summer camp teaching checks were petering out, I found a job as an assistant at the office of a well-respected independent film production company. They had produced movies I revered, and, hungry for the opportunity to be in the proximity of people reputed to have made actually artful movies, I tracked down their phone number when the website only provided e-mail addresses. I called and was granted an in-person interview. When I visited, climbing a long, dim stairwell to the second story on Worth Street in Tribeca, the once-dilapidated Lower Manhattan neighborhood that had grown chic with development, I found a disheveled office and slender black woman with tight braids who wore a red dress and specs. This was KiKi, the current assistant to the couple who owned the company. KiKi seemed cheerfully disgruntled from the moment I met her. She quit within weeks of hiring me; and like that I was the office manager.

The Triangle Below Canal (Street) had been a run-down Manhattan backwater in the Ed Koch years when *Ghostbusters* was filmed there, but by the time I began working there it was a hub for the city's financial and artistic elite, its industrial space long demolished or converted into handsome modern housing, its streets lined with restaurants that attracted celebrities and bankers. Many of the most significant production companies and distributors were based in the area, from Harvey Weinstein's Miramax and Mark Cuban's HDNet Films to Robert De Niro's Tribeca Film Institute; De Niro had long been a major investor in and ambassador for the neighborhood, starting the Tribeca Film Festival in the wake of 9/11.

I was told to make myself quietly indispensable at my subminimum-wage "office manager" job that fall, which mostly required that I field pushy phone calls from unpaid vendors, manage the ego of a former Wall Street character from Great Neck who was paying the company's overhead in exchange for developing his rock-and-roll movie that no one thought was good, and reading scripts for other pictures that, a decade later, mostly still haven't been made, regardless of their quality. The financier of a Harvey Keitel movie the company worked on had skipped town owing $125,000 to various individuals and businesses that had all been contracted through us—European co-productions such as this were part of the production company's lifeblood—and the hard-to-reach Frenchman with a yacht who was responsible for cutting the checks was conspicuously absent when my bosses, through his amiable but clueless line producer, came calling for him. We were always "waiting on the tax credit to roll in," the percentage of the movie the city and state were willing to pay for in exchange for the shoot being in New York, to make the rest of the vendors whole. No one seemed to have any idea how long that would take.

Amid the torrent of angry dog trainers and caterers, best boys and script supervisors who wanted their wages, I watched videos on YouTube (then in its first year of popularity) and scanned the office for paraphernalia from the Golden Age of Indie Film—Harmony Korine's underwear, so the legend went among the junior staff, was an item of particular interest, resting as it allegedly did in a cardboard box amid detritus from the set of one of his earliest films—while submitting my own *Evan-*

geleo to film festivals. I used my office manager job to my own ends, having meetings for productions I was doing on the side, faxing copies of my own script to other producers, ordering padded envelopes for DVD screeners of my thesis film. *Evangeleo* got accepted to a student festival in Los Angeles, where I squandered my world premiere status back before I knew that was a big no-no, and then the Slamdance Film Festival in Park City, Utah. Founded in the shadow of Sundance, which ultimately produced the likes of Christopher Nolan, Slamdance was a big deal for me. My bosses were impressed enough to help me get the legendary rock band Sonic Youth, with whom they'd worked on a foreign film soundtrack, to let me use their music in the film for free. For the first time I felt, however small and powerless, a part of the world of independent film I'd read and thought so much about as a young man.

But disillusionment soon set in. After I took over from KiKi, the company agreed to pay me only $800 a month, well below minimum wage. It was, in theory, enough to pay for my apartment, assuming I didn't eat and walked four miles each way to work. Although it felt like my life could quickly become like the ones sold to me in the film school brochures, even if I was working for less than minimum wage at the office of a production company I revered, "independent film" seemed to operate almost solely on graft and exploitation. I had passed up the chance for a much-better-paid job at an agency that specialized in representing theatrical performers because I wanted to be close to the action of making movies of the type I had spent my late adolescence and young adulthood idolizing. Tribeca was still nicknamed "Indiewood," given the number of production companies and distributors based in the neighborhood back then. To work on the periphery of the scene for what amounted to $26 a day plus lunch, which I paid for with petty cash, was the first, and in my infinite insecurity, perhaps only way to get a foothold.

Independent film producers are notoriously fickle, ego driven, and occasionally, in the case of Scott Rudin, prone to throwing phones, but my bosses never treated me that way. The two principals would be temperamental occasionally, in vastly different ways from each other, but in the short time I worked for them as their office manager, they taught me a lot without trying at all. But they were too busy surviving the end of the golden years of independent film to worry about my development, and unlike my peers working as barely paid quasi-interns at similarly sized indie outfits, I didn't get to work on any movies that actually got made.

In a climate in which hedge fund investors and venture capitalists were by and large pulling out of indie film, I marveled at how they stayed in business despite lacking trust funds. Part of it was partnering with a well-known music supervisor and once-prominent movie star to share office space. (His perpetually stoned lackey came in once a week to gather the mail and stare at the wall.) But another way was to limit their labor costs to unpaid interns. During the first week of 2007 I was told that they would no longer pay me $800 to run the office.

I had been spending too much of my time on my own film, on the verge of its major festival premiere in Park City, I was told. I was welcome to hang out at 1 Worth Street anyway, given the affection they had built up for me, but they had decided to hand over the reins of office management to my intern Frank White, a skinny, wild-eyed actor/musician/whatever I knew from making movies in college. I had hired him after seeing him at a photo exhibit upstate, while at the Woodstock Film Festival with one of the company's films, which had played at Sundance and was directed by someone scarcely older than me. "You'll be a better employer than employee," one of my bosses said with odd affection, claiming I wasn't meant to "clean the brushes" but was supposed to go and be an artist myself. She allowed me to keep the keys and use their office for casting or taking a meeting. I had no idea I'd be doing just that, and a lot more, at 1 Worth Street for another half decade.

My mother paid for my ticket to Park City, beaming with pride. I found lodging on Craigslist, traveling with my cinematographer, David, and another ex-roommate, but I quickly learned that as a young man traveling from party to party on those snowy mountain streets, one may end up sleeping in all sorts of places, from hilltop mansions to the hotel rooms of ginger-haired Canadian journalists. While in bed at the latter locale, I discovered it was an inopportune time to be wearing the swag underwear I received from a Slamdance filmmaker as a keepsake to remember his film by, especially when the garment in question was tighty-whiteys branded with the film's inelegant logo. I was suddenly flirting with young starlets and sharing bathroom line conversations with television actors, competing for girls with Jeff Dowd, the inspiration for the legendary Jeff Bridges character in *The Big Lebowski*. "Lay off my lady friend," he told me, with the utmost seriousness, in the refrigerated-drinks aisle of a 7-Eleven well after midnight, before we shared a cab with the Canadian redhead. If only he had taken my advice to let me be dropped off first!

It felt glamorous, that initial Park City, even if I was playing the minor league festival with the rest of the Sundance rejects, such as a pudgy college girl from Oberlin named Lena Dunham, whom I had met on the plane to Salt Lake and later shared a van with to Park City. When I got home, even though I was still broke, I had some more swagger in my step and was sure it was just the beginning of a swift ascent into directorhood. I supposed, after Slamdance, that I was about to take off on a long and prosperous festival run; but following its acceptance in Park City, *Evangeleo* was rejected from twenty straight festivals. I was humbled, to say the least.

I had to keep making a living, especially without the production company money covering my rent at Taaffe Place every month. Although I wasn't a technician, I took jobs on sets in my spare time, driving trucks for $100 a day on bad indie movies that would sell at Sundance for millions, or assistant directing disastrous short films for first-timers dipping into their trust funds for a taste of the indie film life. I still did work from time to time at a production company, driving around the art director of a Manoel de Oliveira movie as he scouted Staten Island locations, or serving as a production assistant on a CNN commercial, but money was getting increasingly short and my mother was, at the time, increasingly unwilling to help. Another executive at the production company was also a journalist who ran one of the more respected magazines covering the world of independent film. He offered to let me write for his publication and I accepted, but I wasn't aware at the time that this wasn't actually a job, it was simply a means of acquiring free travel and lodging in exotic places by writing for the house organ of a nonprofit. It was just a more glamorous means of scraping by.

IT WAS A BARREL-CHESTED BOUNCER AND SOCIAL worker named Bo, a fellow resident of 227–241 Taaffe, who became the second person after my Independence Day assailant to tell me we didn't live in Clinton Hill. "This is Bed-Stuy," Bo said, a cynical smile crossing his lips as I pondered this. It was probably sometime in late 2006. He had told others, mostly whites who had recently moved into the building, this same thing many times, explaining that calling this block of Taaffe Place "Clinton Hill" was just a branding effort. In those dreary middle aughts, Bed-Stuy was propelled endlessly back into itself by Craigslist housing ads. Every year, before Bed-Stuy was hip among the developer set and the people they shepherded into gussied-up brownstones and recently converted lofts, another street on Bedford-Stuyvesant's western or northern fronts would be digitally rechristened as part of a different neighborhood entirely. Bed-Stuy was a place that many Caucasians, aware of its reputation and history only from rap songs and television news crime reports, didn't want to live.

Bo and I never really became close the entire time I lived there, never stepped into each other's home; he nodded even when he was in a hurry and generally was happy to share an elongated anecdote in front of the building or outside the elevator, but wasn't interested in playing host or coming over to watch the game. He was an excellent talker, loquacious and descriptive, but he carried a sadness with him, a sense that he was witnessing a transformation he wasn't comfortable with. Bo was the first person I met who was actually from Bed-Stuy, who had grown up just a stone's throw away, and who was one of only a couple of black men I got to know on the block of "newly renovated lofts," the other being Mike Rolston, a filmmaker and electrician who lived down the hallway from Tony and me on the seventh floor and eventually moved into a houseboat on the Hudson River. He doesn't have to worry about being a gentrifier there.

Back then, the idea that an amorphous, systematic conspiracy concerning the geography of central Brooklyn was afoot seemed implausible. I wasn't deluded enough to think that lofts inhabited by kids with mysteriously inexhaustible checking accounts and spliff-smoking wannabe filmmakers had always existed on Taaffe Place, across the street from the Lafayette Houses and catercorner to the police station where

Spike Lee shot exteriors for the underrated Brooklyn hood/cop/ drug/redemption Harvey Keitel drama *Clockers* (that cop station rests on the Clinton Hill side of Classon Avenue, BTW), but what was wrong with them being here now? I didn't much think about it, and even if I did, I wouldn't have been able to articulate it.

My roommate spent increasingly more time inside our home with his bass, trying to attain perfect pitch by playing incredibly slow chord progressions over and over and over, to the great, unending annoyance of his roommate, who was trying to figure out how the hell to make a living. He suggested, in low mumbles over his cereal, that he was looking for a job, but the vulnerability that we had shared with each other in shards throughout our late boyhood, despite the tough, taciturn personae we also sometimes wore, began to disappear, replaced by an unrelenting sense that our selves lacked worth without vocation. There was never any specificity to his desire in those years, and for someone as driven as myself, I judged him, seeing it as a waste of his advantages. I tried to help in whatever small ways my underemployed self could, attempting to have him meet one person or another who worked at cool culture industry company X or Y.

Underneath our civility, however, I began to feel a slow, creeping desire to avoid him, to keep away the great silences that suddenly began to mar our time together. His subtle dominance of our living space, engendered by the two-thirds of our rent his parents were paying, floated just under the surface of our domestic unease, casting a terrible pall over our conversations. Everything that had once been easy between us became stilted, loaded, a dizzying vertigo that caused me to choose my words carefully and feel easily embarrassed—was I ashamed of the entry-level labor I was doing, work that Tony had the luxury to avoid? Not necessarily, but I began to feel that the world was not designed for us to have anything resembling equality of opportunity in our pursuits. I don't doubt that Tony knew this. He was, then and now, too wise not to, even if he doesn't see anything particularly wrong with that. One night, he came home drunk and, after a conversation about a Thomas Mann novel of outsized fortunes and destinies born into instead of made, he said, savagely, "Do you think it's any other way now?"

It shook me, that assertion, but of course he was right— regardless of the possibilities the wealthiest country in the history of the world provided for transcendence, his fortunes would be tied to, in no small part, his family wealth, just as mine would be tied to my own family's fortunes, ones that would not prove immune to the tumult the housing market was just beginning to undergo at that time. America was, we were discovering—regardless of the increasingly porous cultural divisions between high-, middle-, and lowbrow—no longer so good at class mobility. According to a study by Pablo Mitnik and David Grusky at Stanford's Center on Poverty and Inequality, "the amount of money one makes can be roughly predicted by how much money one's parents made, and that only gets truer as one moves along the earnings spectrum," claimed *The*

Atlantic in 2015. This seemed obvious to me a decade earlier. Tony's assertion that "It's their money" wasn't quite true in the America we lived in—when the rubber hit the road, the real advantages of familial wealth were ones that he was just beginning to experience, his debt-free $50,000-a-year college education being just the tip of the iceberg.

At first it really didn't seem possible that he would never get a job in the two years I lived there, or even so much as appear to be looking for one, eventually allowing the sheer fact of his effortless affluence to overwhelm our shared space and, in the end, our friendship. For one thing, I didn't think his parents would allow it. I saw the same looks of exasperation on their faces that Christmas holiday when they asked me about his job prospects as they had shown during the previous fall, when his mother came to New York for Tony's birthday and treated us to steak at Peter Luger. I would suggest, disingenuously but with unfailing faux sincerity whenever she would pull me aside, that he was working really hard to find a job. Making some reference to what a terrible job market it was for millennials would usually cinch it; Tony could leave in good stead yet again, free to play his bass or listen to soul records or sip Sapporos while reading Thomas Mann novels with a friend to vouch for his tough luck.

When I would see posts about internships at *The Village Voice* I would print them and give them to him or leave them on our kitchen table. They would sit there for days, unfussed at. Where was the good ol' boys' club when you needed it? Surely this intelligent young man, who read real literature and thought about things with seriousness, would find his way in the world. Regardless, such proximity to the advantages of time undisturbed by the pressure to earn, a luxury he had and I didn't, began to weigh heavily on me.

I continued to try to help him find work but I spent more time wishing I simply had the support to attempt to make meaningful art of my own. I had produced a short—poorly— late that winter, by the friend whom I was speaking to when I was mugged the summer before, but it hadn't gone well and I was increasingly relying on cheap anesthetization to put up with all the newfound stresses of adulthood in the unforgiving city. I found affordable weed (my drug of choice since a dangerous bout with acute liver failure in high school made alcohol anathema) wherever I could—in fact, I couldn't sleep without it. I'm not quite sure when I became so dependent; it more or less coincided with the onset of adulthood.

While collecting the mail from the lobby of my building, I noticed some very young brown children across the street. The boys wore white T-shirts and carried themselves in a way that suggested they were harder than they had any business being at their age. When I saw them conduct a transaction from the opposite sidewalk one afternoon later that summer, I had an inkling they carried. One day I worked up the gumption to approach one of them. "You got herb?" I asked gently as he sat on a nearby stoop. He eyed me hard, his irises green like mine, his skin a delicate caramel. He nodded and told me to call him Little G.

The boy couldn't have been more than thirteen. He was probably no younger than ten. I could never really tell and I was certainly too afraid to ask. He didn't say much, this young yellow child. I couldn't stop looking at him, probably in a way that made him slightly uncomfortable; he looked so much like me. It was as if I were scooping buds from a skinny younger brother of mine, one that as an only child I had never had. He was too young and inexperienced to know the danger he was constantly putting himself in, dealing nickels to loft-dwelling gentrifiers and bangers and desperate folks like me less than a hundred yards from a police precinct. Yet he took on the air of an experienced hustler, projecting an edgy confidence you knew was not hard-won but a mere pose, out of a desperate need to reject the fears that a childhood in the projects brings, let alone those known to affect the willful, abject criminal, servicing the desires of the emergent leisure class just to get over.

I was so relieved to meet someone who would sell me nickels; Little G remained my primary pot dealer for much of that year. I occasionally saw another guy named Clay, a Jewish teenager in a Yankees hat who spoke a thick, almost throw-back New Yorkese. In a year in which I swooned in and out of poverty despite my lush, subsidized-for-one-tenant-only pad, I was rarely able to justify the twenty dollars for his product. I'd known him for years, always walking his fluffy dog while he dealt; he lived with his mom in the Fifties, amid a row of elaborate old town houses and gleaming apartment buildings with red-coated doormen, just north of the United Nations headquarters on the far east side of Manhattan. I'd have to go there to score his product, which reserved it for outings that demanded Manhattan-quality headies.

Clay would meet me on the street, walking his dog the whole time as he spoke a mile a minute, slipping the pot into my jacket pocket while I retrieved a twenty-dollar bill. One time, while waiting for Clay on the sidewalk in the middle of a winter snowstorm, I ran into Gordon Parks, the revered African-American photographer and the first black man to direct a studio film, walking toward his home. I stopped him—we shared a birthday, after all—and quickly told him of my great admiration. "Thank you, young man," he said, but before he could ask me about myself or I could tell him about how we shared a birthday, Clay came barreling across the street and I had to end the conversation to settle my fix.

I worried about Little G, sure, and knew not how to process the marked immorality of buying drugs from a child this young, regardless of my poverty. The Ryan Gosling character from *Half Nelson*, a dope-addicted youth basketball coach and junior high school teacher, was a sorry one to identify with, but identify I did. He's genial, handsome, and reckless in all the same ways I aspired to be at the time. When he gets caught freebasing in a school bathroom by one of his players after a game, a twinge of guilt always touches my features. The movie, which won Gosling an Oscar nomination, climaxes with him in a seedy motel room buying drugs off that same youngster, played by the remarkable Shareeka Epps, who has been needled into the underworld by Anthony Mackie's pusher-with-a-conscience. I always thought a less charming but more honest actor would have made that character more ambiguous and potentially unlikable; regardless, I had the pervading sense we were in the same class of douche bag.

Little G, like most children his age, wasn't reliable, and caution didn't come easy to him. At first he refused to come up into the building to sell, afraid as he was of leaving a well-traversed street in broad daylight to be caught on camera in the confines of an empty hallway. I eventually convinced him the latter was a safer bet than his normal spots. He was frequently late and his weeks-long disappearances caused me to occasionally call one of the Mexican delivery services that ran through much of the city, the ones I swore off because of their less-than-stellar quality. Getting high on marijuana in Brooklyn in this era meant, without the capital to consistently afford the high end, indoor-grown delivery weed produced and sold by middle-class, mostly white New Yorkers in Manhattan and the nicer precincts of Brooklyn, that I was forced to choose between black juvenile delinquency or murderous Mexican cartels. Bad faith everywhere you looked.

Eventually I started going to an illegal speakeasy I was introduced to by some tatted-up girl I met outside of Sputnik, where a surer bet was to be found on a nightcap spliff. That night she took me to 729 Myrtle, where, behind a black security screen door and below a bank of discreet video cameras, was the door to Percy's, an unlicensed bar where one could watch the NBA playoffs and buy cocaine, bud, and spirits. It was the underground Cheers of Bedford-Stuyvesant. Most nights the crowd was relatively sparse, though on certain weekend late nights one could find a hundred cokeheads and sundry on-lookers in that illegal bar, the smell of crack wafting out of the bathrooms, trannies and johns and gangbangers all operating in harmony. Although I became something of a regular, I was always a bit terrified when I entered on the busier nights, as-suming in my infinite bad luck that I would be there when the place finally got raided.

Although upon entering one encountered a three-hundred-pound, thirty-something, hard-eyed black man standing by a bank of security monitors, Percy's was run by elderly Negroes who qualified for social security and seemed like odd, gentle survivors from the blaxploitation movies I had endlessly pon-tificated about to unsuspecting classmates in college. I bought weed from them regularly, especially a woman who would sit in the corner and squint until I leaned over and asked her for a twenty. Frank White, who had taken my job at the production company, went even more often than I did, the rare white reg-ular in that mostly brown milieu.

I thought often of Little G when I would see him hustling out on the street. I gradually stopped buying from him once I found Percy's, but would still see him wandering around the neighborhood from time to time, and witness his transactions with others in gloom, ruminating upon what few opportunities the child had. Was school a place where, as it was for me, the opportunity to learn and grow was made to seem commonplace for him? Did he have parents who went to PTA meetings and who read to him at night while he drifted off into Gulf War nightmares fueled by the CNN-fed triumphalism of the first Bush era? Did he see white people as his peers or his oppressors? Were there other plausible options for him, from his point of view, besides dealing dope before he could legally drive? Who took care of him in that ramshackle building across the street from my loft, near where he spent his days ducking in and out of the gentrifiers' lobbies, slinging bags in stairwells?

Little G faded away before I had the chance to figure it out. I stopped seeing him effortlessly roam the project courtyards, the ones my roommate always declined to cross, regardless of whether it was the quickest way to our apartment from the G train and despite the fact that the police station was always in view. A rumor of juvie caught wind among Little G's friends from the block. A brief sighting as I walked along the projects, north on Classon, cops across the street at the Eighty-eighth Precinct joking on the sidewalk behind me, made me think not. His eyes, green as mine, flashed toward me for a second, a wetness in them I'd never seen. I forced a smile, but G didn't return it. And then he was gone.

I HAD BY FAR A NICER APARTMENT THAN ANY OF MY friends and I was miserable whenever I was there. It felt like it was hardly mine at all even if half the furniture had come with me from home in a giant haul from one of my hoarder mother's troves of model-home-ready furnishings. The nicest items had been ordered from catalogs by Tony's mother; the sinewy South Asian rug, the coffee table Tony insisted we use coasters on, the elegant black bookshelves and dinner table, the green Danish couch that was ultimately broken at a party I held, while Tony was out of town, by a drunk woman, also from Cincinnati, whose body had come between us several New Year's Eves before.

Still, while underemployed and paying my own rent and eating the cheapest food I could muster, I too had something of a safety net. In an emergency, my mother could, and would, and did, in those less strident years, send me money, her staunch desire to see me grow independent of her out in the world giving way to a form of financial sympathy engendered by unconditional love. She sent me several thousand dollars that year, enough for me to make my rent many times when the till ran nearly dry. A shame in my heart, engendered by the help from home, lingered still. Depression would reign during these seasons, even as I thought, with a measure of unchecked optimism, that surely one day soon I would be able to make a living in the movies. It must have been even worse for Tony, who completely relied on such assistance from our earliest time together as postgraduates. But when I would glimpse an errant ATM receipt he'd leave on the countertop that separated our kitchen from the living room and see that he had $10,000 in his account following a $200 withdrawal, the difference in what constituted "assistance from home" for both of us became overwhelmingly apparent and my sympathy for him dried up.

As the year wore on, most of the free time I did have I passed smoking weed in my stairwell or Fort Greene Park, all in order to avoid the increasingly melancholic vibe of our apartment. For the bulk of that summer, I walked from Bed-Stuy to Manhattan's Chinatown, an hour away, in order to eat lunch. I couldn't afford subway fare, refused to ask my mother for (more) money that she wouldn't give me anyway, and Eldridge Street's Dumpling House was the only place I knew where I could eat a fully satisfying lunch for $1.75. I'd pass Pratt Institute and the increasingly gentrifying precincts of Fort Greene, where Spike Lee's old office, a converted firehouse, sits on the corner of the neighborhood's grand park. Sauntering past the Carol's Daughter outlet not far from it, I imagined I'd buy my mother, or a wife I'd have someday, body-care products when scurrying for a last-minute gift from the parkside residence I'd have one day. Turning toward the bridge once I reached Flatbush, sailing near Junior's and in the process encountering the smell of cheesecake wafting from the doors, the first pangs of exhaustion would set in—I was terribly out of shape back then; the poverty was always forcing me to settle for Kennedy Fried Chicken for dinner. I'd enter the colossus of Manhattan from its southeastern flank, seeing the towering city in front of me for the twenty minutes I'd spend walking over the Manhattan Bridge, B and D trains fluttering by. Once I descended into

Chinatown I'd go north on the Bowery, past the shop where I used to buy Chinese-region DVDs, soaking in Zhang Yimou's *Hero* and Wong Kar-wai's *2046* long before they were released stateside, and then I'd dart over to Eldridge Street on Grand, passing the pickup soccer games that take place on the pitches within the skinny park that separates Chrystie and Forsyth Streets between Houston and Canal. I ate at Dumpling House on many a summer weekday afternoon, at the lunch counter or on a nearby stoop, trying to figure out how to make a buck or two with a camera and always plotting another film, despite the obviously dire financial straits I was in.

Over time, signaled by the ways in which my roommate and I began to wear kid gloves around each other, neglecting to broach subjects that would summon his thinly veiled shame at being unequipped to find a job that he didn't feel was beneath him, we stopped hanging out at all. I would go weeks without talking to him, preferring solitude when I could find it in a loft in which you heard everything the other was doing regardless of the drywall. The reality of our disconnection became an altogether undeniable force in our lives, as we grew too far apart to spend nearly any comfortable time together. I would often stay in Harlem at our childhood friend Ray's roach-infested home or with a film school buddy, a tall, rail-thin, and devastatingly intelligent gay Jew named Jimmy who lived in the spare room of an elderly couple on the Upper West Side. He turned tricks on Craigslist for kicks and spare dollars when we weren't kvetching about some film or album we found unworthy, two kids who had hardly made a thing. Whatever I could do to absent myself from my "Clinton Hill" apartment, I would.

Tony and I never once admitted to each other that we lived in an overpriced *Bedford-Stuyvesant* loft, one that was slowly choking away my solvency and our friendship. And I never once admitted, to him or to myself at the time, that despite all this, I loved my roommate, so much. I'd never had a brother, and over a decade he had become one to me. I didn't want to move out. So I kept borrowing money on credit cards and deferring my student loans. "But now you enter the world a poor Negro for the first time in your life" wasn't quite true, but lifelines from home were not, unlike Tony's, seemingly unlimited.

Neither was my shame. In the '90s, just as my interest in indie film was emerging right along with my mother's career in real estate development, she would ask me how much I'd need to make a first film. Even in high school, I was savvy enough to say $200,000. She said she'd get it for me; my mother's prescience didn't extend to the lean times that would emerge in the housing market in which she planned on making a fortune, times that would permanently shelve that promise. I'm sure she thought, given how everything was growing in those halcyon days of centrist liberalism and cheap debt, that by the time I came of age and transformed my teenage dreams into the legitimate ambitions of a grown man, helping me raise such a sum wouldn't be difficult.

Acknowledging several realities, not just about geography and history but relative privilege and shared values, was impossible for me to avoid in the long run, but in my unwillingness to confront the obvious at the time, my inability to work up enough gumption to say to my friend, "Look, I'm drowning. Either we find a cheaper place to live, or help me with my rent. I know you can," I inadvertently doomed any chance of mutual recognition on our part, of the love I had for him growing into the type of friendship I had always imagined for us, gruff old cats like Morgan Freeman and Clint Eastwood in *Unforgiven*, one of our favorite movies, telling ghost-laden stories about the past for a laugh and a sigh.

At the nadir of my postproduction-company-job scouring during the final months with Tony, I had been an overnight production assistant on the first season of *I Want to Work for Diddy*. My whole job was to stay up all night, in the control room of an unfinished set that was being constructed on the fourth story of a large, ex-industrial building on Duane Street, of which the production had reserved three floors just to stage lights and crafty, wardrobe, and production. The sheer amount of money that went in service of this flimsy and tasteless premise could have funded dozens of indie films, I was sure. It paid me $100 a day to stay up all night and eat snacks. Situated in Tribeca, only a few blocks from where the production company office still was, I'd sneak off to the offices of my former employer and nap on the couch not far from what used to be my desk until dawn came and the possibility of being discovered posed a threat. The one time Sean Combs did visit the set during my stint there, a gleeful panic rose through the entire six-story

Tribeca edifice in such a profoundly silly way as to suggest the Christian rapture had dawned on a sect of Satanists.

In the fall of 2007, I temporarily moved out of 227–241 Taaffe Place. Tony and I had a lease, so we moved someone in to sublet while I traveled, but at the time I had no real intention of coming back. I spent a couple of months in Ohio, writing cold pitches to indie film production companies about a movie I wanted to make in Cincinnati, before heading to Martha's Vineyard, where my aunt had a home and I thought I'd write a *Manchurian Candidate*–esque thriller set in a future America where war with Iran is imminent and climate change is out of control. When I arrived back in New York just after Thanksgiving, it was to live in Ocean Hill, east of Bed-Stuy, with a film school classmate, his boyfriend, and their leggy, somewhat unhinged performance artist roommate from Florida. Eventually I moved back to 227–241 Taaffe in early 2008, shortly after Obama won the Iowa caucuses.

Tony and I tried again, but the same baggage was there and I couldn't keep paying $800 a month; it had been over a year since I had stopped getting paid by the production company, and although I was taking on more writing jobs, writing online dispatches from film festivals for *Filmmaker* magazine and *Variety* and applying for grants feverishly, I had yet to consistently replace the income. Still, as soon as I moved back in, I spent about $1,200, mostly on credit, making a new short film, an adaptation of a couple of Jonathan Lethem short stories that he was encouraging people to option for free. It was about a couple who speak in metaphors to each other about biospheres being interjected with new elements instead of having the more frank conversation about infidelity that they are avoiding. It wasn't very good, that film, but it was a strange monument to where I had lived and what had happened to me there. I fled shortly after making it, telling him of my plans only days before, as our communication had grown nonexistent. He didn't help me move out—sitting in his room petulantly and listening to the sounds of furniture being pushed or hauled—as our place in each other's life came to an end.

Would it have mattered if we'd known we were in Bed-Stuy? I don't know. It might not have meant much to me then. But "Clinton Hill" was bullshit, so I thought, and Bed-Stuy was a place of black history. Somewhere in that painful time I was beginning to understand that where I lived had an importance beyond what I had previously grasped, one that my relationship with Tony, and our very presence in the space, potentially threatened. When I see Tony on the street now, coming out of a soul food joint on Nostrand or on the opposite side of an F train car, I avoid him. It's too much to bear, the burden of what Bedford-Stuyvesant revealed about us that we dare not speak of.

551 KOSCIUSZKO STREET

When the great recession hit, in the fall of 2008, I was living at 551 Kosciuszko Street, between Malcolm X and Stuyvesant, just a block and a half south of the Bushwick border. My new digs were located in one of the poorest zip codes in the borough. Much of the neighborhood was dominated by a series of decaying row houses and brick walk-ups filled with immigrants from the western hemisphere's most impoverished countries. I had moved into the four-bedroom town house at the behest of my hard-drinking, New Hampshire–born lighting technician friend—M&M—who had lived with me four summers earlier at 166 Throop. We were talking about "hope" back then, but by the summer before Obama was elected, M&M, who showed promise as an experimental filmmaker in his youth, had given up on making art of his own, having taken on the blue-collar persona of a set electrician. A man who smiled at the mention of twelve-hour turnarounds and dreamed of joining the IATSE Local 52 film and theater technicians union, aesthetics didn't mean much to him in and of themselves anymore. The sausage making that went into finding someone to believe in and pay for your work wasn't for him either. The movies will do that to you, break a working-class kid's heart.

We lived together among an assortment of other clowns from various stages of our lives, throwing raging BBQs and endless poker nights, hosting young actresses for brunch and young actors for opioids and beer. It cost half of what I'd paid in "Clinton Hill," and, when it was good, I was having double the fun. My apartment no longer took on the air of a mausoleum. The constant, unspoken, low-simmering antagonism that had taken hold of me and my old friend from Cincinnati no longer existed. Now I paid $450 for a basement room with a view into a crummy, rock-strewn backyard and tiny carport. I was content with what my poverty could provide at the time.

A significant contingent of the folks M&M knew in the neighborhood were refugees from post-Katrina New Orleans, crust punk street kids in their early twenties who played brass in renegade Second Line bands, had smelly dogs, and came from broken, impoverished homes. M&M was hosting several of them when I arrived with my truck full of furniture on an early June day. It was a musty space, one a lover of mine would later describe as a place "with dirt on every surface." A hole had been smashed at about eye level through the drywall on the stairwell landing, the wall darkened and fraying along the half wall that separated the stairwell from the galley kitchen. Sweeping clearly wasn't much of a priority. The living room ashtray, a large marble affair stationed on a rotting wooden table that was surrounded by well-worn couches, was beyond full and leaking butts.

When I first descended the stairs into the basement where I was renting a room, I immediately came upon a couple lying in a bed under the stairwell, fucking. One of them was the sister of a friend of mine from college. I watched her for a moment, mouth agape, before they noticed me. We both said hi sheepishly, flush with our mutual embarrassment and mild awe. She and her lover—one of the gutter punks, who had a large dog, and a sweet nature, and would be a frequent guest—got decent hastily.

There was another couple sleeping in my room when I arrived, but they, too, dressed and removed themselves, although they didn't take the filth on the floor with them. I stripped a putrid rug, a thin black affair that was encrusted in grime, swept and mopped the floor. The place had the sensibility of a flophouse but I was, in my youthful naïveté, determined to change that. I remember embracing M&M shortly after I arrived, smiling, and saying, "We'll class the joint up," in my most arrogant of tones. My assumption was that it would be effortless.

My room was right next to that belonging to M&M, who bathed sparingly and smoked indoors often. His was an irritable odor of body funk and unwashed clothing, one that often

97

emanated from his room even when he wasn't around. After a Latin punk rocker who lived in one of the two bedrooms on the first floor moved out under duress, another friend from film school, a chain-smoking, cardigan-wearing Italian-American animator named Kevin, moved in upstairs. Liam, tall, morose, and seemingly both too mature and self-contained for this kind of living arrangement, was next to Kevin in the largest bedroom, the one that had a back entrance leading into the small, weed-strewn yard that my bedroom window looked out on.

Liam was the oldest of us and the longest-standing roommate. He seemed wary of me at first, but soon I learned that this was his way with almost everyone. Over time his presence grew more gregarious and less frequent; he'd stay at his girlfriend's place for weeks at a time. I had a girlfriend too, a dancer I had met while at SUNY Purchase whom I'd kept running into near our mutual subway stop at Classon Avenue, but by the end of my first summer there we had both cheated on each other and were mutually moving in opposite directions. It was the last relatively sanguine breakup I've had, no hurled words or trembling days—besides, I'd moved into a bachelor pad and planned to embrace it.

Or so I thought. That summer, despite the newfound social possibilities, was filled with lonely afternoons. M&M's friends in these parts, save some of the neighborhood kids he spoke to on the stoop, were uniformly Caucasian, but they were also among the working poor and blended into the neighborhood somewhat seamlessly. Most of the people I was beginning to

know in the filmmaking community, the hotshot young producers and directors who went to NYU or Columbia for $150,000
but had no student debt to keep them tethered to creativity-
sapping jobs, still found Bedford-Stuyvesant foreign and dangerous. "Discovered a surefire way to make sure people don't
come hang out with you (even when they say they will)—move
to Bed-Stuy," I wrote on my Facebook page late that June.

The local hangout of choice among our crew was Goodbye
Blue Monday, on Broadway, underneath the J train. A dark,
high-ceilinged affair busy with trinkets, scavenged streetlights,
and paintings of gospel choirs in mid-performance, the bar had
a gonzo vibe. I was still teetotaling nearly a decade after my
bout with liver disease, but the GBM backyard, which had the
feel of an active auto garage and a shantytown at the same time,
was 420-friendly when the crowd was sparse. The cheap beer
and sangria, the only beverages available since it never got a
full liquor license, made enough for Goodbye Blue Monday to
keep the lights on and keep the rent paid. The owner, Steve, a
diminutive, middle-aged hipster with long, graying hair he kept
in a ponytail, usually pottered around with both a dour expression and a pit bull in tow. He had opened it as a DIY music
venue that would be easy to book and entice all sorts of characters with, from random crusts to Steve Buscemi, who once
broke up a fight there while catching a set by his son's band.

M&M was a regular, drinking his off days away in those
dark environs when he wasn't taking shifts at the bar itself. Our
whole social orbit gravitated around the place, with friends

from college often drifting through, especially during the summers, when the venue would host daylong parties with dozens of bands, several active DIY grills, and, pre-Tinder, copious possibilities for the random hookup. Deals were easy to come by: Vernon, the boyfriend of my cinematographer from college, bartended there, as did a tall transgender Negro named Reginald. Gifted musicians in their own right, they performed in a band called the Marionettes of Satan. Its reputation steadily grew—by the time I began to go there regularly in those early Obama years, their legend had already been hatched well enough that the New Year's 2008–2009 party they threw was picked by *The Village Voice* as the can't-miss, deep-Brooklyn post-ball-drop freakout of the evening. It was the fourth or fifth party my friends and I went to, long after 2009 had been officially brought in, and the Marionettes were still putting on a remarkable noise show well past 2:00 a.m., with Vernon dancing about rhythmically, intermittently covered by a cape delicately tended to by several women, body pulsating like a punk James Brown. Reginald, who had a greasy seductiveness about him, his heavily processed hair swooshing this way and that, proved to be the ultimate utility infielder for the space, on nights like this tending bar one minute and on stage pounding a keyboard the next.

Having lived in Brooklyn for several years now, I couldn't have made more than 150 percent of my rent the whole time. Learning to live cheaply and simply was essential. At a greasy-spoon Dominican restaurant on Malcolm X, just a block and a half away, one could get an entire serving of rice, beans, and chicken for $2.50. At Seven Flags, a Jamaican restaurant on DeKalb near its intersection with Malcolm X, a whole meal of oxtail, plantains, rice, and stew peas cost just $5. The proprietor, a skinny man in his forties named Wilson, was a gregarious dreamer. He always talked about how he planned to renovate the place and open up the backyard space for eating and dancing. When he needed the help, in the restaurant's halcyon days prerecession, he hired not just West Indians but many of the early adopting hipsters, gutter punks and true bohemians and pot dealers, such as Emilia, a green-eyed, gravel-voiced young woman who was one of my many bud dealers for a time.

It was only just beginning to dawn on me, in the wake of a record number of daily and weekly film critic firings at major newspapers and magazines, which began in 2006 and hadn't let up two summers later, that film journalism might not be much of a career either. I thought I'd acquitted myself well enough while traveling to film festivals and interviewing directors for magazines like *Variety* and *Filmmaker*, reviewing films for long-defunct or mostly forgotten blogs like *Spout* and *Hammer to Nail*. Yet I could hardly earn rent anywhere in Brooklyn primarily writing $50- and $100-a-movie reviews, going to festivals for one $100 blog post where I would easily spend $200 in a week just eating.

My spare time that summer went into editing the short film based on the Jonathan Lethem short stories, which I'd shot in my last months with Tony. My resistance against venturing out into the straight world for a non-film-industry job held strong despite my persistent poverty; the only compromises I would cotton to at the time were teaching jobs related to film, feeling certain that were I to begin down another path, I would quickly get trapped making money and being comfortable instead of making art. That summer, I reluctantly went back to film education briefly, teaching a course in the basics of production for underprivileged black and Latin kids in the Bronx.

I liked the work, and teaching media literacy and production skills to young people of color who were more likely to be shamed or erased in motion pictures than the children I had taught two summers before in Long Island felt relevant and worthwhile. The programming aspect of the job was the most interesting, choosing which films to show them and why. Interesting guests whom I had met going to festivals—the Oscar-nominated director Benh Zeitlin, then a nearly crippled short-film maker, was among them—would drop by to chat and share their work. But it didn't last long. On the very first assignment, one of the children lost a camera and the administrators at the DreamYard ACTION Center put the kibosh on my curriculum. After I was told I wouldn't be allowed to have the kids take the cameras into their own communities and film themselves and their lives, I quit in a huff; what's the point of trying to train young people to represent themselves and their communities cinematically if they can't venture out into the spaces that make them who they are? Immature and restless, I had abandoned the kids, the type of brown folks I told myself

I was out here to pay it forward to, as quickly and efficiently as I had fled Tony just months before. The betrayal was real and it wasn't my last.

After DreamYard I had taken two film-producing jobs in short order. Both paid little, but enough in combination with some festival prize money and a couple of journalism jobs to pay my rent. One of them, Judy Adler's *New Media*, played at Sundance, and the other, Eric Juhola's *Nowhere Kids*, at Tribeca, but both experiences ended somewhat acrimoniously. I wasn't along for the festival ride for either, my name relegated to the "special thanks" on the Sundance title; I was fired after the other producer, who had attended Columbia University's graduate film school with the director, lost the keys to the fifteen-passenger van we were using for the shoot and threw me under the bus for it. I had so neglected *Nowhere Kids* in the midst of the other production that, even after all the prep and casting work I had done, I was told I wasn't needed anymore.

My proximity to what I perceived as "success" in indie film kept me going, even as the setbacks piled up. Hadn't I just had a film in Park City? When I went home to face those who raised me, I would bore them to death with my tales of the filmmaker's plight, always hustling, begging for money. They perked up when I would relate stories of encountering the rich and famous, feeling like they were getting a peek behind the curtain that separates celebrities from the rest of us. I would regale them with tales of nervously approaching Actor X after a National Board of Review screening or Director Y at the

Magnolia Pictures Christmas party. My favorite was encountering Spike Lee after the screening of *Miracle at St. Anna*. "Hey,
Spike, where'd you find that T-shirt you wore to the Democratic
Convention, the one with Obama dunking?" I asked him, genuinely curious. I had caught a glimpse of him on MSNBC during
one of the afternoons of nonstop coverage I would consume
ad nauseam now that I lived somewhere with cable TV. The
shirt he'd worn, when interviewed by one fetching flake or another, depicted a soaring, Jordanesque Barack Obama, wearing
a U.S.A. basketball jersey, mid-dunk on a hapless, suit-wearing
John McCain. "If I had a nickel for every time someone asked
me that, I'd be a rich man," Lee, who already appeared to be a
rich man, told me, before hastily giving me the e-mail address
of someone from a company called Undrcrwn. "Tell them I sent
you," he instructed, before departing our conversation without
another word.

AS SUMMER WENT DOWN AND FALL CREPT IN, THE EN-
tire apparatus of American wealth was threatened by the
bundling and selling of less-than-savory mortgages as collat-
eralized debt. We turned on the TV early that fall, staring into
the apocalyptic gloom that came over the pale, makeup-covered
faces of the anchors for FOX News and CNBC with something
approaching glee. Bailouts for unaccountable financial institutions was the order of the day, but talk of helping "Main Street"
was constant. We wondered, but what of Malcolm X Boulevard

and Stuyvesant Avenue? The kids I encountered in my new corner of the neighborhood had never known any of this prosperity
the television told us was slipping away from normal folks as
the Dow Jones plummeted. The gap between the people bringing us this news and the people receiving it couldn't have been
starker. Schadenfreude is a powerful emotion, common among
those with nothing, and we could have bottled it by the liter
early that fall.

We'd been raised on *Fight Club* and Howard Zinn, all of
us, M&M, Kevin, Liam, and I, and saw strange dignity, if not a
poetic justice, in the potential collapse of capitalist institutions.
Now it was real—every day the hole seemed to get bigger as
the NASDAQ continued to tank. The brinksmanship of Bush's
Republican Congress initially refusing to prop up the banks
they'd let run amok—along with an antiregulation Democratic
president in the go-go '90s—seemed deeply irresponsible to all
of us, even if we liked to watch Rome burn. The economic abyss
of a major depression, like the one our grandparents had lived
through, was intangible to us, but we were egging it on. At least
we'd have something worth living through. Anyway, Obama
was right around the corner, ready to save the day. In those
heady days of 2008, the promise of Barack was irresistible.

Just as so many African Americans did, I identified with the
Democratic nominee for president in a more visceral way than
most of the electorate. He had been, like many young people of
my political persuasion, enraged and embittered by the Bush
presidency. At an antiwar rally in Chicago in October 2002, he

said, "I am opposed to the cynical attempt by Richard Perle and Paul Wolfowitz and other armchair, weekend warriors in this administration to shove their own ideological agendas down our throats, irrespective of the costs in lives lost and in hardships borne," in reference to the forthcoming Iraq War. Here was a man who was on the same side as me, who perhaps hadn't been standing next to a burning effigy of George W. Bush, protesting the war in D.C.'s Farragut Square as I had during the fall of 2002, but he at least understood why I might have been standing there, putting my liberty on the line for what I believed. Unable to say the same about nearly any candidate I had ever encountered, he represented Change I Could Believe In.

Although Obama didn't necessarily seem perturbed by the military-industrial complex and wasn't much interested in single-payer health care, he preached a commitment to transparency and exuded a searching intelligence that excited me. Not surprisingly, for many black folks I encountered, Obama's policies were of little import. They just liked that he was one of us. Or at least looked like one of us. He was a tabula rasa that way; in Obama, whites had a seemingly "transcendent" figure onto which they could project their best intentions, liberal desires for a sleek, multicultural, postracial America, while blacks could be happy that we were finally gonna have a nigga up in the White House running the show. I drank the Kool-Aid like everyone else, going door to door for him in Cincinnati, working phone banks, sharing cookies and pie with old ladies at Ohio for Obama HQ. I thought we were doing something special. I thought we would indelibly change America. I was still thinking magically.

SHORTLY AFTER OBAMA WAS ELECTED, I SIGNED UP FOR food stamps, now known as the Supplemental Nutrition Assistance Program. The mordant-looking, mostly windowless five-story brick structure at 500 DeKalb Avenue would have been at home in 1970s Minsk. It was a stone's throw from our old loft on Taaffe Place.

I waited among the multiple strollers, pushed by either Hasidic women or blacks from various Caribbean nations, a few slumming hipsters in beat-up New Balances, a few tatted-up Crips in throwback Brooklyn Dodgers hats, and then the polo-wearing men with unshakably weary faces, faces that had seen two- and three-hour waits at 500 DeKalb many times. This collection of diverse human misery and mundane suffering was mostly muted by the white cinder-block walls and the seemingly sterile, almost clinical quality of the building, but occasionally an eruption of emotion, usually over denied benefits due to a lost wages report or a botched falsification of income, jolted us all back into consciousness, away from our private tales of trying and failing to make it in a new, winner-take-all America.

As 2009 began, there was a dizzying polarity between the social capital granted me by independent film and my dire economic straits. After receiving admittance to a training program for young film critics sponsored by the International Film Festival Rotterdam, I traveled to a major foreign festival for the first time, beholding a world of movies that remains behind a veil for most nominally cinema-savvy Americans. Fed a steady diet of our own parochial fever dreams in an unending and brutal loop of electronic propaganda from which few escape, it was refreshing to feel like I was glimpsing the world of cinema I had been told, when I was sitting in my film school reviews, would make a place for me, being assured by humble white people, failed artists themselves (they were teaching, after all), that I would be one of the lucky ones.

Yet the clock eventually always struck midnight on my festival trips and my luxury carriage, now a pumpkin, always found its way back to Bed-Stuy, usually in some sort of financial desperation, even if I wasn't paying for the trips. The money from the 800-word Web pieces usually didn't cover my travel and dining expenses while in those pricey locales, so I spent many a night scouring the hallways of five-star hotels, looking for half-eaten room service meals I could pilfer. It was no way to keep paying the rent in Bed-Stuy, wherever I lived in the neighborhood; Jimmy McMillan hadn't run for mayor yet, but I already knew the rent was too damn high.

I would spend afternoons having "lunch" on the pool deck of SoHo House with Lena Dunham and Jaime, a friend from Cincinnati who lived in SoHo and made the *Forbes* "30 Under 30" entrepreneur list for her personal chef staffing and cookbook enterprises, wondering if I could pay for anything besides celery sticks. We'd gawk at Rod Stewart's harem of possibly eighteen-year-old girls a few couches away, then I'd scrounge for change to get back to Brooklyn on the A train. At the Tribeca pastry shop Pécan, where Lena and I liked to go to talk about making $25,000 movies or a piece she wanted to write for my criticism blog, the *Cinema Echo Chamber*—her first published postcollegiate writing appeared there—I established something resembling a line of credit with a sympathetic employee. It created a dissonance, a twenty-first-century double consciousness, interviewing the French auteur Olivier Assayas about his newest film in a lofty Central Park West hotel room before schlumping back to the ghetto with my food stamp card to poach for deals at the only organic market that existed at the Bushwick/Bed-Stuy nexus at the time, Mr. Kiwi's.

The Korean-owned grocery was just beneath the Market Hotel, then an illegal concert venue that, until it was shut down and subsequently reopened as an aboveboard operation, was the premier place to see the slightly bigger acts, from Bishop Allen to Willis Earl Beal, who were still into DIY spaces but not slumming it at Goodbye Blue Monday. The field adjacent to the building that contained both spaces was used one night early the next summer for a concert by Dan Deacon. He'd come a long way since throwing parties in his G Street condo on the Purchase campus a decade before. It was then that I thought I knew the dam had broken and the hipsters had taken Bed-Stuy.

Three years after leaving school, and I hadn't even made my first feature. My own sense of entitlement made me feel like this was some kind of moral failure, that I was listing, but my peers were still encouraging me to soldier on, Lena especially. "Saw your peep show screened tonite at the jane hotel and it was AMAZING. i think my favorite of them all," she remarked to me in an e-mail that July, after our friend Ry Russo-Young, who had starred in my Lethem short and went on to direct a movie, *Nobody Walks*, that Lena cowrote, had shown Lena a short of hers that I had appeared in, fully naked. "i'm so sry to hear about dicey financial times/stresses. i really relate—money is so tight these days, one canceled day of work and i'm way over my head. you're such a resourceful dude, and so talented, that I don't worry for you in the long run :) but i do know how exhausting it is now."

I spent the summer of 2009 trying and failing to finance movies. A couple of features I had lined up to produce fell through; we couldn't find the money for them and the directors wanted to move on to something else. The short I had made the previous summer wasn't getting into the same festivals *Evangeleo* had. Meanwhile, my friends from my trip to Slamdance— like the brothers Josh and Benny Safdie or Lena—were going on to their second features. Children of privilege who also happened to be very talented, they were more easily able to navigate the financing aspect of independent movies than I. "Indie film is a rich kids' game," a rich kid had told me at my summer film camp, way back in high school. His often-absent dad had produced Michael Bay's *Armageddon* and occasionally stuffed $1,000 in his son's boots. My dad was often absent too, but he'd never even allowed me to borrow $100, let alone given me $1,000.

Any hope of receiving even a modicum of this kind of support in adulthood was put to rest by the housing crisis. It had engulfed my mother's savings and business, as well as the black middle class as a whole. My father's financial prospects had come to ruin a decade before, after his janitorial firm lost a key contract, but neither I nor she could have imagined how home-building for the black middle class would disappear overnight for reasons that remained mysterious and unyielding. The idyll of prosperity that was my mother's subdivision, sitting amid malaise-ridden, postindustrial central Cincinnati neighborhoods, was beginning to show its cracks. No financial help from home would ever be forthcoming again. No first feature was creeping out of any checkbook from my relatives either, all of whom found my work both interesting and odd.

AS 2009 WORE ON IT SEEMED THE GREAT RECESSION would neither morph into a great depression nor end anytime soon. 551 Kosciuszko grew a bit more ramshackle, entropy allowing it to revert back to its messy, grease- and dust-ridden self. M&M increasingly invited half a dozen of his musty friends from New Orleans to stay at our place for weeks at a time. I was never sure if the odor was from their unshowered bodies or their equally rancid dogs. Liam moved out in protest late that summer, and Milton, a middle-class Jew from

Michigan who was the only McCain voter I knew in Bed-Stuy, replaced him.

The need to save money was ever more paramount, which meant that once again I was in search of ever-cheaper weed. I began buying nickels from some of the teenage Haitian or Dominican boys I'd see around our hood. Eventually a lanky, gold-grilled, thirtyish black dealer named G, who lived around the corner on Pulaski with his two kids and Spanish wife, became my primary means of acquiring bud—he sold a nickel bag that one could roll three spliffs from, despite the numerous seeds one might find in his low-quality schwag. He was a good man to know in the neighborhood.

G was from South Carolina. He had fled poverty there, but had not acquired many skills besides dope dealing to lift him out of it. He was popular on his end of Pulaski Street, where he'd often play basketball with other young hustlers from his block, with a rickety hoop stationed at the edge of the street in front of a fire hydrant. I'd frequently spy him walking his children home from P.S. 48 a few blocks away; he'd routinely buy an empanada or a grape soda for the youngsters at the bodega on the corner of Stuyvesant and Pulaski on their route, beaming at the youngsters. G loved his kids and was neatly tied into the fabric of the neighborhood, a trusted figure among many people. These folks were just hanging on in conditions many would refer to as grim, but where they took some warmth and comfort in community.

G didn't have a cell phone that worked consistently, so more often than not I would go looking for him in his building, where the front door was usually open. The putrid stairwell leading up to his third-floor apartment was infested with rotting wood and fast-food detritus. Usually I would find him in his apartment, playing video games or watching football. Sometimes, when he wasn't around, Patty, a light brown woman who lived on the first floor, her shock of thinning white hair premature for being so early in middle age, would sell to me instead.

I had been introduced to him by PJ, a charismatic Haitian teenager who lived with his mother and younger brothers in a squalid apartment across the street. Crackheads lived in the basement apartment beneath PJ and his family. I'd spy them from my window sweeping the sidewalk or taking out the trash gingerly each dawn before their morning beer, leering at one another and the new day outside in that serene, docile way they seem to have when they aren't screaming their heads off. From my window I once watched PJ, who couldn't have been much older than eighteen when I met him, dropkick one of them, as I entertained a friend from college.

Despite his ability to end a fight with decisive violence, PJ was an infectious lightning rod of activity and good humor. He would watch football with M&M and me on Sundays, bouncing in and out of our always-open door and the bustling street that awaited him. Frequently looking for work in security or maintenance jobs that just didn't exist, we tried to employ him with occasional jobs as best we could. Liam would occasionally find some more consistent employment for him, painting or doing manual labor of some sort. We all sensed he would need some help staying out of trouble. But being a runner for the tatted-up white girls that lived across the street flipping weed was the most stable job he could keep.

PJ had two younger brothers, Roger and Pierre, and they became regulars in our home as well. Neither of them could have been older than twelve. In the absence of their father, who by all accounts was still in Haiti, PJ, at nineteen unemployed and with a child of his own, was the only male authority figure those boys had. One day early that fall, PJ was nowhere to be seen. Even his younger brothers, who idolized him, had no idea where he was. Several days later, the rumors had been confirmed true: PJ was in lockup.

A whisper campaign of who-knew-what began concerning PJ. Word spread that he and another boy had mugged a white man, tasing him while he was on the ground. Many said PJ had been put up to the mugging by his friend Grimy, slightly older, to whom the police Taser "belonged." When Liam visited him in lockup, PJ claimed he hadn't tased anyone; his friend was the sole assailant of a drunk kid, one who didn't have any money on him when they accosted him. Feeling threatened, he agreed to go to a laundromat on Broadway between Kosciuszko and Lafayette and fetch some money from the ATM. PJ, in the altercation, had lost his cell phone. After getting the money, the man was kind or scared enough, likely both, to walk back to where they had tased him and call PJ's phone. The young Haitian hadn't played out the consequences of that request in his mind beforehand, but was still given an opportunity to weasel out of his comeuppance. "He was like, if you get me some weed, I'll forget all about this," PJ said. PJ and Grimy took the money and promised to bring him back a nickel bag, but they never did. The man gave PJ's number to the cops and the rest was history.

Two years of his life snatched away, for forty dollars. When he went to jail after assaulting the drunk white kid, a pall came over our section of Kosciuszko Street. Kevin took it upon himself to babysit PJ's two younger brothers, and a new responsibility fell on our decrepit bachelor pad. Roger and Pierre's mother—a short, stout woman who spoke little English, and would often leave her sons out in the freezing cold while she prayed at the nearby French-language church—refused to give them keys to their building. They needed someone to look after them. By the end of 2009, the boys became a seemingly inextricable part of our lives. Kevin, from a prominent grocery family from Chappaqua, who smoked rolled cigarettes and wore the same uniform of blue cardigans and wingtips every day, had settled into the life of the mostly poor West Indians in the neighborhood with a grace among the lowly I rarely glimpsed in white people who came from means. He took a special interest in the boys, spending inordinate amounts of time with them. I would return home from work to find the tiny Haitians watching television with Kevin or standing around one of M&M's frequent low-stakes poker games. If no one was home, they would wait patiently on the stoop across the street for either one of us or their mother to arrive. This occurred through a sort of osmosis, as little by little they began to rely on Kevin and me for after-school care and meals, help with their homework, and late-night shelter during the evenings when their mother wouldn't return until after midnight from the storefront church up the street. I never spoke to her more than two or three times during that whole year and change while her boys were such fixtures at our place. She never said "thank you," and I never asked her why she raised them the way she did. It was clear that she had had an experience of poverty, and a desire to transcend it through the Lord, if not through responsibility to her children, that I couldn't grasp with my all-too-finite empathy.

FORECLOSURES POPPED UP ALL OVER OUR END OF THE neighborhood during the first full winter of the Obama presidency. In the stretches of Bed-Stuy where I lived, it didn't so much matter that we were already more than a year into a recession. The economy was already wrecked before. What's the point of a recession if there is little economy to recess? The bodega and Dominican food joints and hair salons were all still going to make their money. People held no illusions—the rich would recover and the already vulnerable wouldn't. The conniving speculators who bet against the very financial products they created—instruments that had driven so many people, especially in our neighborhood, into subprime mortgages that they didn't require—would not go to jail.

The majority of black home owners steered into subprime

loans in the Bush years qualified for better loans, but weren't offered them by predatory banks. The ongoing American legislative and commercial impulse to keep Negroes poor and lumped together had inspired redlining, the practice by which investors in these same black postwar neighborhoods were ineligible for FHA-secured loans. This new tactic, where banks use fancy marketing campaigns to seek out low-information home investors, in neighborhoods where it had previously been impossible to get a loan from a major financial institution, and offer them loans with high-baseline interest rates that shoot up even higher with just one missed repayment deadline, is referred to as reverse redlining. This is what Bush's "ownership society" wrought in our corner of Brooklyn, a generation of aspiring black home owners whose dreams were left in tatters. Our home was not immune.

The rapper Lil' Kim's younger brother Bo was my third Bed-Stuy landlord. I was always meeting Bos and Gs back then. By 2010, this Bo found himself significantly underwater. We were served with eviction papers somewhat routinely starting in the fall of 2009, always accompanied by Bo's easygoing assurances that his lawyers were "handling it." I noticed the mid-six-figure number the bank claimed he owed them and thought there was no surer sign the country had lost its collective mind than the idea that this crumbling home was worth that much to anyone. Especially, I'd think (in bad faith, I knew), in this neighborhood.

Shortly after we received yet another eviction notice, early in the spring of 2010, the calamities at 551 Kosciuszko started to pile up. I was constantly ill in those last few months; at one point, I spent an entire month and a half thinking I had Lou Gehrig's disease. My neurologist bills piled up in short order. When Lena won South by Southwest with her second feature, *Tiny Furniture*, I texted her congrats from my room, in between trips to the bathroom with an irritable bowel brought on by a ten-day cleanse I had been on, hoping to rid myself of ALS; the saltwater colon flush portion of it wasn't going so hot. "Thanks, Brandon!" she texted late that night, from the first few hours of her new life as a darling of the indie film world, and soon-to-be New York celebrity the likes of which our generation had yet to produce. It was the last text she ever sent me.

A few weeks later the entire basement flooded, allegedly because our upstairs neighbor had fallen asleep while trying to thaw a frozen piece of meat in hot running water. The rugs my mother had given me, in much more hopeful times when I first moved to Taaffe Place, were destroyed, as were the fabric-bound sofa chairs and my printer, which rested on the floor near my desk. This happened just after the house had been robbed while I was away at a festival in Poland. When I returned, dozens of my DVDs had been taken, along with several hundred dollars belonging to Amelia, the redhead punk rock chick from across the street who was now crashing in M&M's room while he was away on a film shoot. She had left the door unlocked, disobeying house protocol, and a band of kids, likely led by Roger and Pierre, had left the place in shambles.

We were devastated. Very quickly the children stopped coming around, disappearing from our lives in short order. They'd avoid me when I saw them on the street. When approached by Kevin about what happened, Roger grew taciturn and claimed he didn't know anything. Before their brother PJ was released from jail, the family moved out of the dilapidated building across the street. I have not seen or heard from them since.

M&M planned to move Amelia in permanently when Milton decided to move in with his girlfriend. After spending the better part of the year in New Orleans, she was looking for a fresh start. Amelia's boyfriend had recently blown his head off with a shotgun. In light of this, it was tough to reprimand her for not locking the door. Especially when, even if she didn't officially live with us, it was mostly her belongings that had been taken. Still, I objected to her joining our home; I didn't find her trustworthy and thought M&M wanted her to move in simply so that he could crawl into her bed himself.

We got into a long, accusatory argument, fueled by different visions of what the place should be. I knew if she moved in, M&M's crust punk friends were sure to follow. After alluding to this in a way that was less than generous, suggesting that no sane woman would want to live surrounded by the filth M&M cultivated, he told me to move out. He had no authority, legal or otherwise, to do this. But I didn't want a fight and within a few months I complied.

IN MY LAST DAYS AT 551 KOSCIUSZKO, I HAD WANTED, very badly, to ask Bo about Biggie Smalls, aka the Notorious B.I.G., aka Christopher Wallace, but I couldn't figure out how. Bo had grown up in the neighborhood, knew Biggie personally, and, like many a young man I got to know in my time there, was from a broken home. Along with his more famous sister, he had come of age on those unforgiving north Bed-Stuy corners, but Bo had long since decamped for Queens by the time I met him. Early each month he'd sail by in his Lexus SUV, one with rims that spin on their own, to collect our rent. It was kind of a shock when I first met him—he's diminutive, like his sister, but with a warm manner, speaking New Yorkese with a velocity that rivals Korean. He counted cash, which is how we paid for the place, faster than any human being I'd ever seen.

Never once did he replace or fix anything in our crumbling Brooklyn digs; we'd simply do it ourselves and take money out of the rent for it. Still, I thought it was neat having a black landlord in our mostly black neighborhood. I was beginning to think that by law you had to be a Hasidic Jew to own a piece of property in this part of town. In general he was a very open guy, but I knew he was guarded about (a) the status of our ever-impending eviction and (b) his family. His sister Lil' Kim had a rocky relationship with Wallace, and had been involved in a well-publicized love triangle involving Wallace and the singer Faith Evans, whom he'd married in 1994. All this was dramatized in *Notorious*, a 2009 biopic about Biggie, and I had to content myself with watching that, several times, while living under Bo's roof.

It's not a great movie, or even a good one. Keeping a biopic of a tragic public figure hopeful and reverent, especially one about a hip-hop musician who met with such a swift rise and violent end, is a troubling proposition. In the case of the largely compromised but never less than fascinating *Notorious*, it's one that pretty much sinks the entire enterprise. Still, before the phony redemption tale, there are some good scenes of life in Bed-Stuy circa 1990. We see a young Biggie rocking headphones as he sits listlessly on his building's stairwell, consuming the jams of DJ Marley Marl and Slick Rick. As he gets older, as with so many youth in my zip code, the lure of easy money proves too much, too quickly. Wallace begins dealing crack (in front of the Fat Albert's on Broadway, under the elevated tracks, no less!), but after a brief stint in jail and the birth of his first child, he tries his hand at rapping. Pretty soon his demo draws the attention of an ambitious young producer and promoter (Derek Luke gets the dubious honor of portraying Sean "Puffy" Combs, the film's executive producer and the picture's voice of personal growth/moral reasoning, in a truly astounding, sickening performance: "We gonna change the world, Big, but first, we gotta change ourselves") and the rest is history.

As the film draws to a close, Biggie, in "generating cinematic tragedy 101" fashion, proves what a stand-up guy he is, realizing the faults of his ways and making amends with everyone he's fucked over. This includes his first girlfriend: overweight and dark brown with nappy hair, she's the jilted mother of his largely ignored child. That he left her for a thinner, lighter-skinned woman (my landlord's sister!), whom he then left for a prettier, even lighter-skinned woman, whom he then cheated on with a blond white woman (who, in the film's only legitimately gruesome scene of violence, is beaten up by Faith Evans after she catches Biggie in the act), is never explored as a symptom of the sexual neurosis probably suffered by the darker-than-midnight Wallace. Then, on a March night in Los Angeles, Biggie is shot. Suge Knight, as in Nick Broomfield's documentary *Biggie and Tupac* (2002), makes an easy fall guy, while Puffy gets to be a mentor and executive producer of this film. The winners do get to write history.

But does *Notorious* do any injustice to Biggie's memory? Yes . . . and no. Because it was, unfortunately, exactly how Biggie would have wanted it. Have a look, if you can, at some old rap videos from the '90s online. It was the golden age of the genre, with real auteurs emerging in the format, and lavish production values, totally unimaginable in our era of austerity, being put to use in their making. Watching them again, it's clear how governed by a type of repression, a persistent need to deny social reality, Wallace and his handlers were—much more so than their counterparts on the West Coast in the early '90s, who were much more interested in displaying that social reality in their own three-minute MTV fever dreams. The music videos for Wallace's tracks from that era, the ones that also introduced young teenagers like me to more enduring, unmartyred, now remarkably wealthy rap icons like Shawn Carter and Sean Combs, never dwell on the realities of the streets from which these men came. They're always too busy depicting themselves throwing money around some impossibly well-lit island night-club stuffed with beautiful barely dressed women or lip synching on a yacht while some well-dressed but clearly overmatched goons on Kawasaki Jet Skis chase Mariah Carey to no avail.

It was Biggie's great achievement in his remarkably dexterous lyrics to express this other kind of double consciousness. The songs are rife with tales of Bed-Stuy's violence and social decay, even as Biggie clearly yearns for a different kind of world—one that he claims to have reached already by robbing and drug dealing, but actually hopes to reach through his art.

It wasn't just the Craigslist hustlers and neighborhood-inventing real estate brokers who had an agenda of obfuscation. Come to think of it, Biggie was from Clinton Hill.

158 BUFFALO AVENUE

In the first months that I lived at 551 Kosciuszko, in a bout of wanderlust, I strolled south and east for miles, wanting, as I often desired back then, to know not where I was. On the endless concrete I passed derelict town houses and ragamuffin storefront churches, deli-less bodegas and nascent wood-fire pizza joints, crossing Atlantic as the LIRR shuttled Montauk-bound overhead. Although I didn't know it at the time, I had entered Crown Heights. I continued south, past projects and parks, until I came across a large green field that led to four elegant nineteenth-century houses, which sat at the end of the clearing, an unlikely beacon from a past I couldn't have fathomed. At first I thought they were an apparition, so out of sync were they with their surroundings, but walking along Bergen Street to see them closer, I discovered that they were in fact a real and true thing, resting along what no longer appeared to be a street, but certainly in a pattern that suggested one.

These days the Weeksville Heritage Center, dedicated to the memory of what was likely the most significant free black community in the pre–Civil War era, takes up that half a city block where I, on a hot summer day in 2008, first pondered those strange, anomalous houses. Just three blocks from the neighborhood's northern border with Bedford-Stuyvesant, the WHC is hard to miss. The new building's exterior, of patterned slate tile and golden-hued ipe wood, couldn't stand in starker contrast to the World War II–era NYCHA housing projects it sits next to; on cloudless mornings, the six-story buildings that make up the Kingsborough Houses, across the street, cast a shadow on the center's immaculate lawn. Self-consciously stylish architecture is an oddity in these parts, where housing projects of red brick and faded row houses of cheap beige vinyl dominate the topography.

A two-story, 23,000-square-foot modernist structure that makes elegant use of African design motifs, it houses about 10,000 artifacts from the Weeksville settlement. At present, however, only a fraction of the collection is on display.

Opened in December 2013, the new building is "Brooklyn's largest African-American cultural institution," according to its website. It was built, for $34 million, by the City of New York's Department of Cultural Affairs in collaboration with the city council and the Brooklyn Borough president's office; the city owns the building, and the Weeksville Center is its tenant.

The center takes its name from the nineteenth-century African-American community that flourished in this part of Crown Heights and Bedford-Stuyvesant; it is widely believed to have been the only free black community of its size and renown in the country at the time. Along with Stuyvesant Heights, Ocean Hill, and Bedford, contemporary Weeksville is one of the four distinctive parts of Bed-Stuy, bordered by Atlantic Avenue to the north, Ralph Avenue to the east, and East New York Avenue to the south, but the new Weeksville Center is on the same property as four homes built sometime between 1830 and 1883 in what was then known as Crow Hill. They are the only houses that remain from the Weeksville era, sitting on the site of a former colonial road named Hunterfly; before the construction of the new building, the center was run out of these former homes.

Three of them are restored originals; the other is a replica built after the original caught fire. They once belonged to Frederick Volckening, a German immigrant who acquired the land at the height of the Civil War in 1863, from Samuel Bouton, a local Democratic politician who had bought them from the estate of the Dutch farmer Samuel Garrittsen. Volckening, a carpenter himself, likely moved the four houses onto the property from other segments of the neighborhood. They may have been built as early as 1830, perhaps by James LeGrant, a nephew of the Denmark Vesey rebellion conspirator and prosperous Weeksville landowner Francis Graham. As of 1850, he was the only carpenter, white or black, to appear in the area's census records, while the style of the homes themselves—two-story wood-frame structures with gable roofs on the hall, and a parlor plan with a chimney at the high, split end—recalls the houses along the Eastern Seaboard where a South Carolina–bred carpenter such as LeGrant would have learned his trade.

Remnants of the nascent black society in Weeksville remained largely forgotten until nearly a century after LeGrant's death. James Hurley, head of the Long Island Historical Society, frequently gave tours of Brooklyn neighborhoods sponsored by the Museum of the City of New York. He had begun a search for surviving Weeksville structures in 1968 while teaching a workshop at Pratt Institute's Center for Community Development entitled "Exploring Bedford-Stuyvesant and New York City." Hurley had done aerial photography in Pakistan for the U.S. consulate and navy and so quite naturally, after failing to locate any while walking through the area, he enlisted Joseph Haynes, a professional pilot who also worked as an engineer for the Metropolitan Transit Authority, to fly him over Crown Heights and Bedford-Stuyvesant. At low altitude he was able to take several aerial photographs that revealed four wood-frame houses, hidden in an overgrown alley once known as Hunterfly Road. These houses had sat there, decaying and out of sight but still inhabited, even as housing projects went up around them in the early years of World War II. By the time Hurley visited, only one woman remained in one of the houses, Muriel Williams; it had belonged to her family since the early years of the century.

Hurley was part of a growing community engaged in recovering African-American roots in central Brooklyn. Inspired by the discovery of the houses, the artist Joan Maynard and the activists Patricia Johnson and Dolores McCullough founded the Society for the Preservation of Weeksville and Bedford-Stuyvesant History in 1968, with Hurley, whose workshop they had attended at Pratt, as its initial director. Several members complained that Hurley, who is white, was an inappropriate choice to lead the organization, and that a black person should be found to replace him. Initial efforts to help oust him were rebuffed by Congresswoman Shirley Chisholm, who represented the district in the era before and after her historical 1972 presidential run and was influential in the community. Eventually Maynard, who had worked as a graphic artist for the publisher McGraw-Hill and the NAACP magazine *The Crisis*, became president of the organization in 1972, and devoted the next thirty years to preserving the homes and to founding a cultural center on the site.

Much of Maynard's early support came from nearby P.S. 243. In 1970, children from a third-grade class raised $900 toward the restoration of what they called "the houses in the alley." At Hurley's behest, the children also participated in an archaeological dig that unearthed several artifacts from Weeksville, among them slave shackles that had presumably belonged to a Weeksville resident who had escaped southern bondage. Later that year, a busload of P.S. 243 students and teachers accompanied Maynard as she delivered a petition to the New York City Landmarks Preservation Commission to grant the Hunterfly houses landmark status, which would protect them, despite their condition, from being razed for development. A few years later, the Weeksville houses were added to the National Register of Historic Places.

Maynard's group wasn't incorporated, and it didn't have the resources to restore the properties, so she appealed to the Bedford-Stuyvesant Restoration Corporation, an early model of combined public and private support for community development that had been championed by Robert Kennedy in his final months as a senator. After the students at P.S. 243 raised the initial $900 toward purchasing the homes from the Volckening estate, several financiers, including the Restoration Corporation, helped in purchasing three of the four homes; the state's Historic Preservation Office contribution, matched by private individuals recruited by Maynard, provided financing for the fourth. All were wrapped in corrugated tin in order to prevent further damage, while Maynard's group raised money to repair them, which was badly needed; one house had been vandalized, a car had struck another, and a third had been so severely compromised by neglect that it would need to be rebuilt almost from scratch. Only the house that had remained a residence was fully intact.

For the next two decades, Maynard's group tried and failed to raise the money to complete the renovation, although the houses were restored in the early '80s to something resembling their original character. Difficulty raising money to pay adequate tribute to the history of the community, and to study its lasting cultural significance, had been commonplace from the start. Over the years, Maynard was able to win financial support from the New York Landmarks Conservancy, the Downtown Brooklyn Association, the Vincent Astor Foundation, the Sheffield Rehabilitation Corporation, the National Trust for Historic Preservation, and the Mary Flagler Cary Charitable Trust among other institutions, but major federal funding for the emerging project's efforts dried up after 1973.

For some time, violence in the surrounding neighborhood had prevented restoration efforts from gaining traction. Fencing was installed with guard dogs to separate the homes from the crack-infested streets. The house closest to Bergen Street, 1706–1708 Hunterfly, burned down in 1980 for unexplained reasons and took a decade to rebuild, and just as it was being finished, another house was vandalized. But in the early aughts, just as gentrification was beginning to creep into Bedford-Stuyvesant and Crown Heights, a $400,000 grant from the federal program Save America's Treasures made it possible to restore the houses at long last. In 2005, after contributions from Goldman Sachs and the City of New York helped in getting the restoration process to the finish line, they were finally opened to the public. Ground was broken for the Heritage Center's new building just months before the financial collapse of 2008, a catastrophe largely engineered by the new center's benefactors, the federal government and Too Big to Fail banks.

WEEKSVILLE WAS ULTIMATELY UNDONE AS A PREDOM-
inantly black enclave by forces that aren't so different from
those threatening to once again undo the wider area's particularly Negro character; the community was swallowed by
Brooklyn as its urban grid and transportation infrastructure
moved eastward, bringing waves of white immigration with
it, just as rising housing prices and high demand are driving
upper-middle-class whites, and the brokers and developers
who serve them, eastward into black Brooklyn. Its semirural
texture quickly eroded along with the black population as developers began buying up plots of land, leveling out the deep
hills and laying down street patterns that would cast various
existing houses at bizarre angles to the new grid. The wooden
frame houses that had existed amid these hills, along with the
forests and ponds that lined them, were gradually replaced by
Italianate row houses, often made of brick, designed for the
dense urban living that the city fathers foresaw for the area.

Weeksville's black enclave had long accepted whites; for
instance, its school, Colored School No. 2, was one of America's first integrated educational institutions, both among its
students and its teaching staff. White teachers taught under
the guidance of Junius C. Morel as early as 1869, and perhaps
even earlier. In 1851, long before European immigrants began
moving to the area en masse, twelve of its forty students were
Caucasian. Although Weeksville had been referred to as a black
backwater, a "terra incognito to most of the people of Brooklyn,"
according to the *Brooklyn Eagle* in 1868, that same year the

city of Brooklyn began developing its street grid eastward at an exponentially increasing clip. By this point, Weeksville had already lost its mostly African-American majority; by 1860, on the eve of the Civil War, blacks made up only 36.9 percent of its population. While at the time they remained more concentrated in Weeksville than anywhere else in New York City, the deluge of whites moving into the area continued unabated.

With the new infrastructure investments in place, by the late 1860s and early 1870s city services that had not been provided by the city to the colored people of Weeksville began to appear in the area. Gas lanterns and light posts were installed on Schenectady Avenue and Fulton Street. Drains and a well and pump went in on Rochester. Both Rochester and Buffalo Avenues, along the route where the Weeksville Heritage Center rests today, received pavement. Herkimer Street got sewers. The modern city came to Weeksville and swallowed it whole, although as late as 1883, Weeksville, which was more a loose collection of neighborhoods than a contiguous community, was off the grid enough that between settlements there were no paved roads, let alone sidewalks or street lamps.

All of these changes resulted in a significant power shift, along with unforeseen changes to the social landscape of the place. Increased crime came with the white influx; according to accounts by local police from the early 1870s, houses of gambling and alcohol became more rampant while the area saw an increase in robberies and murders. Police in the Crow Hill area noted that colored persons made up only 55 of the 674 arrests made in the area in 1883, well below a proportionate number given their dwindling but still significant population.

The black population had been declining in Weeksville even before the Civil War; it dropped by 9.8 percent from 1855 to 1865 as newly arrived Germans and Irish began to live alongside blacks in the area when the Brooklyn City Railroad Company's Fulton Street line to East New York was completed in 1857.

In short order, strife ensued over integration of local institutions. The Brooklyn school board ruled, in 1869, that the former Colored School No. 2, then known as P.S. 68, could no longer instruct the forty Caucasians who made up nearly half of the school's student body because it was unhealthy for black and white students to have the "intimate relationship" of attending classes together. Eminent Weeksville citizens were rebuffed by the school board when trying to send their kids to nearby schools made up mostly of Caucasians. Three other cases of educational segregation reached the state Supreme Court in the 1870s. The black plaintiffs lost them all, although a similar case was finally won in the 1880s and P.S. 83 (it had been Colored School No. 2, P.S. 68, and these days is known as P.S. 243, the Weeksville School) eventually became a fully integrated public school.

By the 1890s, after the construction of the Brooklyn Bridge allowed for foot traffic to flow from Manhattan to Brooklyn, the surrounding area was almost entirely European-American dominant. The community and rural infrastructure laid down by the generation of James Weeks and Francis Graham in the 1830s were demolished and largely forgotten. Meanwhile, the mostly middle-class families that moved in were, by and large, living in handsome modern housing. Many of these town houses and brownstones, built for a previous marauding gentry class, are being redeveloped today for another wave of mostly white immigrants.

Many of those moving to these black spaces, both then and now, didn't want their children in integrated schools at all, at least ones with the blacks they found in Brooklyn; once whites had a majority, they needn't play nice with Negroes any longer. In the 1890s, when the school board that governed Weeksville acquired the land at the corner of Bergen Street and Schenectady Avenue to rebuild P.S. 68, they received a petition from many white residents who opposed the school being located there, only a block from the old one, because it would "be attended by colored children" whose presence would "depreciate the surrounding property." Other white parents offered testimony to the board that "the development of the neighborhood assures an immediately useful future for the school if it be devoted to the use of white children alone."

These individuals sound not so different from the Hasidic speculators, interviewed by *New York* magazine's *Daily Intelligencer* blog in May 2015, who spoke about their desire to remove black tenants from Bedford-Stuyvesant, claiming they bring property values down. "Everyone wants them to leave," said one speculator, "not because we don't like them, it's just they're messing up." Another young landlord claimed that black tenants "bring everything down," but in saying so opted to remain anonymous in fear of losing his reputation. They sound not so different from the parents at P.S. 8 in modern, affluent Brooklyn Heights, described by *The New York Times* as "anxious about their children's being part of a racial minority," who have resisted efforts, aimed at reducing overcrowding, that would move their children to nearby and predominantly Negro P.S. 307. Efforts to integrate the area in a way that honors and maintains the hard-won semisovereignty blacks have periodically found in central Brooklyn, from the time of Weeksville onward, have always proven unsuccessful. P.S. 243, the Weeksville School, the direct descendant of Colored School No. 2, whose students stood with Joan Maynard to have this space of black sovereignty remembered and protected, has, as of today, a student body that is 97 percent people of color, with white students making up less than 1 percent of its population. It is, very obviously, like much of the surrounding area, more segregated in 2015 than 1851. It is likely to stay this way, until another wave of racially coded change inevitably comes and tears it asunder, remaking the school and the surrounding community in its own image.

730 DEKALB AVENUE

With little money, a green crew, and a lead actor who would threaten to kill himself, arching his body high off a walking bridge on the Ohio River, if I didn't shoot a scene the way he demanded, I produced and directed *Redlegs*, my feature film debut, in the summer of 2010. A comedic drama about the aftermath of an untimely death in Ohio, it was greatly inspired by John Cassavetes's seminal 1970 film, *Husbands*. The night Lena's film *Tiny Furniture* won the grand jury prize at SXSW, it had been deliriously conceived while viewing, on YouTube with Kevin, a *Dick Cavett Show* episode in which the *Husbands* cast drunkenly promoted the film. Five months later, surrounded by people who had known me from many different walks of life, we began the first day of shooting on a farm in Alexandria, Kentucky.

It was a calamitous, fly-by-night process from the start. The money was raised from drug dealers, art nonprofits, and crowdsourcing, the cameras and many of the locations given to us in kind, the labor of recent college graduates from Wright State University's nearby film school duly exploited. During one take that begins in Ohio and ends in Kentucky, we were breaking six laws simultaneously. I'm not sure if shooting well past midnight in a moving vehicle driven by an unlicensed driver while drugs and far too many people are crowded into a Jeep is ever a wise thing to do but it resulted in an electric scene, one of my favorite in the film.

My first editor, a friend from film school who is the daughter of a nun, broke down and cried when I first sat down at the editing table in the upstairs parlor of her home in Sunnyside, Queens, that fall. She had decided only days before not to leave her rock star husband, another ex-classmate of ours who was always on tour and rarely if ever made much money despite his band's growing reputation and top-shelf national press clippings. The reason? She wanted to edit my film on his gear. I was inadvertently keeping a broken marriage together, but our own working relationship couldn't withstand the pressure. The full-time job she held down cutting the Tom Selleck cop show *Blue Bloods* meant we could only cut during evenings, and after four difficult months we parted ways, friends no more.

I had spent much of that year living in a tiny front room of a former Crown Heights meth den with an EMT named Monty for $500 a month and a South Slope two-bedroom with a graf-

fiti artist named Flo, the star of ι
charged me $800. I could hardly at
unsurprisingly, neither ended well: both
to move in women with whom they were sι

Unfinished versions of *Redlegs* were rej
2011 by SXSW, Sundance, Rotterdam, the Los
Festival, and, with great heartbreak, Slamdance, m⟩   ⸱ mater. My sound mixers took four months to do three days' worth
of work on the film. It wasn't until early in the spring of 2012
that I was able to give the film the shape it needed, largely due
to my roommate Jake's editing equipment. For the entirety of
that year when I released a movie and America reelected a black
president, I lived in a hallway separating the two sides of a two-
bedroom railroad in Bushwick, sleeping on a raised platform
that allowed me to squeeze a skinny dresser and the fraying
white leather love seat underneath it. Along with my mattress,
it was all the furniture that remained from my relatively opu-
lent dwelling with Tony a half decade before.

Despite the cramped quarters, the Bushwick residence
had been felicitous creatively in ways none of the other places
proved to be—it's where I finished *Redlegs*, largely in my pa-
jamas or with a spliff in my hand. One of the stars of the film
moved in that spring after yet another broken housing situation
of his own had collapsed. He shared that hallway with me for
the better part of the year, sleeping on the love seat beneath my
bunk when we were both in town. When the film was done,
having squandered my chances with bigger festivals, I passed

opportunity to play at smaller fests, hoping the Tribeca Film Festival would take the film. It didn't, and all my options seemed exhausted. But leveraging a few relationships I had made as a journalist, I arranged a small premiere at a festival of no repute in Brooklyn and four-walled the smallest cinema in town, the ReRun Theater in Dumbo, Brooklyn, during the final weekend in May of that year.

Redlegs received, truly out of nowhere, glowing reviews from *The New York Times* and *The Washington Post* and largely supportive notices from *Variety* and *The Hollywood Reporter*. It was carried by word of mouth to more weeklong releases, festival bookings, and a no-advance distribution deal from Cinetic FilmBuff. But, ultimately, few cared. Through a quirk in the movie release schedule, only six movies were opened that week (it's routinely four times that amount most weekends in New York these days), allowing our reviews to garner some traction. But two of the other films opening that week were *Moonrise Kingdom* and *Men in Black II*, both bound to vastly overshadow my modest, self-distributed effort. *Redlegs* made less than $5,000 theatrically and disappeared, like most of the 800 or so movies released in 2012, into the digital cloud of iTunes and Amazon. It only irks me when I remember the film hasn't even inspired pirates to torrent-stream it. A year and a half after they put it out on DVD and VOD, FilmBuff sent me a check for $497.

This shouldn't have surprised me. Ninety-five percent of independent movies lose money, even critically successful ones that play at Sundance and sell for millions of dollars. The world of movies I worked in nebulously was equally in flux; I had learned to roll with punches coming from all directions. In the years since I had entered the industry, the old-guard New York indie producers had watched as venture capital and hedge fund investing pulled out of the sector, their sense of a stable livelihood disappearing. By the time *Redlegs* was released, episodic television was the only growth sector in the industry, and the publications that had devoted themselves to independent film were routinely running episode recaps and clickbait listicles that had little to do with the enduring difficulty of making movies in an unusual way. Anyone who aspired simply to be an uncompromising film artist was being told to drop dead (or get rich) by the official organs of indie film.

Even for those filmmakers whose works premiered at reputable festivals and were acquired by companies whose logo one's Ohio mother may have seen before a movie she liked at the just-barely-getting-by local art house, the advances were dwindling, the sense that one could really break out seeming ever smaller. Lena had done it, acquiring powerful mentors such as Judd Apatow and leveraging her $25,000 indie movie for more clout within the industry than anyone had ever done before. But she had a sensibility, self-effacing but narcissistic, privileged but portly, postmodern but disarmingly approachable (for whites), that could sell. No one knew it would become a new Brooklyn zeitgeist unto itself, this sensibility of Lena's, especially Lena herself.

"What I wanted this to be no longer exists," said a mutual friend and prominent female director, lauded in *The New Yorker* and most of the publications that matter in indie film, just before her picture won an acting prize at the Tribeca Film Festival. She wanted to be the new Lena, or something akin to that, and had in her short career already made better films than Dunham ever had, but that type of stardom would remain out of reach. There were people that crossed over every year, but the expectation was now that, like Ryan Coogler, they would go make work for the man, somehow rejiggering an ancient franchise like *Rocky* into a work of personal expression as brand rehabilitation, such as *Creed*. Selling out had simply become a way of life.

My debut feature film was released on DVD and VOD the following year, after I had moved back to Bed-Stuy, broke again. It fell like a tree falling in an empty forest where no one was around to hear. My writing was appearing in more well-known or respected places, from *The Daily Beast* to *The Brooklyn Rail*, but often for amounts that made it impossible to take the subway let alone rent an apartment. The $750 a month I paid to live with Liam, the most stolid and reliable of the roommates at 551 Kosciuszko, and his buddy Simon, also a former Kosciuszko tenant and gifted illustrator, was more than I could really afford. I had squandered my momentum, one agent told me, joining without quite knowing it that list of black directors with promising first features who struggled to leverage them into something bigger. I wasn't twice as good, but even if I was, would it be good enough?

I knew thousands of filmmakers who would kill to get the reviews I had gotten. One of my actors got an agent and some other film roles. I was suddenly a credible candidate for teaching jobs. But my circumstances had not changed. "Success" wasn't what I had thought it could be. My life was still not the stuff of those film school brochures. The dream they sold, even for the most successful independent filmmakers, largely didn't exist anymore.

And I still didn't have a stable home. When this newest Bed-Stuy dwelling ran its course, it didn't sting as hard as some of the others; there were no hurled words or quivering days, and not too much avoidance. It was the second Bedford-Stuyvesant and fourth Brooklyn apartment I was thrown out of by a white man, in this case after eight months of intermittent subletting and never being late with the rent. Liam was a good man and a decent roommate, quick-witted and mostly fair, even if he confided to friends and ex-girlfriends of mine that he had fucked me over. When I journeyed back to Ohio for a long stretch of the summer to look after my ailing father—a lifelong smoker and poor eater who didn't quit cigarettes before or after the double bypass surgery he had in July of that year—the newest subletter, a friend of theirs, took hold of the place and I was asked to leave permanently, cast back into the anxiety and destabilization of the undomiciled. But I was old enough to know that there were no idylls to be had in Bed-Stuy, and happily ripped off some of the subletter's magic mushrooms with the keys I still had, from the room I still considered mine, while removing my belongings. The dudes doing the evicting were looking out for their own convenience, pursuing the American Way; who was I to blame them, really?

ON THE EVE OF MY THIRTIETH BIRTHDAY, IN NOVEMBER 2013, I was an adjunct college professor who relied on food stamps for duck bacon and homegrown kale sandwiches while paying $750 a month for the honor of living with a skinny pot dealer who once dabbled in shady real estate and had deep ties to Brooklyn's Orthodox Jewish community, a peak oil survivalist from Newton, Massachusetts, with a horror-movie-ready skin problem, and yet another mild-mannered, fair-eyed Cincinnatian.

Everywhere on the streets of Bed-Stuy now, I saw a breed of young upwardly mobile professionals that had strollers and expensive jackets, designer bags, running lycra. A great social experiment was suddenly unfolding in our midst. Restaurants were popping up on Nostrand Avenue that served ten-dollar tater tots and were lauded in *The New York Times* for their adventurous cocktail lists. Organic markets sprang up where mere bodegas had once stood, seven-dollar breakfast sandwiches the norm. Realty firms such as the Corcoran Group displayed their signs ever more prominently, on an increasing number of the neighborhood's handsome brownstones.

We seemed to be immune to it at 551 Kosciuszko. I lived with Jews, one of whom had grown up Orthodox and knew the landlord from the Hasidic community. Only within the auspices of their solidarity could I receive a submarket rent in this black part of town anymore. For this I was grateful; while it was a bit ragamuffin, the place had a rough-hewn charm. There was a nice garden in the back of the split-level property. I had the room right near the front door, the only one without a closet; it was listed as the office within a three-bedroom, two-bath, two-story apartment. The four of us paid $2,800 for the place in total and knew it was a pretty good deal. It was also illegal, technically; dwellings of this sort could not contain four people. Neftali, our landlord, was a mild-mannered redheaded Hasidic man who worked with Brooks, the Cincinnatian, at B&H Camera in Hell's Kitchen. "The nice thing about this place is it's stable," said Albert, the pot dealer. "You know he'll never raise the rent that much."

I took to the place. Andrew, the survivalist with the bad skin, kept a garden out back of organic vegetables that he almost never harvested. I was happy to pick up the slack, hosting dinner parties powered by the fresh cucumbers and Swiss chard, tomatoes and kale that he grew in our backyard. Albert and I converted the common area into a screening room, painting one whole wall the proper silver color to maximize reflectiveness and purchasing a BenQ projector using Brooks's discount at B&H. It took us one long afternoon, breezing in and out of the room to the rickety wooden back stairwell that led into the garden to catch some fresh air, Kendrick Lamar's "Money Trees" emanating in waves from the portable iPhone stereo. We went back and forth over the white wall, trying to achieve just the right even silver sheen to bounce light off. Andrew, the longest-tenured tenant, was nonplussed about the change at first. Despite being consumed with prepping for a dystopian future, he really hated household change. Once the screening room was set up, however, he never failed to happily watch *Game of Thrones* on the rig whenever he could.

We entertained people on a weekly basis, throwing massive barbecues in the garden, creating a social mix that few in this quickly gentrifying and self-segregating neighborhood would have fathomed. Kids like Rudy, an underemployed Dominican twenty-something who hung out at the barbershop across the street, would tend to a fire that warmed pot-gorging Hasidic guys and prudish Argentinian women, journalists from august magazines and directors of hit movies. Ours was an unusual groove, but we made the most of it, seeing the $750 each of us paid for the $2,800-a-month place as a last refuge amid the storm of rising rents.

At some point in the years previous I had become the stuff of Grover Norquist's nightmares, scraping by in central Brooklyn with the accoutrements of both the destitute and the refined. The newfound delicacies at the Metropolitan Market— which was a drab, pedestrian ghetto grocer when Tony and I would wander past it in 2006, and had morphed into a place that carried kombucha and kefir in the interim—felt like the only responsible way to spend my welfare money. My $160 in food stamps, increased by the Obama stimulus from $120, went not just to daily sustenance, but to barbecues for dozens of people powered by state-sponsored D'Artagnan duck breast and lamb chops.

I had never had much of a foothold in the middle class as an adult, chasing the hazy dream of making a living directing movies, but that fall I saw the glimpse of one down a corridor I had studiously avoided. Based largely on the critical success *Redlegs* had received, I was asked to teach at my alma mater, SUNY Purchase. The adjunct position called for me to co-teach the senior-level production course in which the BFA thesis films were made, and paid $9,000 for the whole year, just little enough for me to stay on food stamps. I took it in a heartbeat, just like I said I never would.

TONY WOULD APPEAR IN FRONT OF ME FROM TIME TO time, on the streets of Bed-Stuy or in front of a café in Bushwick, on the F train toward Manhattan or next to the elliptical machines at the Bed-Stuy YMCA. We'd generally ignore each other, although at the YMCA that was too hard, so we'd make terse if seemingly friendly conversation before going back to ignoring each other. He was mustached early that fall, heavier in that way men get when they eat potatoes and wheat. We were standing on the stoop of his building, one his parents had in the five years since we stopped living together bought for him to reside in and manage near the corner of Jefferson and Bedford Avenues. He had just turned thirty and his brother, in town from Cincinnati, insisted we all get together. We were uncomfortable. The booze, at a '70s-themed dive bar called One Last Shag, had helped. But by the time we got to his property, things had gently soured again.

He told me, with a weird matter-of-fact quality, "If blacks just stopped shooting each other, we'd have a murder rate that was the same as Sweden's." It was a little under a year after Jordan Davis was killed by a white man for playing his music too loud, a little less than a year before Eric Garner was choked to death by a white cop trying to arrest him for selling loose cigarettes a short drive away from us, in Staten Island. His brother, who is, beyond being a much bigger hip-hop fan than I, set to inherit the family's multimillion-dollar real estate and plasma center fortune and collects the rent of Tony's tenants at his Ohio office, echoed his sentiments. They continued belaboring this point, which we may have gotten to via gun control or some other moribund political topic, for some time, long enough to actively bore Tony's newest blonde girlfriend. When she asked to go back inside, Tony complied, adding a "just saying," as he went back in, absentmindedly accidentally locking his brother and me out of the building as we continued smoking a joint.

We rang and rang the doorbell, but when neither Tony nor his girlfriend returned, I left the ex–dope pusher and budding real estate entrepreneur with his equally blonde girlfriend on the stairwell and sauntered in a subtle disquiet back to my own imperiled Bed-Stuy dwelling. Walking through the cool early night, I thought a lot about the ignorance I had just witnessed.

These were crimes, "black on black," that were often committed by *broken* people who are largely motivated by fear and rage and hopelessness and material desperation. The materially and spiritually oppressive policies and mores of white men concerning this country's Negroes had nothing to do with any of that fear and rage and hopelessness, went the logic I had heard from my well-meaning friends, people who had never known the petty unfairness of class from the bottom or the middle, let alone the societally enforced dread of growing up poor and brown in our most dangerous inner cities. Neither did I, of course. But, even if I didn't know that life from experience, I knew its contours intimately and had begun to choose solidarity instead of aspiration. To refuse the "loyalties of my class," as Tony would have once put it. Problem was, I didn't know what my class was anymore.

THE LOVERS AT THE CENTER OF SHAKA KING'S WON-derful and unfortunately titled film *Newlyweeds*, which opened that fall I lived at 730 DeKalb, are young, black dreamers of Bed-Stuy. The two are flatmates drifting through a romance both chemical and genuine: Amari Cheatom's Lyle is a repo man for a rent-to-own electronics and appliance store, while Trae Harris's Nina is a museum tour guide; both spend most of their adult lives stoned. He's a little angry and she's not; neither of them, it turns out, is a particularly good listener (she dreamily talks of going to the Galápagos, for instance—Lyle isn't savvy enough to realize she's serious). Despite this, they're funny together and create a blazed-out cocoon where they can mutually blot out the troublesome world around them. There is plenty to blot out.

Class tensions exist on the periphery of the relationship. She's a member of the black bourgeois of Brownstone Brooklyn and he is not. The unspoken context of much of their interpersonal troubles throughout the picture, especially those pertaining to her *Cosby*-ready Brooklynite parents, is that his work and class background are somehow beneath her. They proceed with their affairs, undaunted by this possibility until the law's dark hand descends on both of them for blunders that bespeak not just the consequences of pot on otherwise nimble minds, but also the lot of any two young black people caught in a justice system that now often functions as a revenue generator for the prison industrial complex. The two face a crossroads long prescribed, and not just by her penchant for bringing by seemingly affable scholarly brothers who hit on her, or her inability to keep her fresh-baked pot brownies out of the hands of nosy grade-schoolers on a museum tour.

The movie asks the question: do the ties that bind these young potheads, for better and for worse, appear stronger than the forces of increasingly entrenched economic immobility that might otherwise drive them apart? Toward the end, the narrative eventually forces them to ask these questions of themselves in a series of quite beautiful scenes that are simultaneously satisfying and ambiguous. Even if they do remain together, what future do they have? By film's end, our heroes, like most young black couples in Bed-Stuy, don't have a definitive answer and neither do we.

While Nina has the support structure of a traditionally middle-to-upper-middle-class black family to lean on, Lyle has none of this, and is subtly looked down upon by Nina's elders for it. After watching this film, you're inclined to ask, "Are black people looking out for each other in Obama's America, regardless of class and creed?" What new horizon could possibly await Lyle? He's not a particularly cunning or deft character, one whose entire conception of adult happiness revolves around marijuana, but is nevertheless honest and compassionate, someone who tries—often with disastrous results—to give the benefit of the doubt to poor people whose debt-laden goods it's his job to take. This is a man who, at sixty, if the world continues as it is these days, will need basic income guarantees to support himself; the skills he's acquired will surely be automated in the years to come. He lives in a borough that will soon be beset by the rising oceans. He is, in effect, fucked. With all of this to worry about, he still must also be concerned with his liberty being taken, all because he likes to inhale the smoke of a naturally grown and remarkably popular plant while living in a brown body.

In these dying days of marijuana prohibition, when even John McCain can muse on national TV about the possibility of the war on marijuana being abandoned (he dare not speak of disastrous consequences for large swathes of his fellow citizens directly), Barack Obama, former middle-class member of a stoner circle called the "Choom gang," still believes, at least publicly, that people like Lyle and Nina belong in jail. Of course, a reasonable person must assume in order to retain their sanity that he doesn't actually believe that. It's less depressing to assume that he just doesn't find it politically expedient to claim he doesn't. But this might have been the least of our disappointments at the time.

As good as he was at allowing us to imagine a better future, at least way back then (way back in 2008!), Barack Obama was incapable of leading us there. Or at taking stands that were the logical and difficult extension of his pretenses toward justice (legal, economic, global) and inclusion and a better world for all. Nowhere in the homilies of '08 do I recall hearing about unaccountable drone warfare and southern blacks being unable to share in the benefits of the Affordable Care Act because it didn't protect them from the malfeasance of their state legislatures. These were things I had, by casting a ballot twice for Barack Obama and progressive legislators, imagined I was voting for. In the specter of the obfuscatory and naked racist nonsense propagated by Americans who still consider themselves "conservative," it's easy to forget the hope of those halcyon days of 2008, especially since I was high for most of it. Now it's almost like all of us have forgotten to believe in our ability to effect change in a profound way, to reach for utopia in our time. We also do this, the forgetting, at our great peril.

But not Neil Drumming. He remembers. In his debut feature film, *Big Words*, a dramedy about three ex-rappers that had come out the previous July from black cinema darling Ava DuVernay's African-American Film Festival Releasing Movement, the filmmaker grapples with that historic day and night when more than a hundred million of us turned out to the polls to defeat a failed status quo and made Barack Obama the first nonwhite president of the United States. Drumming examines that day by meditating on the lives of three mildly broken-spirited black men of Brooklyn, each of them struggling with or making excuses for ignoring Election Day 2008 in Kings County. This proves a valuable way to frame a narrative about the difficulties of overcoming the past and of forging new identities for yourself when you're an American black man.

This same spirit of a failed status quo punctuates the drama in *Big Words*. John, one of Drumming's three ex-rappers who have grown apart in the fifteen years since the dissolution of their critically praised rap group, is an ex-con and gifted lyricist. He's been fired from his tech job when we meet him and told to suck it up by his white employer because, after all, the country was going to elect Barack Obama, black president #1—everything was going to be better. John spends the day navigating a strip club and having a meeting with a very attractive black woman, but he is simultaneously emotionally needy and unavailable, and more damningly, he has a past to suppress, one that is getting in the way of him changing into the person he needs to become to be happy. That he can't tell her he's been to jail, that he wants to play down his past as a rapper, for this welcoming but still slightly classier-than-thou girl, throws into stark relief a petty drama of Negro status anxiety that the movies rarely capture. And when it isn't stress, or dementia, or torture, or true poverty, that drives most people slowly out of their minds, it's status anxiety. It wasn't for no reason that the late, great black crime novelist Chester Himes once opined, "Obviously and unavoidably, the black American is the most neurotic, complicated, schizophrenic, unanalyzed, anthropologically advanced specimen of mankind in the history of the world."

A difficult past with contemporary consequences, ones we're shamed into not acknowledging, or into forgetting, or at least not being too loud about, is the lot of many black men in *Big Words*, including John's cousin James, who is gay and out of the closet, albeit mostly so in the context of his well-heeled publishing industry gig. He spends the day like Mrs. Dalloway, unhappily preparing for his election party, Caucasian assistant in tow—one who, surprisingly in the white-collar world in which he's advanced himself, knows all about his exploits as a hip-hop wunderkind a decade and a half before, seeing as he's the son of a hip-hop scholar who is indulging in a bit of it himself. Not just any hip-hop wunderkind, mind you. The type who spewed the vitriolic antihomosexual lyrics that were—and in many quarters still are—a dominant feature of popular rap music. A romance brews just under one of their interactions, as they drive around Brooklyn in suits in the black gay man's nice car. There is an election party to prepare for, however, and a likely mildly jealous boyfriend, and a number of white lesbians, all of whom are privileged in myriad ways beyond their homosexuality, who will be waiting to celebrate in reverence and tears. Things remain on the platonic tip. No blown covers, no suppressed past exposed.

The other character in *Big Words* still plies his trade as a barely employed hip-hop artist, burning the candle for a bygone era of the form like some latter-day Brand Nubian, headphones constantly wrapped around his neck. He gets involved in various hijinks during the day: he flirts with a bartender, manages his crumbling relationship with a girlfriend who rightly thinks him no good, and floats amiably throughout Brooklyn, in neighborhoods once more chocolate than Hershey's, where these days you can't throw a stone without hitting a gentrifier.

None of them is through with the past, or with each other, and the mutual disaffection they share is palpable, even as the film's tone hews mostly toward light dramedy. At the film's end, much like in Kelly Reichardt's 2006 film *Old Joy*, we know these men will never be as close as they were. Ultimately what they'll reveal to each other is how little difference their solidarity would make, and how the disappointments of the past are all bound up with their present.

THE CRACKS IN THE FACADE OF STABILITY AT 730 DeKalb became too prominent to ignore as 2013 became 2014. On the first Sunday of 2014, a record cold swept the city; I'd smoked at dawn on the landing of the rickety wooden staircase leading into the garden and felt the sensation of a thousand pins pressing against my flushed skin with each gust. I had planned to host a soiree to coincide with the Cincinnati Bengals' NFL playoff game against the San Diego Chargers that day. The affair never went off, however; I awoke to a strong knock on the front door, just outside my room, and an overwhelmingly humid sensation. My downstairs neighbor, a Mexican cabdriver who spoke little English, gesticulated wildly. "Agua! Agua," he exclaimed, "from the ceiling!"

Pipes had burst all over our apartment that morning. My bed, an orthopedic number that had been a graduation present from my eldest aunt, lay on the floor alongside a wall that contained a burst pipe. It had been soaking in warm water all morning but I didn't notice until I returned to my room with my animated neighbor and discovered a long trail of water leading across my floor. The paint along the wall near my bed had bubbled up, distending over the bed, and was warm to the touch.

Before long there was water all over the house as uninsulated pipes throughout the property began to burst. I spent much of the afternoon ladling water from strategically placed pans along the walls into buckets, hoping Neftali would return our calls for a plumber. He never did, and ultimately we called our own. I had started a batch of Cincinnati-style chili in our Crock-Pot in hopes the party could be salvaged, but once it became clear that finding a plumber on short notice in Bed-

Stuy on the coldest day of the year was damn near impossible, I called it off, slurping chili and bourbon alone as I frantically scooped water and watched the Bengals lose. When a plumber did arrive to stop the bleeding, much of the flooring and walls had been terribly damaged. A jagged hole, larger than a square foot, sat right next to my new waterbed.

The heat went out the following week. It stayed off for a full seven days, the absurdity of the situation compounded when Neftali brought by some completely inadequate space heaters and said it would be taken care of soon. You get what you pay for. I was a food-stamp-collecting adjunct professor and I knew I'd never find rent this cheap again, in the only neighborhood I'd ever really thought of as home in New York. The episode was weirdly assuring, though; he's not going to raise the rent, not after this, I must have thought.

It was going up across the street, however. All over the neighborhood, whenever I ran into my friends, often in the new bars that seemed to be springing up everywhere, our once-interesting conversations would naturally drift to the subject of pricing Negroes and first-wave hipsters out. Feeling secure that such a thing wouldn't happen to me here was foolhardy, of course, especially when I withheld my rent in order to get the hole in my wall fixed, a risky move for someone who didn't have a binding lease; we paid Neftali, as I had Bo, in cash. I thought I had little other recourse than to get the wall fixed and my bed paid for. "Nafty," as we called him, didn't take kindly to this. A contentious phone call ("Sorry about the pipes, the bed is not my problem") led to a meeting, a full clearing of the air, in late February.

Neftali showed up with another man, a skinny and wiry Hasid named Dell. My roommates and I were all surprised by his presence, but immediately we recognized him. He owned, or perhaps only managed, the building across the street. They spoke in Hebrew between themselves for a second, Neftali pointing at various places in our foyer and hallway, living room and kitchen, Dell nodding in agreement and occasionally casting the four of us a sideways glance. "So it's been a difficult winter," Neftali began, solemnly, standing next to our makeshift movie-screen wall, next to a giant indoor growing chamber Andrew used for raising cannabis. "And we have to make some repairs to make sure this type of thing never happens again." We all nodded in agreement. Damned right! Neftali's face darkened after saying this. Dell looked at us with a nervous intensity. Something was awry.

"When are you thinking about making the repairs?" I asked. "Because I just feel very strongly that I shouldn't pay rent until my bed is replaced and the hole in my wall fixed."

Dell shot daggers at me with his eyes. My roommates looked on warily. We each paid rent separately to Neftali, not as a collective, so my withholding rent didn't mean so much to them. Albert had abruptly left in the weeks preceding, having taken a job in the medical marijuana business in Northern California. Formerly a member of the community himself, his departure, even if Alan, too, was Jewish, eliminated the bridge between us and Neftali. He had no reason to remain loyal.

"We need to do them immediately," Neftali replied, ignoring my complaint, which had been left at an impasse in our phone conversation.

"You need to pay your rent immediately!" Dell intoned, shocking all of us a bit with his aggression. I stared daggers right back at him. I didn't trust this motherfucker for a second. The two men standing before us shuffled their feet uncomfortably.

"But when we begin, you all can't live here when we do the repairs," Neftali said, claiming they'd be too invasive. Brooks, who worked with Neftali in Manhattan and had heretofore remained stoic during the whole thing, awoke suddenly. "Well, you have other apartments we can move into during that time, right?" Neftali shook his head, claiming he didn't have anything else for the time being. "When can we move back in?" Alan asked, already knowing the answer but still in denial about what was happening.

Neftali blushed a bit. One could have cooked an egg on his pink, sweaty forehead. This was stressing him out. "That remains to be seen," he said. "When it's finished, it will probably be in the hands of a management company."

I let out a guffaw.

"Oh, I see, we're getting kicked out," Al lamented, with a rueful laugh. Dell looked at us hard, a fire in his eyes. Neftali's eyes went to his shoes, but he couldn't hide his intentions from us any longer, didn't want us to keep the place and was willing to forgo our rent in order to get us out. The winds of change, and the money that rode in on them, were too much to resist.

We had seen the writing on the wall. By the dawn of winter, a new group of Caucasian hipsters that had moved next door to us, with their blow-up baby swimming pool and Adele songs and Christmas tree lights in the backyard, were paying much more than the African-American family that had lived next door to us in the fall. In January of that year, the New York *Daily News* ran a story claiming the price of one-bedroom apartments in the neighborhood had climbed 15 percent in 2013, from $1,587 to $1,835. It reported on graffiti artists who had taken to spray-painting "Gentrify Here" on the walls of the new luxury tower going up a few blocks east of us on DeKalb, and landlords who "bully tenants out of affordable housing, only to flip the property and lease it at a market rate—often at more than $2,000 for a one bedroom." What had once been a surgical strike was growing into a full-scale invasion.

The bullying began in short order. Neftali would frequently call, asking if we had made plans to leave. I would find Dell peering up at my window late at night, menace in his eyes. "Let me come in to fix the wall," he would say, unannounced, near midnight. "Why won't you let me come in and fix the wall, huh?" he repeated again, when he and Neftali cornered me in my room another day and questioned my character. Dell said something about how "you people" always behave in the process. I asked them to buy me out but they refused; they knew I had no lease and they were not inclined to help me out in any way, shape, or form. So I continued to withhold rent, daring them to begin eviction proceedings.

I had learned, through a housing lawyer named Marty Needleman, that those proceedings could take up to eight months but that in no uncertain terms, unless they continued to harass me with documented illegality (a strong possibility), there was no way in which I could keep the place. At first we were defiant in our desire to stay, but slowly my roommates each peeled off. Albert was already gone; he had moved to California in February to work in the aboveboard medical marijuana industry. Brooks, not wanting to cause undue ire at work, where he was subordinate to Neftali and in need of his help to advance in the largely Hasidic domain of B&H Camera and Video, decided to leave in short order as well. Al and I seemed determined to stick it out, but eventually he folded too. Instead of looking for a new place, I wrote a screenplay, in a sort of desperation, that mirrored various elements from the affair. I hoped to shoot it in the apartment, planning to stay as long as I could.

But no money materialized to do it and my mother, in Ohio, nervous for my well-being, insisted I leave. It was mildly terrifying, being alone in the apartment at night, looking out the blinds to find the Hasidic answer to one of Ray Liotta's cinematic tough guys ominously staring up from the street below, but even if this was exactly the type of situation my mother hoped to have me avoid, I found it sort of thrilling, too. Fuck these guys. The piss-and-vinegar side of me kept saying, "You have as much a right to live here as anyone else."

I threw a party for my students upon the completion of their senior year and invited thirty years' worth of Purchase film alumni to celebrate their graduation, but in a way it was also a goodbye. Structuralist experimental movies played in the screening room we had fashioned out of the common area, and the state-sponsored French-cut duck breast flowed. Had I become what I set out not to become: a man of broken dreams, at the end of the party, a misbegotten mentor to others?

In spite, we gleefully kicked a larger hole in the wall of my room. The next day I pilfered as much of the furniture that had been left there by Albert, Brooks, and Al as I could and left the beer bottles and trash where they were on the way out, giving the keys to Rudy, a Dominican kid from across the street with whom Albert and I would smoke and watch football during 730 DeKalb's all-too-brief halcyon days. I told him to squat if he liked; if he held out a month and started to get his mail there, potentially he could stay as long as eight, given the city's relatively protective rules for tenants of all sorts. He took me up on the offer.

75 SOUTH ELLIOTT PLACE

Whenever I brought up where I lived with my family in Ohio, they always mentioned Spike Lee. He was synonymous with Bed-Stuy, even if he'd never actually lived there. And I'm sure the worlds of *Crooklyn* and *Joe's Bed-Stuy Barbershop: We Cut Heads*, forty and thirty years gone, respectively, have some bearing on the Bed-Stuy I've lived in, but I haven't found it. The black barbers and jazz musicians I know don't live in such elegance, nor do they have such striver-centric social anxiety. Why would they? The brownstone on Arlington Place where Spike and Co. shot *Crooklyn* recently sold for $1.7 million. In these days of the form's increasing cultural irrelevance, there isn't a hit jazz record on earth that would sustain for its creator that kind of mortgage. Or a haircut.

In the years I had lived at 551 Kosciuszko Street, I frequently walked down Stuyvesant between Lexington and Quincy, the block where *Do the Right Thing*, Lee's sole narrative masterpiece, was shot. Whenever I'd ask a young man who was more or less the age Martin Lawrence was in that film if he'd ever seen it, he'd shake his head no or pass me by without a word. It's almost always empty in the middle of the summer, that block. The busy and bustling community depicted in that film was a fantasy. Which is not to say those early Lee films don't represent a certain reality of the place. But it was a vision of Bed-Stuy as much less poor and desperate and sad than it actually must have been in those years, a Bed-Stuy that was more like the liberal, middle-class neighborhood where Lee himself grew up: Fort Greene.

When *Do the Right Thing* came out in the summer of 1989, the media worried that it would cause race riots. They shouldn't have. In Lee's films—like in the blaxploitation films he generally found wanting despite his affection for some of the performers—the nationalists, the Muslim rabble-rousers, the dudes who "want some brothers on the wall," always get short shrift at the end: they are embarrassed, or jailed, or, in the case of Radio Raheem in *Do the Right Thing*, they die a violent death. In his more nuanced films (including *Malcolm X*), they transform into more complicated individuals, people willing to grasp the ambivalence of Negro existence and understand that the white man is only part of the problem and, naturally, an even bigger part of any lasting solution. Watch the films. That's actually what's in them, from *Joe's Bed-Stuy Barbershop* (Mr. Lovejoy, the sharply dressed black nationalist gangster antagonist, is seen as a shark and charlatan) through *Bamboo-zled* (where Mos Def's nationalist meets a violent, undignified end). The revolution never comes, only imperfect compromise with the nefarious forces of racial animus or institutional corruption. Those forces are rendered benign not through greater understanding but through mutual resignation to the status quo. Neither Lee nor his cinema has ever been revolutionary. The resilient but embattled Negro middle class consumed Lee's images for years, letting him give the nationalists just enough rope to hang themselves. Lee was the middle class's champion no less than Bill Cosby, a child of their aspirations and the troubadour of their anxieties. But they didn't show up for his more difficult Brooklyn tales, like *He Got Game* and *Clockers*. And eventually he was begging all of us for money on Kickstarter.

ON A SUNDAY NIGHT LATE IN JUNE 2014, A FEW WEEKS after I moved out of 730 DeKalb Avenue, I stepped into the School of Visual Arts Theatre in Manhattan for the world premiere of Spike Lee's *Da Sweet Blood of Jesus* with a sense of foreboding. It was in the air of the place, a mild gloom, despite being packed with well-dressed and excited Negroes of every shape and size and color, the ebony and the high yellow, most of them notably well off. For my part, I was less than casket sharp, as they say in parts of the South, but playing the schlubby journalist at festivals is something I've grown accustomed to. Soon enough I spotted other members of our sartorially challenged tribe, in T-shirts and poorly fitting jackets, clutching their press tickets. Those pale journalists and a smattering of indie film folks, lackeys for the small and midsize distributors still interested in a new Spike Lee Joint, made up most of the whites in attendance. In these parts, they seemed exotic.

It was the American Black Film Festival's first year in New York, and it had a lot riding on this screening, perhaps even more than Mr. Lee had. One of the country's most venerable auteur brands, Spike Lee is the most famous African-American filmmaker the United States has yet produced. He doesn't need the American Black Film Festival to survive, but the festival does need him. No one gives a shit about the American Black Film Festival. For most people, Spike Lee is American black film, and where he goes, critics will follow.

Da Sweet Blood of Jesus was financed largely through a controversial Kickstarter campaign that Lee, who is reportedly worth $40 million, undertook the previous summer. His bankroll padded by $1,418,910 from more than six thousand contributors, Lee made the film quickly and without fanfare. He needed a comeback. His previous feature, a 2013 remake of Park Chan-wook's elegant and hyperviolent Korean grindhouse hit *Oldboy*, skipped festivals altogether, probably because its distributors didn't want it to be thought of as a "festival circuit" film. Lee seemed unhappy with the effort; he dropped the "Joint" branding at the end of his credit for the first time since his earliest films.

Except for the commercial success of his first foray into

pure genre filmmaking, 2006's heist-and-hostage thriller *Inside Man*, Lee has not had a real hit since 1998's *He Got Game*, which debuted at number one at the box office and grossed $21 million in theaters. Since then, returns, both financial and aesthetic, have been diminishing. Is Spike Lee still a major American artist? Was he ever? The self-satisfaction and intellectual malaise of his most recent works are troubling enough to warrant some skepticism and soul-searching, even among his fans.

In the '80s, Lee found his niche speaking for black middle-class audiences in pictures that seemed, given the climate of the industry, more or less impossible before his arrival. No one was making movies about middle-class black hipsters (*She's Gotta Have It*, 1986), Greek life at historically black colleges (*School Daze*, 1988), or the causes of Brooklyn riots (*Do the Right Thing*, 1989). Displaying a black-American-centric sensibility absent from the indie sector and the studio world, these films signaled the dawn of a career unlike any American film had ever seen. Along with the Nike commercials he was making a fortune on, these films gave Lee an importance few directors achieve in a lifetime, much less after three features.

His next three films, *Mo' Better Blues* (1990), *Jungle Fever* (1991), and *Malcolm X* (1992), the last of which I saw on the big screen as a nine-year-old with my entire family, elevated Lee to the first rank of American auteurs. These films are not just lasting contributions to the cinema of the black diaspora, canonical works in that realm, but movies of lasting importance to American society as a whole—the ugly mythology that hangs over American miscegenation had never, before or since, seen a motion picture treatment as penetrating as *Jungle Fever*, while before *Malcolm X* no black revolutionary life had ever been the subject of a sprawling, and sympathetic, Oscar-bait movie produced and released by a major studio. His studio work to that point dwarfed that of any other black director who had ever worked in the system; not one had ever been able to make something even remotely like *School Daze* or *Malcolm X* with house money; indeed, James Baldwin's first draft of a screenplay languished, unmade, for more than twenty years before Spike wrested the opportunity to make the film from Norman Jewison.

Yet he was far from done; Lee continued with the lucrative side gigs, and continued to make movies of interest and quality—*Clockers* (1995), *Get on the Bus* (1996), *He Got Game* (1998), *Summer of Sam* (1999), *Bamboozled* (2000), and *25th Hour* (2002), while not masterpieces, are all fantastic movies—until just after the towers fell. *25th Hour*, about a convicted drug dealer (Edward Norton) making the rounds on his last day of freedom before serving a seven-year sentence, is shot through with disorientation, fear, and uncertainty. It remains one of the most evocative American films to grapple with the larger urban mood in the wake of September 11 and is perhaps Lee's best movie not named *Do the Right Thing*.

It is hard to overstate the importance of Lee's career in the annals of American cinema. Had he never made another film, like so many other black directors who showed early promise, I might still think of Lee as the greatest black American director; his career is still assuredly the most far-reaching, the most groundbreaking. His run from 1986 to 2002 is rightfully legendary, a career for which black and brown and many white people the world over, regardless of how silly his hats are or how outlandish his public commentary, still revere him.

Which makes what has come after seem so incongruous, and so consistently disappointing. Tragic, really.

Inside Man, the last financial success and first deeply impersonal work of Lee's career, was well made but slight, with purely commercial aspirations. The troika of *Miracle at St. Anna* (2008), *Red Hook Summer* (2012), and *Oldboy* (2013) have few partisans; meandering, overlong, and unfocused, they're all hampered by a sensibility that feels wrong for the material. *Miracle*, Lee's picture about black GIs, has scenes of great emotional weight, but its structural coherence is torpedoed by a silly present-day framing device that makes the film a Russian doll of flashbacks. It's also overburdened by self-righteous writing ("We served our country too," one character says, in one of the many speeches about racial injustice), and, in what's since become a bad habit for Lee, excessive musical cues. Lee's bombastic style—already straining against his material in *She Hate Me*, with its animated sperm shooting out of Anthony Mackie's cock—overwhelms *Miracle* with sentimentality and smugness.

In the '90s, Lee was too big for festivals. Not anymore. In 2012, *Red Hook Summer* premiered to mixed notices at Sundance, a place Lee had never felt the need to take his narrative films before. It was the first Lee shot digitally without a name cinematographer, and his crew consisted largely of recent alums from his NYU graduate filmmaking class, not the union vets he was used to. He came to Sundance with something to sell, but no one wanted to buy it: *Red Hook Summer* was released through a service deal with a small start-up distributor called Variance Films, to whom Lee paid an undisclosed sum to distribute the film. There were subway ads, but no televised trailers, no billboards. The movie quietly disappeared from view in a way none of Lee's narrative films had since the dawn of his career.

DA SWEET BLOOD OF JESUS MIGHT BE JUST ANOTHER dud if it weren't also a remake of Bill Gunn's *Ganja & Hess* (1973), a legendary film in certain cinephile circles, especially black ones—the mere fact of a remake represents a bold claim by Lee. Rumored to be the lover of several white-boy starlets of the '50s, such as Montgomery Clift and James Dean, Bill Gunn was for a short while a darling of the New York theater world before he began his varied career as a novelist, playwright, and filmmaker. Like so many fascinating black actors from the era, Gunn was never blessed with roles that spoke to his talents. Nor was his motion picture work granted the distribution and cultural platform it deserved. After adapting Kristin Hunter's novel *The Landlord* for Hal Ashby to direct (resulting in one of the earliest narrative films to document the gentrification of Brooklyn), Gunn made his directorial debut with *Stop* (1970), which made him one of the first four African Americans to direct studio films, alongside Melvin Van Peebles, Ossie Davis, and Gordon Parks. That of those four filmmakers' work only Gunn's is now unavailable is no accident of history. Beloved in neither gay nor black circles, *Stop* has all but disappeared. It was pulled from theaters following a brief run in 1970 and never released on home video. It last screened in its original 35mm format in 1990, following Gunn's death, at a Whitney Museum retrospective of his work curated by his publisher and collaborator Ishmael Reed.

In retrospect, Gunn's next feature, *Ganja & Hess*, should have made him America's first broadly celebrated black auteur. The first film directed by a black American to screen at Cannes, the 1973 picture was, like *Stop*, vigorously suppressed before it could make an impression. Its backers anticipated a *Blacula* (1972) redux, a cheap vampire movie with brown faces to satisfy the grindhouse crowd. What Gunn delivered instead was a brooding and mysterious film built on erotic lyricism and the parochial aspects of black American life. At Cannes it was greeted by a standing ovation, but its backers at home were less enthusiastic. They angrily seized the film from Gunn, and it was recut several times into bastardized versions that later crept into B-movie cinemas and home video under lurid titles such as *Blood Couples* and *Double Possession*. *Stop* was rereleased in the late '90s at the behest of *Ganja & Hess's* producer Chiz Schultz, who spearheaded a reconstruction of the director's cut from materials found in the attic of the film's editor. By then the legend of *Ganja & Hess* had spread, though its stylings and concerns were still too baroque, and too Negro, for the sort who put the cult in "cult film" to latch on to completely.

Like Gunn himself, *Ganja & Hess* is an unclassifiable piece of work. Gunn's symbol-heavy narrative creates a world in which the word "vampire" is never used, and the usual tropes of the genre are discarded (daytime really ain't no thang for Negro bloodsuckers). Shot in hazy Super 16, the opening sequences glide from frozen tableaux of neoclassical European sculpture to extended, documentary-like scenes of a Pentecostal church, replete with speaking in tongues and lustily belted spirituals. It's a vampire movie that feels at once like a vaguely remembered daydream concerning Negro church life, post–civil rights black class consciousness, and lucid erotic nightmares. While *Ganja & Hess* focuses on a wealthy black man, and so raises questions about the travails and wages of black assimilation, its interests are opaque and only incidentally political. Bill Gunn, unlike the most prominent black American directors of his era or afterward, had no desire to make everybody's protest movie.

In the film, Duane Jones is memorably assertive and taciturn as Dr. Hess Green, an anthropologist living in a gothic Hudson Valley mansion and studying a long-vanished (and fictional) African civilization known as Myrthia. Hess reads as self-made, a man with one foot in and one foot out of the larger black community. Though he attends a black church where his chauffeur, played by the musician Sam Waymon (better known as the little brother of Nina Simone), is a pastor, he also has a self-consciously aristocratic mien and a son, expensively educated in private schools, who is most comfortable speaking to his father in French.

Trouble begins when the local archaeological museum assigns him a new research assistant named George Meda, played by Gunn himself in a memorably animated and feline manner: his high-pitched voice and unruly shock of Negro hair make him come across like a haunted, less-Jheri-curled Lionel Richie. After spending an odd evening together getting acquainted, Hess discovers Meda sitting in a tree behind his home with a noose in his hand, threatening to hang himself. Convincing the man not to kill himself on his property is paramount to Hess. "Mr. Meda," he pleads, "I am the only black man who lives in this neighborhood, so if another black washes up ashore I can assure you the authorities will drag me in for questioning."

The drunken Meda comes down from the tree and, after indulging Meda's bizarre, self-revelatory conversation for a while, Hess goes to bed, crisis seemingly averted. In the middle of the night, however, the formerly suicidal Meda turns homicidal, bursting into Hess's room and stabbing him with a Myrthian dagger. Meda follows his attack with a bath, after which he shoots himself in the chest. Hess wakes up following the attack unharmed, with a dead research assistant in his bathroom and a new thirst for blood, which he immediately whets by licking Meda's off his bathroom floor. At first he robs blood banks to feed his thirst, but soon his cravings lead him to the seedier parts of New York City—the Negro night spaces in which so many blaxploitation fantasies were lived out—to seduce victims for his fix.

When Meda's wife, Ganja (Marlene Clark), a nouveau riche arriviste, comes looking for her husband, she falls swiftly in love with Hess and his haut-bourgeois lifestyle. "I'm very valuable," is how she introduces herself to Hess, and when he asks her straightforwardly why she came to his estate, she replies, "Money." They begin a torrid relationship, and even after she discovers her husband's body, hung frozen in Hess's cellar, she marries Hess in front of a small crowd of mostly white people. (One of them is the writer William Gaddis, a friend of Gunn's.) In the midst of one of their sexual encounters, Hess makes Ganja into a vampire. They soon find themselves luring young men to their home to extract their blood.

Hess comes to rue his lifestyle. It's a lonely and morally degrading slog, killing for blood, not to mention the tedium of being physically cold all the time. Despite what might promise to be the eternal companionship of Ganja, he finds himself seeking redemption in the arms of the Christian God. Standing shirtless in his basement, in the shadow of a cross that hangs from the ceiling, he drops dead. Gunn, whose film treats both the teaching of black Protestantism and the myth of vampirism literally, saw the irony of casting the salvation of Christ as freedom from immortality as opposed to the doctrinaire Christian reading. Ganja, however, lives on, and the last image of the film is of a new young man rising, undead, to join her.

The association of the vampire with the aristocrat is as old as Dracula, and has always implied the extraction of vital life forces by the wealthy. *Ganja & Hess* adds another layer by making its well-heeled vampire a serial perpetrator of black-on-black crime. In Gunn's film, when Hess exclusively attacks poorer Negroes, images from pastiched African ("Myrthian") rituals flood the screen, accompanied by an ominous, horror-movie drone of synth strings; it's as if Hess's vampirism were a way of forming a connection to an atavistic past, one he could only study at a cold distance as long as he was fully human. It is as strange a portrait of the black bourgeoisie as has ever been offered on film, and for his pains the film brought Gunn obscurity and neglect.

NO SUCH FATE WILL LIKELY VISIT SPIKE LEE. IT TOOK A combination of luck, talent, and unyielding ambition for him to become the face of whatever we speak of when we speak of black cinema. Lee is now etched permanently in the national memory as a rabble-rousing cultural touchstone. As he has grown older and richer, his relevance as a media persona hasn't waned as much as his reach as a filmmaker. Lee's increasingly tone-deaf and heavy-handed narrative filmmaking is antithet-ical to Gunn's mix of lyrical, moving camerawork and biting cynicism. A telling contrast lies in their use of music: where *Ganja & Hess* unfolds largely without a score, *Da Sweet Blood of Jesus* is plagued by desperate underscoring through-music—a never-ending soundtrack of neo-soul and neo-Tropicália, crowdsourced through Twitter, that strains to save the movie from its jerky pacing.

Things are similarly awry in the design and aesthetic of the film: what's veiled or suggestively opaque in Gunn's film is dialed up and garish in Lee's. Lee's overly crisp, wide-depth-of-field digital sheen replaces the gauzy Super 16 of Gunn's gloomier telling. A modern beach house on the shores of Martha's Vineyard—the island where Mr. Lee and many other members of the Negro elite, including the forty-fourth president, "summer" in the wispy confines of Oak Bluffs—stands in for the Hudson Valley mansion. The home becomes something to scrutinize (how much those curtains must have cost!), and the lush colors of the décor, lighting, and costumes—deep browns, reds, blues, and yellows—provide too much visual information, running counter to the mystery of the story. In *Da Sweet Blood of Jesus*, Hess is played by the Broadway actor Stephen Tyrone Williams, and Ganja by the British-Iraqi actress Zaraah Abrahams, ten or so years younger than in *Ganja & Hess*, and much more flamboyant. They get married wrapped in kente cloth, ride in private jets, and put on designer clothes even to go to the bathroom. Where Hess in the original was ecumenical in his tastes, Lee's version makes him out to be a high-class pan-Africanist only interested in collecting African art. Even the recondite "Myrthia" is transformed into the real—and therefore implausible—Ashanti.

What Lee's remake handles most clumsily is class. It is as if Lee's own significant wealth has blinded him to its essential meaning. Lee's need to underline everything with a thick political marker gets in the way of the point he appears to be making. In the original, Hess's wealth was shrouded in mystery; in the new version, it turns out that his family owned "the first black firm on Wall Street." On his large estate, which Hess claims to measure "about forty acres," he holds forth about the ills of contemporary society: "We do live in a blood society. The United States is the most violent country in the world." But violence appears not to be the issue so much as "addiction"—as vague an idea as Lee has ever put on screen. "Change is impossible because we're addicted to our society," one white woman tells Hess at a party, "especially the upper middle class, because they've taken the damn thing in such large doses." "What decides whether one is a criminal or not is which side of the law your fix is on," says another. Lee has always been heavy-handed, but in the past he tempered his didacticism by threading through ambiguities and political impasses that made lessons hard to extract. It's hard to view *Da Sweet Blood of Jesus* and remember the deeply felt paradoxes that made his best work so watchable.

Lee's sloppy approach to class issues ends up straining the plausibility of his film. In *Da Sweet Blood of Jesus*, as in Gunn's *Ganja & Hess*, Hess seduces and kills ghetto women, but here all of them are light skinned and well dressed. The scenes of seduction and murder reach such queasy unreality that it's clear Lee sees these events as simply fodder for an exploitation flick he can commit to only halfheartedly. Hess meets one victim, a crisply enunciating mother—she unspools dialogue like "You ask mad questions! Dang!" without a shard of credibility—minding her own business on a park bench outside the projects with a baby in her arms. Inexplicably, he convinces her with little difficulty to go upstairs with him so he can bleed her. It's hard to believe a child-rearing, light-skinned, stately-looking black woman would be sitting on that park bench in the first place, let alone allow a total stranger into her home to fuck in the presence of her child. Nor does it seem plausible that Lee's Hess, fed with silver spoons since childhood, would know the first thing about the Fort Greene projects where he scores his victims.

After the ABFF screening, the baffled audience stuttered their questions. "What message are we supposed to take from this film, Spike? And my second . . ." one audience member said before he was cut off by the director, who exclaimed, "I don't talk about the meaning of my films anymore, I haven't for fifteen years, I stopped doing that." Lee, with his trademark intimidation, stifled debate over his intentions before it even began. The director was willing, just barely, in the most canned responses, to allude to the film "being about addiction" in an ever more addiction-prone world. Perhaps these banalities hid a deeper problem—that the movie was an allegory of Lee's own addiction to high society, his need to preserve himself above the black filmmakers whose work he wouldn't abide. Or, perhaps, an allegory for the New York he helped turn into a luxury prod- uct he neither desires nor understands.

THE SO-CALLED NEW BLACK CINEMA OF THE EARLY '90S didn't yield many lasting directorial careers, save those of Lee and John Singleton. Where have you gone, Julie Dash? Leslie Harris? Matty Rich? Darnell Martin? These young black film- makers made celebrated debuts in the late Bush or early Clin- ton years only to, for the most part, disappear.

White studio execs were largely to blame. But black au- diences were partly responsible, too; they didn't show up for the best of these films. Charles Burnett's *To Sleep with Anger* (1990), a masterpiece on par with his revelatory student film *Killer of Sheep* (1978), found audiences that were overwhelm- ingly small and white. Burnett, considered by many observers to be the greatest American black filmmaker, has had only one widely distributed feature since 1994's *The Glass Shield*. A flawed but potent movie set in the immediate aftermath of the LA riots, it was taken away from him and recut at the behest of Harvey Weinstein, the head of Miramax Films at the time, likely to its detriment.

Lee's celebrity, which grew exponentially while he shucked and jived with Michael Jordan during his Mars Blackmon years, shielded him from such indignities. For much of his ca- reer in the studio system, Lee received final cut, giving him the authority to make his films as he wished. In an America that seems to prefer a single black arbiter of Negro feelings and beliefs, his career and public persona have eclipsed everyone else's. His persona has also, somewhat dispiritingly, eclipsed his own filmmaking.

In many ways, this state of affairs seems to suit Lee just fine. He, too, seems to prefer a single black arbiter. More than a few young filmmakers Lee has mentored at NYU, black and white, have offered casual anecdotes of his evasiveness and defensiveness when dealing with potential heirs. One ex-student of Lee's once bemoaned at a party how his professor would read the scripts of students who were the sons of white billionaires but not of those like him, who'd grown up on the streets of black Bed-Stuy (unless they were gay and female, a baffling wrinkle). "A sucker move," the student said. Another protégé, a documentary filmmaker, went so far as to say that his mentor was happy to help cinematographers, actors, and documentarians who were black, but male narrative directors were another story: he liked being the only iconic American film director among black males and wished, in his heart of hearts, to stay that way.

The morning after the premiere, I took the subway from my apartment in the Bronx—where I'd settled since deciding Bed-Stuy had become too expensive—to the 40 Acres and a Mule offices in Fort Greene to interview Lee. A neighborhood long lost to most of the middle class through gentrification, Fort Greene is still home to poor folks who reside in the Whitman and Ingersoll Projects just north of Fort Greene Park, where

Lee shot much of *She's Gotta Have It*, and near where his father, a jazz musician, has lived since 1969.

The original home of 40 Acres and a Mule, which relocated five years ago to 75 South Elliott Place, was in a former firehouse on the southwest corner of Fort Greene Park. In my early years in the city, as I would pass it while riding a bus down DeKalb Avenue, its imposing African-themed flag billowing above the street always seemed to me a beacon of hope, the shining star of black filmic achievement. The flag, which had been relocated, too, didn't hold quite the same power in front of 75 South Elliott.

Lee had caused a stir the previous February during a Black History Month–themed appearance at nearby Pratt Institute, where he was asked to address "the other side" of the gentrification debate. In blue Nikes and a hoodie emblazoned with the slogan "DEFEND BROOKLYN," he said: "Why does it take an influx of white New Yorkers in the South Bronx, in Harlem, in Bed-Stuy, in Crown Heights, for the facilities to get better? The garbage wasn't picked up every motherfuckin' day when I was living in 165 Washington Park. . . . What about the people who are renting? They can't afford it anymore! You can't afford it. People want to live in Fort Greene. People want to live in Clinton Hill. The Lower East Side, they move to Williamsburg, they can't even afford fuckin', motherfuckin' Williamsburg now, because of motherfuckin' hipsters. What do they call Bushwick now? What's the word?"

"East Williamsburg," someone called from the audience.

I was ushered into Lee's second-floor rehearsal space, which was serving as a staging area for journalists. I sat at a small table in the middle of a building-length room with wood flooring, its walls stocked with memorabilia: the pizza box Lee carries in and out of Sal's Famous in *Do the Right Thing*, a gargantuan one-sheet from the Italian release of Scorsese's *Mean Streets*, signed by Lee's fellow NYU alum. The other journalists and I made small talk, scanned e-mail on our phones. I checked the early reviews. My pallid interlopers from the night before had mostly given it a pass. Richard Brody praised it on his *Front Row* blog for *The New Yorker*, saying, "Spike Lee has entered his Mannerist period, which, in movie terms, can be defined as making a film on the basis of images rather than experience." No kidding. Scott Foundas from *Variety* had clearly found the film wanting, but he didn't bring the knives out. It was too loaded for anyone outside the tribe to pour salt on the wound of a filmmaker who had so lost his way.

When I arrived on the third floor, it was mostly silent except for Lee yelling at one of his staffers for leaving a stack of boxes unattended in a hallway. He spied me quickly, out of the corner of his eye, and immediately ceased his theatrics—the media was watching. I followed him into the editing room, its blue walls covered, floor to ceiling, with paintings and images of Michael Jackson. It was the single creepiest room I entered in 2014. I sat on a leather couch and produced my laptop, making small talk as I prepared to record the conversation. Mr. Lee's legs were crossed, one orange-Nike-bearing foot perched not far from my computer. "What you got for me?" he asked.

Although he spoke lovingly of Gunn, he spent the better part of the next thirty minutes bobbing and weaving around my questions like Floyd Mayweather. He wouldn't address whether there was latent meaning in Hess's newfound class status and youth, or in his preference for mulatto victims ("I'm just trying to cast the best people, I wasn't trying to find the most light-skinneded actresses I could!"). He cared not to elaborate on how his methods have changed or evolved as he's grown older; whether he enjoys the newfound freedom of not having financiers to answer to; if, indeed, he has any more original stories he's dying to tell, themes he's hankering to explore. He seemed, in many ways, resigned.

It is odd to see Spike Lee, a filmmaker who came to prominence as someone with a bold and uncompromising voice, become, in his mid-fifties, something resembling a hack: a Jay-Z-and-Beyoncé-era rich black navel gazer. Here is an intelligent and remarkably accomplished man who seems to have little or nothing left to say in his films, and has abdicated control of their meaning. I was more than a little sad.

After we mercifully concluded, he grew somewhat more magnanimous, for a second. He stood as I was putting away my computer. "Thanks for coming all this way," he said.

"I used to live down the street in Bed-Stuy until recently," I replied. "Got rent-sabotaged out just last month." He asked where I was currently living, and I told him the northern Bronx.

Suddenly the wall of defensiveness he'd erected as soon as he stopped yelling at his employee fell away. His face softened. I watched him utter a brief but full-throated laugh. I couldn't tell if it was schadenfreude or a jadedness that he normally kept to himself.

"Just give it some time," he said. "Pretty soon, you won't be able to afford to live there either."

THE FINAL IMAGE OF SPIKE LEE'S *CHI-RAQ*—AN ADAPTA-tion of Aristophanes's *Lysistrata* that was released eight months after *Da Sweet Blood of Jesus* and named the best film of 2015 by venerated critics such as Amy Nicholson (formerly of *LA Weekly*) and *The New Yorker*'s Richard Brody—is a shot of the city of Chicago's flag bearing the words "WAKE UP." It's unclear, though, what exactly we're supposed to wake up from: our culture's complacency concerning inner-city gun violence, or the illusion that such violence, often committed by African Americans against other African Americans, isn't deeply con-nected to America's racist legacy. Unfortunately, what one be-comes most conscious of is the largely evasive way Lee portrays this ecosystem of denial and neglect. At a historical moment that requires more hard truths than soothing delusions, *Chi-Raq* and its author seem like preening tourists who—to para-phrase Gil Scott-Heron's legendary verse about the NAACP director Roy Wilkins—stroll through black Chicago in a red, black, and green liberation jumpsuit they've been saving for just the proper occasion.

Chi-Raq is clearly meant to be fantasy, depicting a sex strike by the women of the South Side of Chicago that successfully ends a scourge of gun violence in the Second City and inspires corporations to rain down full employment on ghettos everywhere. But this is a dangerous fantasy, and a shameful one, too: it refuses to acknowledge the real stakes of its narrative, cheapening the cost of black sovereignty and dignity in the face of this country's many failings. Unlike Tarantino's *The Hateful Eight*, which, in its postintermission flashback, makes clear that the disregard for black female life and property is at the root of its revisionist Reconstruction narrative, *Chi-Raq* withholds the violence against black female bodies that is at the heart of its outrage. Lacking the seriousness of intent to contain such verisimilitude, Lee's film is too busy dreaming of a world that never was, one that simply makes a mockery of our own.

Teyonah Parris, of *Dear White People*, plays Lysistrata as a gang leader's mistreated girlfriend who masterminds the strike after holing up with a stern middle-aged neighbor played by Angela Bassett, a strident black intellectual with no TV, a wall full of books, and—like the movie as a whole—sanctimony to burn. Shortly after she becomes homeless and is almost murdered by gang members seeking to assassinate her boyfriend— the gang leader Chi-Raq, played by Nick Cannon—Parris's Lysistrata realizes, in the movie's blundering narrative logic, that she and her sisters can use their sexuality to change the world. Bassett's character hips Lysistrata to Leymah Gbowee, the Liberian villager who in 2003 led a sex strike to bring attention to the violence that threatened her country. Of course, by the time Gbowee accepted the Nobel Prize, she owned up to the fact that the sex strike wasn't effective politics, but simply a publicity stunt in support of effective politics. Lee refuses his characters the intelligence to make the distinction. Instead, *Chi-Raq* takes the act of a sex strike seriously as a political one, without ever examining the ramifications.

While it's clearly not a work of realism, *Chi-Raq* is nonetheless very firmly, from its first frame to its last, situated in the political and material present. Although Lee called the new film "heightened reality" on *Charlie Rose* in 2015, he was quick to disavow any serious consideration of his own film's ideas, saying, "The whole sex strike thing is really a metaphor; in no way, shape, or form are we suggesting the way to stop gun violence in Chicago is to have a sex strike." This isn't fair play. *Chi-Raq* remains unsure of whether it wants to be a polemic or not, and remains coy about what more "realistic" politics its sex strike is intended to symbolize or stand in for. It suggests, very loudly, that it has something important to say, using Lee's familiar Brechtian bag of tricks to do so. Just what that something is remains obscure to most observers, even its most ardent supporters. I simply did not encounter the "comprehensive view of the society-wide reforms surrounding guns and gun violence on which constructive local changes would depend" that Richard

Brody claims to have found in the film. They aren't there, nor should they be.

Lee may have a special burden placed on him among many African Americans to get it right, to be a voice of reason in an American motion-picture world that has often marginalized the talents of African-American film artists and the reach of their films, but an equally troubling byproduct has come to the fore with his most recent releases, that the occasion of each new "joint" becomes a conduit for white critics to exercise their complete ignorance of African-American communities, and the people and psychologies within them, when trying to analyze Lee's mid-to-late career follies. All that seemingly thoughtful Afrocentrism, all those beautiful black bodies gyrating through space in immaculately coiffed hair and costumes that seem like they may have come from a sequel to the Sun Ra freakout *Space Is the Place*, got the better of the pallid, workaday film reviewers. How cool it all is, this hell we're living in.

Working with a real budget and *She Hate Me*'s DP, Matthew Libatique, for the first time since 2006's *Inside Man*, Lee gives *Chi-Raq* a seductive look and feel; from its opening overture of Nick Cannon rapping ("I don't live in Chicago, I live in Chi-Raq"), the lyrics emblazoned on the screen before crescendoing over an American flag made up entirely from guns, one gets the sense the film is meant more for arousal than reflection. The movie isn't in control of its tone, exposition, or much else, however, beyond its ability to titillate. The main characters have just been immersed in a bloody shootout at a South Side night-club, one in which a member of Chi-Raq's gang was killed, but both seem nonplussed or otherwise distracted from the desire for kinkily filmed bump and grind once they get home. The prurient, candy-colored tracking shots that follow Ms. Parris's behind, as she sashays down graffiti-covered and tree-lined streets, are equally tone-deaf and cheaply salacious.

Although the film tells us from the top that "This is a State of Emergency," Mr. Lee has picked a false "emergency" to hip us to. As Jason Harrington pointed out recently while responding to the film in *The New York Times*, gangs are no longer the cause of much gun violence in the Chicago neighborhoods where *Chi-Raq* was shot. Personal beefs—often over the smallest of things, which loom larger when society has cast you into degradation and poverty—rule the day among the underemployed and greatly marginalized. Even as a purely narrative invention, the rivalry between the gangs at the film's heart is drawn in the thinnest of ways; never does the movie seek to explain why the men, young and middle-aged, are shooting at one another. The idea of adapting *Lysistrata* to this environment proves to be a strained one from the conceptual stage alone.

This confusion shouldn't surprise us. Since around the time the Twin Towers fell, the universe of Spike Lee's narrative movies has grown curious, one that requires the extended and uncomfortable suspension of disbelief. As his films have become increasingly untethered from reality, or an aesthetically satisfying or intellectually edifying departure from it, so have his opinions about how to better it. See, for example, his recent comments about campus rape: "What's happening on college campuses today, you know, what happened at the University of Missouri where the football players got together and said unless the president resigned they weren't going to play, I think that a sex strike could really work on college campuses where there's an abundance of sexual harassment and date rape," Lee told Stephen Colbert in the run-up to the film's release, dressed head to toe in the black, green, and red *Chi-Raq* swag he's been peddling on Twitter. One gets the sense that this "State of Emergency" is as much a call to help out Lee's flailing box-office returns or merchandise sell-off as it is to end the violence.

One misses the Spike Lee who once peddled Malcolm X hats and Nikes—the director has always been a savvy self-marketer. It's no small irony, then, that the costumes Lysistrata's militant sex strikers wear—black-and-gray tankinis, boots, and pants, with dark berets—recall the uniforms of the Black Panther Party, which advocated for greater armament in the black community, if not outright insurrection against its oppressors.

Chi-Raq's ideas about what in fact should be done about gun violence remain opaque throughout. Lee punctuates his Chicago gangland sex comedy with overlong scenes of sanctimonious direct address from Samuel L. Jackson's snappily dressed Dolmedes, the film's Greek chorus (and a subtle nod to Rudy Ray Moore's blaxploitation character Dolemite). His haphazard commentary on life in a dangerous ghetto, where neither your neighbors nor the police are to be trusted, is like that of every other underrealized character in Lee's dangerous fable, essentially a mouthpiece for the director. Yet Jackson doesn't offer any perspective that, as a Greek chorus should, allows the tale to resonate from the merely provincial to the universal, nor does it clarify the film's themes—other than suggesting that living without sex, or amid gun violence, is hard.

The structuring absences that allow this to pass are gaps you could drive a Buick through. Where are the scenes of organizing prostitutes, housewives, baby mommas? We get a quick scene of negotiation between female members of the rival gangs, the purple-hued Spartans and orange-tinted Trojans, that begins with a call for "peace and hair grease." A club of "respectable" black ladies, led by Bassett, does eventually take part in the strike too, but Lee never shows us how that affects the rhythm of daily life or the tenor of their relationships. All we get are a couple of intercut scenes of Parris and her Trojan counterpart jilting their gang-member boyfriends. What of the women who would surely be beaten and brutalized due to such a campaign? Would solidarity hold? Would the violence really stop? Would women all over the world, in places with no apparent gun violence such as Copenhagen and Tokyo, also join the sex strike?

Of course not. But in the absurd version of the South Side Lee has conjured, magical realist solutions for black America's burdens are a dime a dozen. A place where 411 murders took place in 2015 and the median income (as John Cusack's Michael Pfleger–inspired preacher didactically reminds us, mid-eulogy, in one of the film's oddest scenes) is $12,000 a year, the South Side of Chicago deserves a more thoughtful and aesthetically honest exploration of its woes. Yet Lee abandons any sort of honest attempt at depicting how protest movements live and die, thrive or flounder, for Hollywood grandstanding—as when a group of mostly disempowered, poor black women storm the Illinois State Armory and find they have no problem subduing its guards, who all end up stripped and bound, before the movie forgets about them. Run by a conspicuously southern-sounding white codger (played by David Patrick Kelly from *The Warriors*) who, at the mere hint of sex with an attractive black woman, strips down to his Confederate flag diapers and mounts an ebony cannon in his office, one is left to assume imbecilic bigots normally run state armories in the Midwest.

The film's profound confusion only grows from there. If it is a satire, as Mr. Lee has said, it knows not what it aims to satirize. *Chi-Raq* seems to take with the utmost seriousness, in its stated plea for us to "wake up," the idea that the ongoing standoff must be settled not by a bloody SWAT team raid, but an organized "sex bout." Staged at the site of an ongoing hostage situation and televised with the full support of the local government (the mayor, played by D. B. Sweeney, wants to get back to intercourse with his black wife, who is also striking), Chi-Raq and Lysistrata get it on in front of everyone, both in the armory and at home. Whoever reaches orgasm first in the Illinois State Armory "sex-off" is the loser. The fate of Chicago's black community hangs in the balance. At some point toward the middle of the sequence, when we finally get the signature Spike Lee dolly shot, I'm pretty sure all the head-scratching I'd done had resulted in a rash.

When defending himself, whether on *Meet the Press* or black radio, Lee has made much of the nonactors from Chicago, including many victims of gun violence, who are in the film. Why would they be in a film, he angrily intones, that doesn't treat their pain with the utmost care and seriousness? Probably because no one but Spike Lee can convince white billionaires and the blinkered indie film execs who represent them to finance an eight-figure, star-laden movie about gun violence in black Chicago. But just because one has the privilege to speak to a major national crisis with expensive public art doesn't mean that it is any good. The one memorable nonactor in the film, a wheelchair-bound ex–gang member who talks to Cannon's title character while he sulks over some purple drink, offers the only moment of gravity and genuine feeling in the whole phony thing, talking about the perils of gang life from what you know is clearly firsthand experience; it makes Lee's actors look even worse. Before the moment can really breathe, though, Lee cuts awkwardly away from it. In its place? A montage of the elevated train circling into the loop that, beyond being a cinematic non sequitur if I've ever seen one, could come straight out of a promotional ad for the chic intra-loop Chicago that no one ever thinks of as "Chi-Raq."

It's a moment that illustrates how *Chi-Raq* is afraid of the power it contains, how it never transcends the infantilized, opportunistic, and irresponsible measure it takes of Chicago's ongoing nightmare. It represents the profound disconnect between the black leadership class, one Lee is very much a part of, and the people living in America's most dangerous urban districts. Topical but not wise, *Chi-Raq* is the moment where Lee, recent recipient of an honorary lifetime-achievement Oscar, has gone the full Kanye: maximum spectacle, minimum coherence.

FUCK GEORGE JEFFERSON, IT'S SPIKE LEE WHO HAS moved on up. He didn't want to be like Melvin Van Peebles, trumpeting the accomplishments of one movie he made forty-five years ago in some tattered sweatshirt he wore around the apartment—a nice one in Columbus Circle, bought with Wall Street speculation money. He didn't want to spend thirty years trying to get his first movie distributed and bumming around Africa, as Charles Burnett has, asking dictators and strongmen for funding. And he didn't want to be like Bill Gunn, thumbing his nose at the genres he was expected to make. He wanted to be noticed, to make a lasting impact on a broader cultural stage. He wanted to gentrify black Brooklyn himself. He didn't want slumming, Sundance-hungry white filmmakers—like the Oscar nominee Benh Zeitlin, or Slamdance winner Keith Miller, or filmmaker brand Quentin Tarantino, or any other white liberal making inauthentic stories about black poverty or bondage or struggle—to do it for him. Then Lee gave up. He moved to the

Upper East Side, the story goes, and got citizenship in the Republic of Jaguar commercials, the brand of "Brooklyn" emblazoned on limited-edition Absolut Vodka bottles with his name underneath.

But these days Lee—minus the fame, fortune, and ritzy address—is just like the rest of us. In mid-January, a full month before its "theatrical release," *Da Sweet Blood of Jesus* was released through Vimeo On Demand for a fraction of what a new videocassette of *Clockers* would have cost in 1995. The film graced a few coastal theaters and faded into oblivion along with most of the other movies given weeklong runs in New York City in 2015, a number that exceeded the 950 the *Times* reviewed the previous year.

It might not feel this way because of the recent successes of Steve McQueen, Ava DuVernay, Barry Jenkins, and Ryan Coogler, interesting black directorial voices all, but black movies by black people who are not beholden to the desires of white imaginations—black films in which the characters are, you know, alive, as opposed to symbolic stand-ins—have always been exceedingly rare. "Black cinema" is truly no better off than it was in 1984, just after Lee debuted his senior thesis film and Gunn finally gave up directing for good just before his novel *Rhinestone Sharecropping*—about how nearly impossible it is for Negroes to make nondegrading work in Hollywood—began gathering dust on bookstore shelves. "I want to say that it is a terrible thing to be a black artist in this country," Gunn wrote in the *Times* in 1973, "for reasons too private to expose to the arrogance of white criticism." How is it possible that this still rings true? How likely is it that Charles Burnett, Haile Gerima, Julie Dash, Wendell B. Harris Jr., Tina Mabry, Dee Rees, Dennis Dortch, Frances Bodomo, Billy Woodberry, Larry Clark (the black one), Leslie Harris, Darnell Martin, Rashaad Ernesto Green, Michael Schultz, Kasi Lemmons, Shaka King, Damon Russell, or Moon Molson will get a directing job on the kind of topical, studio-financed film that Lee, for more than a decade, made seem commonplace?

Without the monumental career of Spike Lee, I am quite certain I would have never taken the idea of becoming a filmmaker seriously. His turn toward hack demagoguery, and the revelation of certain unsavory aspects of his character, at a time when the entire profession is becoming increasingly unsustainable for people who are nonwealthy, regardless of whether they already have the commercial and industrial stain of being black, is on some days almost too much to bear—why should I even try? Your heroes always disappoint you, someone said once. "I can't lie to your students," Charles Burnett told me over lunch in Westchester County a few months after I interviewed Lee. He had flown all the way from Los Angeles to screen *The Glass Shield* for my students. "I can't look them in the eye and tell them they should become filmmakers." This from perhaps the greatest black American director, a man who can't get a feature financed and doesn't think, even though he has made just as many masterpieces as Lee has, that he has had a great career. Heartbreak doesn't even do it justice.

But for those of us with the addiction, we wait. We wait for a black public to find ways to pay for its own media. We wait for wealthy Negroes you and I have never heard of to provide a more muscular financial backing for specialty films with content that speaks to the concerns of the African diaspora, and indie-film prognosticators to stop doubting the ability of films with black characters to perform overseas. We wait for young white studio heads with a love of hip-hop but no middle-class black friends to stop telling seasoned Negro filmmakers something is or isn't "black" enough for their studio to produce, market, and distribute. We wait for dignity we've never been granted and have yet to find the means to take for ourselves.

"When I first came into the 'theatre,' black women who were actresses were referred to as 'great gals' by white directors and critics," recalled Gunn in that same letter he wrote to the *Times* about its review of *Ganja & Hess*. "Marlene Clark, one of the most beautiful women and actresses I have ever known, was referred to as a 'brown-skinned looker' (*New York Post*). That kind of disrespect could not have been cultivated in 110 minutes. It must have taken a good 250 years."

200 GHOLSON AVENUE

A few months after I moved into 730 DeKalb in the fall of 2013, while on assignment writing about a film festival in Memphis, one where *Redlegs* had won a prize the year before, I journeyed to Holly Springs, Mississippi, an antebellum town forty-five miles southeast of the historic and troubled city where Elvis Presley lived, to meet a man named Paul MacLeod. Perhaps the most famous Elvis memorabilia collector of all time, he was certainly the stuff of regional legend, a gun-toting, mile-a-minute talker with a questionable relationship with the truth. The film festival staffers I knew insisted I go to his home and take a tour. So late one Sunday night, in a van full of festival attendees, I found myself in front of Graceland Too, an 1853 antebellum house at the corner of Gholson Avenue and Randolph Street.

On the morning of July 17, 2014, about a month after I moved out of 730 DeKalb, Paul MacLeod was found dead, slumped in a rocking chair on the porch of Graceland Too, the door locked behind him. An air of mystery immediately surrounded his death. No foul play was detected. The local coroner, who suggested initially it might take up to six months to get autopsy results due to a backlog of bodies, claimed Paul had died of natural causes. Some people came and took pictures of his dead body before officials were notified. A picture of his fresh corpse, taken early that Thursday morning, circulated through the town in the weeks to follow, peeked at on smartphones in bars and on street corners. There would have been nothing too mysterious about all this had it not been for the fact that two nights prior, on the same premises, Paul MacLeod had shot and killed a man named Dwight Taylor.

GRACELAND TOO RESEMBLED AN OUTPOST AT THE END of the world; it looked like the last refuge of a bygone southern gentry waiting out an apocalyptic siege, one they would call the "War of Northern Aggression" for generations after. It had been a white frame house entirely at one point, but now the sides were undergoing a pale rust repainting that was yet unfinished. A seemingly unused green ticket booth, decked out with Christmas ornamentation and photos of Elvis plastered on its back wall, sat near the street just ahead of a gated driveway, both reinforced with barbed wire, not far from two statues of lions, also wrapped loosely in barbed wire and adorned with neck bows that seemed to be made of police crime scene tape. They were perched in protection on either side of his low-slung portico.

When I first arrived there, I walked around the house, mostly looking for a dark place to urinate before entering—I had just gotten half-drunk on Tennessee whiskey at the Indie Memphis closing-night reception. This proved prescient since MacLeod didn't, I would learn the following summer, have a working toilet. He used the facilities down the street at the local library for number twos, and his backyard for number ones. While pissing out some of the liquor I'd consumed several hours before along the eastern side of his property, I noticed a Confederate flag hanging from a post reinforced with rocks. It mingled with several American and state of Mississippi flags. Chuck D was right: Elvis was a hero to most, perhaps, but he had never meant shit to me. Here I was, a northern Negro in a southern town I knew nothing about other than that it had been developed as a site for cotton plantations, about to enter the home of a man whose antebellum space I was pissing on and who purportedly brandished guns frequently, some of which he claimed had once belonged to Elvis Presley.

Amy Hoyt, a stocky and square-jawed Tennessee native, sandy blond hair and groovy specs adorning a face that kept one guessing what was on her mind, was the volunteer transportation coordinator for the festival and a "lifetime" member of Graceland Too—she had a card to prove it. Hoyt was the first to walk up onto the porch. It was silent and still on the street, but the house was lit up along the front. The names Elvis Albert, Brenda, Helen, and Mary were emblazoned in raised yellow block letters on the underside of the pediment above, along with a collection of letters that read "TCB."

In his early seventies MacLeod was still an imposing man, with slicked-back white hair and a gleam in his blue eyes that let you know he had long ago lost his mind, or at least wanted you to think he had. Twenty-four hours a day, seven days a week, he offered tours of his home. He did not have the vintage Elvis memorabilia necessary to be taken seriously by other collectors, whose circuit of conventions he shunned. MacLeod claimed to have more than 300,000 photos of Presley along with every conceivable type of memorabilia one could imagine on display in the first floor and backyard of his home. Rugs, mugs, calendars, full-size framed portraits, paintings, dolls, curtains, fabrics, towels, videos, news clippings, trading cards—you name it, he had it—laid out across the six rooms and in an overgrown lot behind them. Like Elvis's home, Graceland, currently a remarkably lucrative international tourist attraction, the upstairs was off-limits; Paul had erected a chain-link fence around the stairwell. But the real draw of Graceland Too was not the immaculately constructed simulacra, the Southern Gothic meltdown vibe of the place that had long ago become the life's work of Paul MacLeod. It was Paul MacLeod himself.

MacLeod wore several dense rings on his large hands as he gave the five-dollar tours, and left the impression that he was not above using them in a dustup. His charm melted away at the edges of a subtle menace he exuded. If he caught a visitor staring off into space as he was talking, he would often grab their shoulder forcefully or pound on it twice with a back-handed closed fist, saying, "Yo, yo!" until he was confident that he had regained their attention.

Paul often told stories about his famed patrons. Muhammad Ali had been there, he said. So had Bill Clinton. Clinton was always visiting Graceland Too. He had always been there just two weeks ago. Paul kept a seemingly comprehensive set of visitor pictures in the "guest room," a hallway decked floor to ceiling with photographs. Neither Ali nor Clinton could be found. In the pictures, people stood in front of the Elvis shrine in the "shrine room" or posed wearing a jacket that Paul claimed Elvis once owned. He claimed he had a lot of things Elvis once owned. Rugs and guns especially.

He used the term "half-nigra president" in the most neutral of ways. MacLeod openly referred to women's cunts, basking in the glow of what he'd have his young Elvis Albert do to a particular woman's private parts, often right to her partner's face, a gun by his side most of the time. MacLeod was not bashful about brandishing guns among the unsuspecting. "If by taking my own life I could bring back Elvis Presley for his millions of fans across God's green earth, I would shoot myself right now in front of all of you here tonight," he exclaimed about halfway through my initial tour. The muzzle of a gun was pressed to his temple. I didn't know if the weapon was loaded, but MacLeod didn't look like he was lying.

I didn't glimpse any famous faces among the visitor pictures, no ex-presidents or heavyweight champions, mostly just college kids, red-faced with booze, smiling. In the "record room," which had once been the room of Paul's mother, Helen, before she passed away, he serenaded us with his own version of one of Elvis's songs, the walls covered with exposed Elvis records and their covers, a microphone and stereo system at the ready. MacLeod was a surprisingly effective crooner, issuing a more than passable series of Elvis tunes at the microphone for his rapt guests toward the beginning of the tour.

In the "portrait room" Paul kept photos of himself as a younger man, sometimes with a female companion, sometimes in the back of a limousine, and sometimes with large assault rifles. Smaller portraits of Elvis lived throughout the space. They were pink framed and occasionally adorned with mistletoe. It's easy to lose track of time in Graceland Too, amid that remarkable volume of detritus, stuffed in closets and bins, often covered in dust. Dolls of aliens or blond angels sat among poster boards covered with photos of Lisa Marie Presley, Britain's royal family, light erotica. MacLeod was, unbeknownst to himself, a postmodernist.

Intermixed with photos of himself as a younger man, Paul kept pictures of his son, Elvis Albert, whom he mentioned frequently but who, along with a wife he also referenced, was nowhere to be found. Legend has it Elvis Albert resides in New Jersey, having left his father, with whom he oversaw Graceland Too for much of the George H. W. Bush and Clinton administrations, due to the love of a woman he met while giving a tour of the space. Almost everyone who recounted that story in the community of Holly Springs, except for Paul, of course, had their doubts as to its veracity.

After pushing through, visitors stood around Paul on all sides, doors leading to other parts of the home behind them, the room's red walls covered in cutout photos of Elvis from periodicals and laminated copies of a front-page news story with the headline "Elvis Presley: He Excites Girls, Terrifies Critics." I kept my eyes on the floor now, exposed, unfinished wood, cluttered with political placards and yard signs, having lost track of the amount of "niggers" Paul had tossed off during the tour. I stood for a while by a placard that was for a mayoral candidate named Kelvin Buck before I finally walked out in the middle of one of Paul's diatribes. I had little doubt that Mr. MacLeod, a man of unmistakable charisma despite his subway loon vibe, was an unparalleled pastiche artist. I wasn't sure if he was genuinely dangerous or not. I didn't want to stick around to find out. Eliza Hittman, a filmmaker who had been the target of some of Paul's sexual innuendo, followed not far behind.

"Are you okay?" I asked her once we got back in the van. She said she was fine. I was the only black person in her party but I feared she may have been traumatized the most; our host had not just cast her as an object of desire but had openly speculated about many uses for her sexual organs in front of all of us. The others filed out and climbed back in the van, and without much talk, we pulled away from the sanctuary for self-obsessed idolatry that had become Paul's oddly poignant life's work, a chilling testament to a man who, like Paul, went on to his reward while sitting down.

SOMETIME AROUND ELEVEN O'CLOCK ON THE NIGHT OF July 15, Paul Bernard MacLeod, aged seventy-one and Caucasian, and Dwight David Taylor, aged twenty-eight and black, found themselves on opposite sides of Paul's front door. Dwight had been seen on Paul's porch earlier in the evening, agitated and chain-smoking, by a man who lived across the street, a local restaurant owner named Tyler Clancy.

A distraught Paul told local law enforcement that Dwight, whom he knew and who had been in his employ from time to time, tried to force his way into the "museum," possibly over money he thought he was owed. A glass pane near the base of a door leading to the foyer had been kicked in, seemingly from the outside. An altercation ensued. Ostensibly fearing for his life, Paul shot Dwight in the right side of the chest, killing him. Less than twenty-four hours later the case was considered closed. The mayor and acting police chief, Kelvin Buck, a sharply dressed, smooth-talking African-American politician and ex-member of the Mississippi House of Representatives, believed that Paul MacLeod had acted in self-defense. That was the official line.

Some members of the community, even before the local police had made their announcement, were not satisfied that justice had been done. The afternoon following the shooting, when Paul had secluded himself inside Graceland Too, various people drove by the property and yelled accusations from their cars. Dwight's mother, Gloria, told Channel 3 news that no one had been in touch with her from the police department about what had happened and why. "All we want is justice for our son," she said.

Dwight was a diminutive man, much smaller than Paul, with an angular brown face, close-cropped hair, and an easy smile. He went by "David" with his closest intimates. Unable to maintain steady employment, he was known to approach people at their homes and ask for work doing anything that could possibly need doing. He was often seen painting Mr. MacLeod's home, which in recent years had been several different colors. Dwight was by all accounts a gifted musician; he both sang and played guitar for the fifty or so parishioners at the Tabernacle of Prayer.

Like his parents, Dwight was desperately poor. The local homeless shelter, a former twelve-room motel in the run-down northern end of town, turned him down because of outsized demand for the few rooms available. But he and his parents were known to use the shelter's food services from time to time. His parents lived in poverty on Valley Street, also in the impoverished northern end of town. Dwight had hoped to bring his father to the church to play music with him on Sunday, July 20, five days after he died.

Less than seventy-two hours after the shooting, Marshall

County district attorney Ben Creekmore confirmed that the investigation into the death of Dwight David Taylor was ongoing and that the results were to be presented to a grand jury on October 1. That grand jury, the proceedings of which remain sealed, didn't result in an indictment.

It isn't common, one imagines, for unarmed young black men, regardless of how desperate they are, to break into the homes of heavily armed white men in a place long riven by the ghosts of human ownership and the hundred-year state-sponsored terror campaign that followed in its wake. What was Dwight Taylor really doing there that night?

I ARRIVED, WITH A PHOTOGRAPHER NAMED LEVIN, IN Holly Springs for a second time early on the afternoon of August 10, a few weeks after the shooting, to figure out what happened to Paul, and to Dwight, for *Harper's Magazine*. I had a lot riding on the story, as it was the most lucrative piece of journalism I had ever been assigned. Given that I still qualified for food stamps, I was hoping it would, for at least a little while, elevate me out of the chic poverty I had known since my adjunct teaching checks stopped coming in during summer break. My things were in storage and I had spent much of the summer shuttling back and forth to and from the Bronx, where I was subletting a cheap and tiny studio while I figured out what I could afford and where. I had run out of money that summer again, subsisting on the dollar menu at McDonald's for weeks at a time in July once my food stamps expired. A lucrative story in an important magazine seemed like a lifeline.

Seeing it in the light of day for the first time, the city of a little under eight thousand had whatever one thinks of when the term "southern charm" is issued. A center for cotton production before the war, it was later home to thirteen Confederate generals, and then played uneasy host to General Grant's command as the Union army invaded. It's home to one of the oldest historically black colleges, Rust, founded in 1866 to educate newly freed slaves. Today, the 70-percent-black population lives integrated with whites on the more genteel southern side of town. Blacks hold the mayoralty and two alderman seats in the city government. On the northern end of town, not far from Rust College, exists a level of poverty and disinvestment that has become forgotten America's calling card, especially in communities of color.

That area was once home to the highway interchange that had been moved south with a rerouted Interstate 78. Cars feed off the three-lane highway there into a seemingly always busy Walmart. Houses that have stood since Jefferson Davis's time line a street that leads from the highway into the town's handsome square. I vaguely recognized it from a movie: Holly Springs is the setting of Robert Altman's 1999 comedy *Cookie's Fortune*. Like many of the other homes from that era in Holly Springs, Strawberry Plains, a mansion used in the Altman film, was spared by Sherman's March. The town legend is that the mansions were too beautiful for the approaching Union army to burn down. Or that someone had a mistress.

You couldn't miss it, Graceland Too, perched on a corner not far from the square, where East Gholson Avenue, mainly a collection of one-story ranches, dead-ends into South Randolph Street. The front porch and surrounding area was covered with hundreds of unopened cans of Coca-Cola, the beverage Paul claimed to drink twenty-four times a day—they'd been left there by well-wishers in memoriam. The Confederate flag I had seen on the edge of the property months before had been removed.

Immediately after we'd parked across the street and stared out at the house for a bit, a van pulled up behind us and parked. In it were Amy Hoyt, the volunteer for the film festival who had first brought me there, and Amy Nicholson, the auburn-haired documentarian from New York who had previously been there with me as well. She was back to film the proceedings of the ensuing week; Paul's funeral was scheduled for the following Tuesday morning. A day of events at the home and a nearby community center, all culminating in a midnight vigil and screening outside the house, were also scheduled.

We were given access to the premises that Sunday by Philip Knecht, a local lawyer who was managing Paul's estate. A stout man in his early thirties, he was dressed as if to parody the image of a genteel country lawyer from yesteryear; his pale, balding pate glistened in the heat.

We walked around for a bit, taking photos, listening to

Knecht recite various aspects of Paul's legend, as we dug through Paul's belongings. In a closet we found a pink shotgun and several other weapons. The police had taken only the weapon Paul used to kill Dwight, and his ammunition. Out behind the house, Paul kept a makeshift electric chair he'd claimed was from *Jailhouse Rock*, as well as a couple of limousines, including a pink one he said had belonged to Presley but which he had actually acquired from a local used-car dealer. I encountered a large and active hornets' nest. A wheelbarrow filled with basketballs, painted black and wrapped in barbed wire, sat not far from it. Near the pink stretch limousine, I found storage bin after storage bin of empty spray cans in half a dozen different colors. It hadn't always been pink.

Paul slept on a rectangular storage box in the "shrine room" of his museum, above which hung a portrait of his idol. A bank of six or so TVs stretched along the far wall. On these televisions Paul, who owned the largest collection of *TV Guide* I will surely ever come across, recorded any mention of Elvis Presley on network television he could find for many years, just a few feet away from where he slept.

In the "portrait room" Amy Hoyt discovered letters from Paul's mother, Helen, who shared a birthday with Elvis Presley. She had sent them from Paul's ancestral home in Michigan and later from a retirement center in Arizona more than twenty years before. In the letters, some of which were written in a script that is nearly impossible to read, she often asked about him and his son, Elvis Albert. Were they okay? In another letter to her son she suggested, quite oddly, that she was as beautiful and alluring as a clearly much younger woman in an attached photograph.

Was it okay for us to be here, rummaging through a dead man's belongings, through a space that had recently seen so much tragedy and dread? "My position has always been, as the attorney for the estate and the attorney for the house, and the person with the keys, I want as many people in here as possible recording, filming, getting his name out, because I am first and foremost Paul's attorney," Knecht said to us. He had issued a press release three weeks previously stating, "Graceland Too, in partnership with the City of Holly Springs, is excited to announce a Memorial and Celebration of the Life of Paul MacLeod on Tuesday, August 12, 2014, during Elvis Presley week." It went on to state that tours of the premises led by "family, friends and lifetime Graceland Too members" would be given that day for five dollars each, even to other lifetime members accustomed to paying nothing, in order to raise money for Paul's "funeral and burial expenses, as well as the expenses and costs of his estate." No mention was made of whether the "expenses and costs of his estate" included fees to Knecht.

But this was still, in many ways, a crime scene. Philip Knecht, despite having a law practice that was only a few blocks away from Graceland Too, first talked to Paul at length the day after he shot Dwight. They spoke at the behest of the local pharmacist and town alderman-at-large, Tim Liddy, who implored Paul to get legal representation. Paul was mainly interested in giving Liddy and Knecht yet another tour of his Elvis museum even as Knecht suggested he could be charged with murder. "In a way, I got the last tour Paul ever gave of Graceland Too," Knecht reflected in his nearby office later that day.

Knecht knew Dwight as well, better than he knew Paul. "He would come by and offer to wash my truck. I usually didn't let him," said Knecht. "I'd let him do a little something and give him some money. Most of the time I would go to the store and buy him food. A lot of people did that around town. They were basically drifters, he and his wife, Cindi." Knecht, who has a gallows sense of humor and a nervous laugh, had known Cindi longer than he had Dwight. He was friendly with her for the most part but was upset about rumors he claimed she had been spreading. "She's been saying some things to other people that were racially insensitive, trying to make it a race issue."

He claimed to have helped both Dwight and Cindi out with legal issues they'd had, pro bono. They were both sent to jail for six months in 2013, almost simultaneously, Dwight for grand larceny after he allegedly stole a grill and Cindi for reneging on back child-support payments from a previous apparently violent marriage. They both faced fines they ultimately couldn't pay. "His family isn't acknowledging this but a lot of people knew Dwight, a lot of people had interactions with him. In the last two weeks of his life, they weren't very good interactions." Knecht alleged that Cindi had filed charges against her husband, whom she had married only months before, claiming he had been abusive toward her. She left him and returned to her family in nearby Ashland. Dwight had told Knecht he was desperate, given that he could go to jail for a long stint with the potential new charges. A silver chain and an iPhone charger were stolen out of Knecht's truck a few days later. The last time Knecht saw Dwight, he says that Dwight admitted to stealing them.

Paul had also previously filed charges against Dwight, who had apparently tried to break in before and, according to the former Holly Springs tourism chief Susan Williams, had beaten Paul up and stolen his car. Allegedly this was becoming a pattern for Dwight; Tom Stewart, who owns a catering company and a restaurant named Southern Eatery on the square, told me a few days later that Dwight, whom he "fed for a year and a half," had tried to break into his home the night after Stewart had refused to deliver five meals to a local motel where Dwight and some of his friends were holed up. When I asked him what Dwight was like, Stewart, a pink-faced, heavyset man in his forties, paused and looked around his restaurant. It was full of black patrons. He clearly did not want to offend anyone who might be listening. "He was not atypical of Holly Springs." He paused again, taking another look around. "He may hit you up for money, he may say, 'You got some work?'"

I suggested Dwight was underemployed. "Severely. Severely undereducated, had some substance problems, fairly moody guy."

Sitting across Knecht's desk, I suggested that rumors had been circling that Paul owed Dwight money, and that that night

Paul had called Dwight to come over to his house and get his back wages, only to kill him in cold blood when he arrived. "Paul didn't own a phone, he couldn't have called anyone," Knecht said in rebuke to that assertion. He suggested Cindi and possibly Dwight's parents, whom he had never met, were behind the rumors. "She has been saying some things to other people that are racially insensitive," he repeated. He admitted that in Holly Springs, Mississippi, it would be easy to make this case a "racial issue," claiming that U.S. attorney Ben Beaverbrook was bringing the case to a grand jury for purely political reasons informed by the racial dynamics of the town. "I think it's political, it's the DAs washing their hands of it, it's political and racial," he said.

Isn't everything, I thought.

SHANNON MCNALLY RESIDES IN AN UNASSUMINGLY gorgeous white frame antebellum house, finished in 1857, that sits high on a hill overlooking a tucked-away corner of Van Dorn Avenue, about a half mile from the town square. "I can only afford this house because it's in Holly Springs, Mississippi. I'm a musician. You can barter here, you can make things happen," she explained shortly after we arrived. She was wearing a black dress, her dark tresses tied back, green eyes a bit sallow. She pulled her legs back beneath her on the porch swing she sat on mournfully as she spoke. Shannon and her husband had lived in New Orleans before being pushed out by Hurricane Katrina.

Now they'd been joined by her parents, native New Yorkers both; her father is an ex–police detective from the Bronx who, along with Shannon's mother, retired to the area when Shannon and her husband, Wallace, settled there.

"This was Wallace's vision," she said gently, in a voice that suggested a mild dissatisfaction with the arrangement. She had adopted the cadences and southern lilt of those around her and there was something slightly put upon about the way she spoke. I'm sure she'd done a lot of adapting; Shannon had been a busker in Paris before finding her way to a major-label record deal with Capitol in the late '90s, back when such a thing still meant something, before the music industry's business model fell apart. Dwight's wife, Cindi, had left, spooked by the possibility of our presence, but she would return, Shannon informed us. "No one's actually talked to her yet. For multiple reasons. She's a little skittish."

Here we were, three Yankees in what Shannon referred to as a "quintessential small southern town," not quite sure what to make of one another. She talked at length about how difficult everything had been for Dwight and Cindi. They had been homeless off and on, struggling with substances. They could both be found on too many nights at the clubs in the alley, a small lane just off the town square that was known as a haven for public boozing and dope for the town's less well-off.

Shannon took an active interest in helping the newlyweds. She had met the couple, as many in the community had, when they knocked on the door asking for work. Over time Shannon began to see them almost every day. "They went everywhere together. They were clearly very in love. I would generally give them whatever work I could actually afford. Everyone else around here took advantage of them."

She suggested that the Taylors were often exploited, given cheap to nonexistent wages by people who would have them wash a car or clean a house. No one did this more than Paul MacLeod. "Paul had him paint that entire house with spray cans and then wouldn't pay him. Dig a ditch and give him fifteen bucks because you're a junkie and I don't want you to spend it on that. Man just worked eight hours or ten hours, whatever he did, who are you to say what he spends his money on?" Shannon said, "It's a tough little town."

Shannon didn't always have work to give them and would offer food instead. During the winter, she'd give them socks, hats, and coats. Eventually Shannon tried to give them things to do that were enriching. She'd invite them to do yoga or some leisurely gardening. Dwight's interest in music mingled with her own; Shannon knew that he sang at church. Eventually Shannon began to try to figure out how to get them into some housing, onto food stamps and Medicaid. A month before he died, Dwight had finally gotten a social security card and hoped he'd be able to get on disability. But they never seemed to be able to get through "the incredible labyrinth of endemic poverty," as Shannon put it. Dwight frequently claimed he couldn't get food stamps because he didn't have an address and he couldn't get an address because he couldn't find enough work to afford one.

Cindi showed up a short time afterward. She's a small woman, not much taller than five foot four, and was dressed in an oversized pink T-shirt, shorts with a plaid design, and a ball cap that read "Chattanooga." We greeted each other gingerly after she climbed up the porch steps. Shannon asked if she felt like talking. Mosquitoes were swarming, actively biting us all. "Let me go get something," she said. Then she asked to go sit in the garage. "I'm from the dust," she said after we had sat down to talk, referring to the homes she grew up in without floors in nearby Ashland, about forty-five miles south.

Cindi confirmed that she was still in touch with her family there and had been in Ashland when her husband had been killed. They were at least temporarily estranged, although she wouldn't discuss the details. None of their problems dampened her feelings of loss. "I miss my husband. Whatever he done, I miss him," she said to us with an earnestness that belied much pain. "What brought me here was Dwight. That's my best friend, my lover, my husband. Me and him had a connection that didn't no one else have in Holly Springs."

Cindi had come here to be with him in 2009, only a month after she had met him, after many late-night phone conversations. She thought she'd just come for the weekend, but she never went back. She referred to herself and Dwight as the "Bonnie and Clyde of Holly Springs" without irony. They'd coordinate their clothing in order to seem more like a unit. Her Christianity assures her that he's now watching over her and that he has no worries. "Every day that we wake up, we got problems. Good, bad, problems," she said, smiling, as if to reiterate that she was almost happy for him not to have to struggle so much anymore. "The average person wouldn't want to live how we live for seven days. You'd want to kill yourself."

Dwight and Cindi met Paul in 2011. He was having trouble digging a ditch on his property as they passed by on a hot day. They offered to help him. Cindi spoke about him with great affection. Her grief wasn't limited to Dwight. "People never knew our struggle. That's how we ended up meeting Paul. Paul has pictures of us on top of his roof all over his house. We took care of Paul when Paul got sick," she said. Paul had fallen off a ladder and broken one of his legs shortly before they met him. It wouldn't stop swelling and got to the point where he could scarcely get around. "Maybe God put us in that man's life for a reason, me and Dwight. We stayed down in Senatobia Hospital a week with that man."

Paul had wanted to shoot the doctors after they had discussed amputating his leg. Fortunately, he improved enough to keep it. "Me, Paul, and Dwight, we was like this," she said, squeezing her fists together. "He was a funny guy, but he was crazy, too, but he was a good person, Paul," Cindi claimed, trying futilely to hold back tears. "I lost two people. We developed a friendship that nobody knew about, for real."

They had painted the house blue, they had painted the house gray. "We painted that house from roof to bottom," she remembered with fondness. "We just happened to come into his life when he wanted it moody blue." When Paul would be in pain and hardly able to give the tours, they would help him out. They provided security when an especially rowdy group would visit late at night. He often would pay them only in Coca-Cola and Budweiser. For a time, they didn't mind. "He was cheap, but he would help us," she said.

Paul and Dwight had fallen out two years before. Cindi wasn't forthcoming about what had compelled Dwight to go to Paul's that night. I asked her if she thought Paul was capable of shooting someone. She said she never had a doubt he was. He would tell everyone who entered the home that he was carrying weapons. She said he was worse when he was drunk. Cindi suggested that Paul could go through a case of beer before noon. Shannon, who was sitting with us while Wallace played with their child nearby, asked Cindi why she thought Paul had shot Dwight.

"Let me tell you somethin': Paul opened the door for Dwight because he knows him," she began. "For real. It was a reason that Dwight went there, that only I know, but I won't say right now. I just want you to know about Dwight and Paul. My best friend and his associate. Paul would never have done that. No, Paul's not the bad guy. And David's not the bad guy either. Whatever happened God intended to happen. He never would have hurt him, no sir." Her voice began to rise a few octaves as her hands trembled. "We stayed at this man's house. Only a few people got to see the upstairs. We got to see what downstairs and the upstairs was like. We had it all. Literally."

Cindi, increasingly emotional, assured us that no break-in had taken place, that the story the police were telling was surely inaccurate. Shannon suggested that maybe Paul didn't recognize him and that's what caused the shooting. Cindi shook her head. I asked if he'd simply gone to Paul's house to talk. She didn't respond to either question.

"It killed Paul. Reality set in that he killed his friend, Dwight D. Eisenhower. He had nicknames for both of us. He called me C. C. Rider," she said, the tears finally escaping down her face. "There is more to this story than people will ever know."

PAUL MACLEOD WANTED TO BE BURIED IN A GOLD SUIT. It didn't happen. He never got life insurance and died with a $17,000 lien on his home that he had taken out just months prior, so his remains ended up in an urn, one decorated with the visage of Elvis Presley. It will be placed in a donated burial plot in Hillcrest Cemetery, not far from his home. A planned monument at Hillcrest will read, "Here Lies the World's Greatest Elvis Fan."

Only about sixty turned up for his funeral on August 12, three weeks after his death, at Christ Episcopal Church. His two daughters were in attendance but his son, Elvis Albert Presley MacLeod, who had tended to the museum with his father for many years, was not. Brenda, the oldest of the children, had visited Paul once at the museum, neglecting to tell him she was his daughter until toward the end of the tour. After that first visit, her husband refused to come in with her; he'd wait in the car while she visited her father.

Rev. Bruce D. McMillan, who had been Paul's preacher for many years, presided over the service. Annie Moffitt, Paul's purple-haired black friend, sang showstopping versions of "Amazing Grace" and "Walking Around Heaven" for the attendees, including more than a few people, young and old, in newly printed Graceland Too T-shirts. Mayor Buck was there too, dapper as he'd been described. The entire thing lasted less than an hour.

It was Elvis Presley week in nearby Memphis. Every August, in the run-up to the anniversary of Presley's death on August 16, the town plays host to parades and conventions, to impersonator contests and singalongs. The goings-on in Holly Springs proved far more telling, however. A spectacle of simultaneous remembrance and denial was in store for all of us. It was in the air. Half a country away, in that very same week, Ferguson, Missouri, had become a police state because an unarmed black man had been struck down by an armed white one; here it was just an opportunity for commerce.

If paying off his outstanding debts meant luring some of those who had converged on Memphis to take a posthumous tour of his home or buy a Graceland Too shot glass, so be it. One can't say the man wouldn't have wanted it this way, wouldn't have indulged in the crassness and opportunism that would inevitably come with his passing. T-shirts and plastic cups were sold at a tent outside Paul's home, dilapidated male and female mannequins displaying the pastel blue and pink T-shirts while various "lifetime members" of the museum gave tours of the space.

I passed Cindi, wearing a black-and-gold Drew Brees #9 T-shirt, a few blocks from the house. She was distraught and claimed she'd been drinking. She had been walking around the neighborhood, working up the courage to go over to Graceland Too while all those strangers were there, touring the place where her husband and her friend had died. Eventually she was given a tour by one of the "lifetime members." She broke down about halfway through.

Jeffrey Joe Jensen, a well-heeled documentary filmmaker who had been making a film about Paul, and a scholar from nearby Oxford who had commissioned Paul to write about his Elvis fandom, traded war stories and hawked their work nearby. Both of them spoke to visitors in the dusty museum and at a larger public memorial held at the town's multipurpose center that evening. After that memorial the crowd grew younger, with the college students that often made up Paul's customer base showing up as the light died over the town. Alcohol flowed freely; later that night, a fistfight broke out between two women.

As this younger set took over the street near Paul's, lining up to get one last look at his property before its uncertain future was sorted out, Elvis Presley songs blared from a PA set up in the middle of the street. Tyler Clancy, the owner of a BBQ joint and café in nearby Red Banks who lives across the street from Graceland Too, set up a stand in his front yard where he sold "The Paul MacLeod": a deep-fried version of the peanut-butter-and-banana sandwich that was Elvis's favorite. A screening was held just after midnight of various short films people had made about Paul over the years. And then the place thinned out. Paul MacLeod had gotten a hero's send-off, no question about it.

"WHAT I CAN'T GET CINDI TO TELL ME IS, WHY DID HE shoot him? I don't know," Shannon McNally said to us a few days later. She was in between blues sets at a fancy wine bar in Oxford and was having a rough day. Her mother had discovered just that morning that her stomach cancer, previously thought to be in remission, was back. Shannon also admitted that she was soon to get divorced. We shared some whiskeys.

Hill country blues was born here, on the guitars of Mississippi Fred McDowell, R. L. Burnside, and Junior Kimbrough. Gary, Burnside's son, is working on an album with Shannon. He was her sole accompaniment that night; her husband, who normally served as her drummer, was nowhere to be found. They went without a rhythm section.

"David was bipolar. He had some kind of bleeding ulcer or stomach cancer, he had something going on in his gut, I don't know what, but it was untreated and it was bad," she continued. "He was suicidal. He was ready to die." Cindi had gone home, leaving him for a couple of weeks because the stress level, exacerbated by their poverty, had gotten out of control. Shannon confirmed Knecht's assertion that Cindi had filed domestic violence charges against him. Given his previous record, he was facing a longer prison stint than he had ever known. According to Shannon, Cindi immediately regretted doing that, knowing it would simply trigger his frequently unhinged emotions. "He really didn't want to go back to jail."

While Cindi was at her parents' place, Shannon had fed him every day and eventually started putting him up. He stayed with her for the three days and nights before the shooting. "I'd spent, like, a hundred dollars just keeping him above water," she recalled. Dwight felt indebted to her. He would do whatever he could to help Shannon around the house. Dwight had spent most of the day the shooting took place at her home. "He was in physical pain, but he was also in mental pain," Shannon remembered. She tried to get him to seek medical help, but he rebuffed her.

When he came around that Tuesday night, ostensibly after being on Paul's porch earlier in the evening, Shannon's daughter and her daughter's friend were at the house. Shannon could tell something was amiss. She thought to ask if he'd like to go inside to sleep, but couldn't. Dwight was agitated. "There was a lot going on with him and his energy. I knew if I brought him in my house and anything went wrong . . ." she said, trailing off.

She offered to get him a room at the Holly Inn, the $45-a-night motel on the increasingly destitute northern end of town. Shannon asked if Dwight wanted to go to the emergency room, but he seemed more concerned with the forty dollars he owed someone he had been staying with off and on. The person had held on to his belongings and wouldn't give him his personal items back until he paid them. She gave him twenty dollars. "I just didn't have that much cash on me," she remembered. "We sat there for an hour and a half. He wasn't hungry. He was in pain. I said, 'David, I need one more day. I'll get you squared away in the morning.'"

The place was filling up behind us. Some folks nearby asked if she was going back on. Our time together was coming to a close. "I trust you, Ms. Shanno," she remembers him saying. He was worried about going back to jail, looking at five years because of the domestic violence charge if it went through. Given what thin ice he was on legally, "anyone could send him back to jail for anything," Shannon suggested. She knew she couldn't help him fast enough. "I knew he was dying. I knew he was dying that night."

In Mississippi, the black poor don't have the institutions of resilience that they do in Bed-Stuy. When the going got tough, there was no city-run, understaffed but reliably open Health and Human Services building full of stern-looking black female civil servants doing God's work. The homeless shelter is a derelict motel. It's really all about who you know. McNally was truly, by the end, all these people had.

When Shannon saw a text from Tim Liddy the next morning, she already knew. Shannon had warned Dwight away from suicide; she feared he might try to provoke a police officer or jump off a nearby bridge. She told him that if he wanted her to take him to the emergency room, to call. Before he left, Dwight said to her, "It's going to be big, Ms. Shannon." And then he was gone.

Soon after, Paul MacLeod was gone too. The broad majority of his collection was auctioned off for $65,000 to an anonymous buyer in Atlanta. The house sits empty now, painted over white so as not to be an eyesore, with nothing likely left in its future than condemnation. Paul's friendship with Dwight and Cindi had transcended class and age, and had scaled the walls of race, in a town riven by the ghosts of the violence that had long reinforced those very walls. But the endearing poverty that gripped both men, and their alienation from the more well-adjusted around them, proved to bring them together and rip them apart. In a way, both of them died of broken hearts.

5920 RHODE ISLAND AVENUE

I was driving to my mother's home in the central Cincinnati neighborhood of Bond Hill one summer night a couple of years ago. I had the windows of her bright orange Volkswagen Beetle down, and had stopped on Bond Hill's main drag, Reading Road, where the pockmarks of shuttered storefronts and crumbling housing are evident from every vantage point. On many a night, seemingly aimless, unemployed Negro boys sit and carp near a Richie's Chicken restaurant, across the street from a long-closed Nation of Islam diner. Although I grew up a few neighborhoods away in slightly leafier and more integrated Kennedy Heights I can remember when the neighborhood wasn't quite like this, before the streets became so hopelessly violent and economically unsalvageable that my father, who'd lived in the heart of the same neighborhood with his most recent wife, decided to get the fuck out. "I'm tired of niggers," he'd said, his processed hair straightened just so, the green eyes we share darting away from each other's. It must be tiring to be tired of yourself.

While stopped at the intersection, I glimpsed out of my eye a tall Negro dressed in a white tank top, his skin high yellow like my own, crossing the street in what seemed like a beeline toward my car. He was coming from a corner where much wasteful bravado and boisterous ennui take place, and I felt it immediately, that familiar sensation, the need to secure my body against potential predators. I was driving an orange car with plastic orange flowers on the dash, the same car I had been driving when held up at gunpoint not far from that corner two summers before.

The man sauntered behind my car, and I locked the door. Hearing this, the electronic click of the door locks snapping into place, he looked back at me and our eyes met as I swiveled my head to watch him. We didn't stop looking at each other the whole time he crossed to the other side of the street. The light turned green, and he said, "I ain't trying to roll up on you, bruh."

"It's all good," I replied, but really, it wasn't. Fear might be the predominant mode of contemporary American life, but that doesn't make it good for you. For the past fifty years or so, Bond Hill has become predominantly African American, and for the last twenty-five or so has been moribund and blighted, as have many Negro communities in Cincinnati. This is a direct result of redlining, blockbusting, and deindustrialization, of racist federal policy and cynical opportunism on the part of white developers—of America not having a clue how to treat its black citizens fairly.

My best friend's father, an intellectual property lawyer, grew up in Bond Hill in the '50s. His family fled with the rest of them, likely told of the coming Negro hordes and the imperative to save themselves from declining property values by huckster slumlords. When I met and befriended his son at Seven Hills School, along with a few coloreds who were nigger-rich like us, his family lived in the tony district of Hyde Park. Bond Hill is now only 7 percent white and just as segregated as it was a half century ago, when blacks first started to seek refuge and opportunity there.

My foot hit the gas, and the encounter ended. As I drove home, back to the rings of suburban simulacra on the outskirts of the neighborhood just a mile away—a suburbia my mother helped build with other Negroes—I couldn't shake the anger and shame. Why should I have to be afraid of my fellow yellow brother, or any brother for that matter, in the fucking first place? My mother, in her desire to protect me, had spent a great portion of her life instructing me to fear the very officers of the law who were supposed to ensure our safety, all while locking her doors and windows, employing an alarm system, and owning several guns, all in fear of the type of niggers (yes, the very word we use) Negroes fear most. At the "Villages at Daybreak," not far from a golf course and a decaying sports arena that hosted the NBA during the Kennedy administration, my mother is trapped in a cycle of fear that white folks of her station in life mostly don't know.

I had returned to the area to take care of my ailing father, a ceiling cleaner and janitor with diabetes, heart disease, chronic back pain, and a menthol cigarette habit he'd stopped trying to kick. After the dissolution of his third marriage, he had first stopped taking all of the nearly two dozen medications he was on. After a stint in the hospital, he began to take his medications liberally, without much rhyme or reason. He spent the summer in rehabilitation. I had never seen him so low.

Unable to keep his apartment in his current condition, his belongings were moved into storage. I was charged with finding him a place to live after he was let loose, but we had no idea when that would be. By summer's end, fearing he'd be put out on the street as his rehab stint was coming to a close, he became a tenant of my mother's, paying rent to live in the room I had called my own in the decade since she built our newest home, at 5920 Rhode Island Avenue in Roselawn. His pride and her comfort weren't as shattered by the development as I had imagined; given that her construction business had seen lean times for many years since the recession, she needed the income and he needed the security. Anyway, she mainly did it for me. Her love knew no bounds.

LATER THAT SUMMER, ON JULY 19, A FEW DAYS AFTER I assumed the worst about the man approaching my car on a humid Bond Hill night, an all-too-real spectacle of violence against a defenseless black motorist sent chills down both of our spines, and that of the entire city. In Mount Auburn, a neighborhood on the steep hill that separates downtown from the University of Cincinnati, Samuel DuBose, a forty-three-year-old father of thirteen, was shot in the head by the University of Cincinnati police officer Raymond Tensing, who had stopped DuBose for not having a front license plate on his Honda Accord. Cincinnati police initially said that Mr. DuBose, who had been arrested sixty previous times, handed Officer Tensing a bottle of alcohol after being asked repeatedly for his license, suggesting he may have been under the influence. Officer Tensing allegedly asked Mr. DuBose to exit the vehicle. After he refused, Lt. Col. James Whalen of the Cincinnati police told reporters on July 22, "There was a struggle at the door with Mr. DuBose in the vehicle and the officer outside the vehicle, and the vehicle sped away," while the police report, written by Officer Eric Weibel, stated that Tensing claimed he was being dragged by DuBose's car and had to fire his weapon as a result. Officer Phillip Kidd, who arrived on the scene just as the shooting took place, backed up Tensing's account, and so did Weibel himself, writing, "Looking at Officer Tensing's uniform, I could see that the back of his pants and shirt looked as if it had been dragged over a rough surface."

As national news outlets pursued the story of Sandra Bland's death in a Waller County, Texas, jail cell following a similarly minor traffic stop, the DuBose mystery picked up momentum locally. The police were in possession of body camera footage of the incident, but the Hamilton County prosecutor, Joe Deters, was unwilling to share it with the public. The Associated Press, *The Cincinnati Enquirer*, and four local news stations filed a joint lawsuit against Hamilton County on Friday, July 24, claiming that Deters's refusal was in defiance of Ohio's open records law. Police Chief Jeffrey Blackwell—who had considered resigning in May, after there were four homicides in ten days and reports of dissension within the police leadership—and City Manager Harry Black were grave when discussing its contents that Tuesday. "It was not a good situation," Black told local news station WLWT. "Someone has died that didn't necessarily have to die, and I will leave it at that." Blackwell added that the police were "prepared for whatever might come out of it."

THE MINI MICROCINEMA, IN CINCINNATI'S OVER-THE-Rhine district, is perhaps the country's only corporate-backed experimental microcinema. Screenings during its initial opening in 2015 were held, for most citizens, on the second floor of the former Globe Furniture building at 1805 Elm Street, a gorgeous structure that dates back to the 1890s. It sits across the street from Ohio's oldest continually operating market. The first floor, adorned with old movie chairs, serves as a gallery and gathering space; its white walls are covered with well-manicured posters for various programs that the Mini, as its supporters call it, had hosted in its inaugural season.

Gentrification works differently back home than it does in New York. In Cincinnati, just like in Mississippi, poor people don't have organizations of resilience that demand political accountability for their needs. While the black community's highest strata have collective clout that can shake city hall, their working-class brethren, out in the neighborhoods, don't. Meanwhile, the city's long-blighted and now suddenly cherished urban quarters are gobbled up and renamed, not by Hasidic developers and unceasing wells of foreign money, but by public-private partnerships in the name of Germanic city heritage.

Over-the-Rhine, with the largest collection of Italianate architecture anywhere in America save Greenwich Village, has recently become a neighborhood of shiny boutiques and fancy restaurant-laden streets, or restored nineteenth-century German beer halls with ten-dollar bratwursts. The Globe Furniture building, along with many of the buildings near it, has been newly renovated at the behest of 3CDC, a private nonprofit that is the constant target of the city's gentrification critics, who bemoan the billion dollars of mostly private money that have gone into remaking the neighborhood to fit the imagination and sensibilities of the elite. James Pogue, writing in *n+1*, suggested that 3CDC has "the money to write the future" in this town where the job of city planning in the once-riot-torn neighborhood just north of downtown has been largely taken over by corporate interests.

Sponsored by a grant from, and housed within the property

of, People's Liberty, a self-described "philanthropic lab" that acquired the building from 3CDC and purports to bring together "civic-minded talent to address challenges and uncover opportunities to accelerate the positive transformation of Greater Cincinnati," the microcinema is really just a large room that was once a showcase for sofas and is now a glass-encased corporate headquarters. With a pulldown screen, some ineffective curtains to shutter its large windows, and a hundred or so portable plastic chairs, the room is converted into a screening space.

The brainchild of C. Jacqueline Wood, a former staffer of the Ann Arbor Film Festival, one of the country's premier venues for avant-garde work, the Mini has some influential supporters. Eric Avner, CEO of People's Liberty, has since 2008 been a vice president of U.S. Bank's Carol Ann and Ralph V. Haile Jr. Foundation, one of the largest arts- and culture-focused philanthropic organizations in the region. Their fingerprints are all over almost every significant cultural institution in the city. They have clearly decided to put their resources, at least temporarily, behind experimental film exhibition.

This is surely unprecedented, at least in this town. Cincinnati, where I grew up and where I hope to continue making films, was once overflowing with cinemas, but by the time I came of age most of those were long closed. Even in its cinematic exhibition heyday, there was no place that catered to experimental movies; those types of pictures had rarely—if ever—reached the northern shores of the Ohio River, and when I shot my feature debut in parts of Over-the-Rhine, not far from the Mini five summers ago, the space was still pockmarked with blight and disinvestment. Although the 3CDC-powered Disneyfication of the area was already under way then, *The New York Times* was typically obtuse when claiming Cincinnati was finding its "artsy swagger." The city and the corporate proxies it had ceded authority to were in fact creating an environment in which a previous generation of low-rent gallery and exhibition spaces where one might encounter experimental film, such as Publico, would no longer exist.

Meanwhile, in some still "undeveloped" parts of Over-the-Rhine, one would be hard pressed to find a young black man who does not have some sort of criminal record, usually for the slightest of offenses. The stakes for second- or third-time offenders from the black underclass, who nearly never have access to their own legal representation other than court-appointed defenders, are high. They are seen as de facto criminals by the city's police establishment and as unemployable by the posh new businesses opening in their neighborhood. Their grievances are many and they have little reason to believe, at the present time, that education and self-enrichment, let alone protest and civil disobedience, are attractive alternatives to crime when navigating the troubled waters of inner-city poverty.

They're certainly not the individuals who were welcomed into free screenings at the Mini Microcinema that summer. All the events were free. So too were the popcorn, beer, wine, and cookies that were served for a half hour before the screenings. Wood talked about the need to educate new audiences, people who had not been exposed to the aesthetics of experimental movies and would, given the conditioning of American television and mainstream film culture and our continued unwillingness to fund K–12 media literacy education, likely find them unreadable. But that didn't seem to include longtime residents from the surrounding neighborhood. I'd seen a lot of strange things in my days, but never experimental cinema hosted by major financial institutions that catered to Negroes. I wasn't holding my breath.

The first program I saw there, of new experimental dance films, began with a short by Maya Deren, the grand doyenne of American experimental cinema, to give historical context to the development of the craft, segueing into more recent works. The whole thing seemed promising. But the next time I visited the microcinema, the most talked about movie in Cincinnati was one none of us were allowed to see, the videotape of Samuel DuBose's murder, which was still being withheld by the prosecutor's office. While waiting for an ultimately underwhelming screening of Detroit-based experimental work at the Mini the following weekend, I discussed the DuBose affair with Peter van Hyning, a volunteer at the theater. While pouring me a glass of rosé, he went on about how he was withholding judgment on the matter until he could see the tape. If we ever had the chance. Censorship was in the air in more places than the prosecutor's office.

Soon the screening started, and hackneyed Motor City experiments washed over us. One film late in the forgettable program, the most ambitious of the lot, focused its attention on the demolition and disrepair of various empty structures in Detroit, interwoven with occasional tongue-in-cheek text detailing who or what we were seeing. The movie, like much of the program, strained for relevance, but what I do recall most from it was a wide shot that included a portion of Detroit's skyline in the background left and, in the mid-ground right, a rooftop where a group of black men were congregated. The building that both they and the filmmaker were standing on was, we were led to believe, condemned. Two sets of text popped up at the top of the screen. "Detroit," with an arrow pointing toward the skyscrapers, appeared on the left. "Gangbangers," with an arrow pointing toward the young Negroes congregated on the rooftop, appeared on the right.

The three other black people besides yours truly who had come to the sparsely attended screening left during the Q&A. At the end of the talkback, Wood announced the screening to be held the following Tuesday, a program concerning the nearly forty-year effort to gentrify the very neighborhood the Mini was located in. Curated by the local documentarian and activist Erick Stoll, one of the key figures in New Left Media, it was sure to be a hot ticket; it had attracted more than 700 confirmed attendees, according to Facebook. (The fire code for the space would prohibit anything more than a fifth of such a crowd.) For the Mini's biggest event yet, Wood planned to hold two screenings in the space, which holds just 140, to accommodate at least a slightly larger portion of the demand. She then suggested that although gentrification was a hot-button topic in the city, the space she oversaw was one where the aesthetics of filmmaking were to be discussed, not their political content. "This isn't the place to complain about 3CDC," she said. No kidding; they used to own the building.

I was dumbfounded by this notion that the director of a cinema would tell her audience what they were allowed to discuss and not discuss in the space in advance of a screening. I spoke to Wood afterward and didn't mention it; everyone was making nice. She was standing next to a local teacher and writer, Danielle Ervin, who also shared an interest in holding screenings and promoting film culture in the city. Ervin had a hand in a documentary film series that had taken root at a meeting space for young artists and activists, Chase Public; perhaps a partnership of some sort could be forged.

Before long, however, three black preteens ambled up the stairs into the space and began making their way around the room in some mixture of confusion and awe; just where the hell were they? I doubted they had ever seen an experimental microcinema. Wood's attention drifted away from our conversation. She approached the children, who were somewhat aimlessly wandering around, and very brusquely told them that they were in a cinema and the screening was over before ushering them back down the stairs and out into the street. A man sitting at the desk on the first floor gave them uninviting looks as they partook in some of the corporate-sponsored cookies that sat on a tray near the welcome desk. Following behind the spectacle in shock and shame, Ervin, who is white, and I made our way out in silence.

"Did you feel that?" she asked.

"Yeah," I said.

Those kids were a menace, based largely on the color of their skin, or they didn't belong in such environs, largely for the same reason, went the logic that suddenly overwhelmed Wood's thinking. Perhaps, as blacks are often told, usually by white Americans, this is simply paranoia, that any children would have been treated with a similar mix of disdain, fear, and annoyance. But it seemed to fit a pattern others noticed too. All this Over-the-Rhine development, my consultant aunt told me one day over sixteen-dollar fried chicken sandwiches at one of the posh new beer halls, "was all about the White Man." How could it be otherwise? In Obama's America, we had not thought through any solution to the poverty within our cities besides handing over most of the buildings to well-to-do whites and the Stuff White People Like. That most of the invaders felt no shame about this, carrying out a class war, block by block, boutique by boutique, bar by bar, displacing people they would never personally evict or have to look in the eyes, made me wonder about the limits of empathy. Could I muster enough myself? Where did my culpability begin and end?

Danielle and I were both upset about the disregard we had seen those children treated with, the presumption of their lack of innocence, the disinterest in "building new audiences" for experimental cinema that had clearly just been displayed. Ervin informed me that many in her local documentary and activist circles had given up on the Mini and said disparaging things about its proprietor and sponsors. Apparently Wood had offered a troubling anecdote at the space's opening event. She had encountered a local family in front of the building who, after glimpsing the sign in front of the Mini, inquired about whether the neighborhood was getting a new movie theater. She told them that it was but it was one where they'd inevitably find the films "hoity-toity." You'd need advanced degrees, such as the one Wood holds from the University of Michigan, to understand them, she offered.

In the telling of Ervin and others, Wood went on to suggest during her opening comments that, in the wake of this encounter, she had decided to screen *Aladdin* for black Over-the-Rhine residents and their children, like the family she had encountered. The insinuation was that such people couldn't be expected to comprehend and engage with the work she planned to screen for the increasingly middle- to upper-class Cincinnatians for whom Over-the-Rhine had recently become all the rage. Experimental movies, in Wood's mind, were ostensibly Stuff White People Like. When she did find some photogenic black children (and one lonely black mother) to invite into the space, she screened *Who Framed Roger Rabbit* for them on the ground floor via flatscreen, not in the cinema above, and posted a photo on Facebook celebrating her own inclusionary impulse. Let them eat cake!

ANOTHER EVEN MORE HAUNTING AUDIOVISUAL TESTI-
mony to radicalized plunder surfaced when video of Samuel
DuBose's killing was released to the media. At the same press
conference in which it was unveiled, Raymond Tensing was
indicted for murder. The video clearly depicts Tensing, who is
twenty-five and Caucasian, shooting DuBose with little provo-
cation. Deters is a Republican who was called "pro-cop at any
cost" by *Cincinnati CityBeat* following his refusal to prosecute
Officer Marty Polk for running over a homeless woman, Joann
Burton, while she slept in the city's recently renovated Washington Park five years earlier. Polk claimed not to see her as
she was lying in a blanket. This was enough for Deters to refrain from prosecution. He was unambiguous, however, in his
condemnation of Tensing during public remarks unveiling the
tape and Tensing's indictment for murder, a move widely cred-
ited with stamping out any potential unrest. "It's an absolute
tragedy that anyone would behave in this manner," Deters said.
"It was senseless. It's just horrible. He purposefully killed him."

In the run-up to the press conference, largely due to Blackwell's and Black's comments and Deters's reticence in releasing the video, fear of riots gripped the city. Cincinnati has a
long history of them; while nineteenth-century riots, such as
those in 1829, 1836, and 1841, often directed their anger at the
city's burgeoning African-American population, the riots of the
past fifty years, such as those in 1967, 1968, and 2001, have
largely been forums for blacks to unleash their own dissatisfac-

tion. Cincinnati was the site of the last major American riot, in the spring of 2001, following the deaths of fourteen African-American men in the five years leading up to the April 7 shooting death of unarmed nineteen-year-old Timothy Thomas during a foot chase in Over-the-Rhine.

On April 9, protesters stormed a city council meeting demanding answers concerning the shooting, in which Thomas had been shot in the back four times by Officer Stephen Roach. Mayor Charlie Luken, part of a political dynasty in the area, was dismissive of their anger and eventually left the chamber before the meeting ended. The local pastor Rev. Damon Lynch III, a senior member of the civil rights organization Cincinnati Black United Front, suggested the protesters bar the doors until they get some answers. The current Cincinnati mayor, John Cranley, then a city councilman who presided over the committee that was holding the meeting, slammed his gavel down and demanded order, but none was to be found. After Councilman Jim Tarbell, long known as one of the key figures in Over-the-Rhine's gentrification, told protesters that the officer had fired his weapon because Roach thought "his life was in danger," the protesters headed for the streets.

Four days of looting and skirmishes with police ensued, largely confined to the Over-the-Rhine neighborhood after police barricaded the neighborhood's southern border to keep the violence from spreading to the central business district. More than $5 million in property damage occurred and a citywide boycott was imposed, but it went largely unenforced in white neighborhoods. In the aftermath, an economic boycott of the city led by various black advocacy groups cost the city an estimated $10 million, leading Luken to call the involved parties "economic terrorists" in the months before 9/11.

A year after the unrest, in the spring of 2002, Cincinnati Black United Front, the ACLU of Ohio, the City of Cincinnati, and the Fraternal Order of Police entered a collaborative agreement to repair the toxic relationship between the police and black communities. Initially, it didn't seem to work; crime spiked in Over-the-Rhine, with the city setting new homicide records in 2003 and 2006. Some citizens felt that the police, in retaliation for the violence, stopped policing violent crime aggressively in Over-the-Rhine. But soon a massive gentrification effort in the neighborhood began, spearheaded by the corporately financed nonprofit 3CDC, and a significant police presence has become a routine feature of Over-the-Rhine and its increasingly upscale population.

The events of 2001 surely informed Blackwell's fears. Yet the streets of the city's Clifton district, where the campus is located, were quiet the Wednesday afternoon after the video of the DuBose killing began playing on local media, nonstop. The University of Cincinnati closed early for the day and armored cars were moved into place in the event chaos spread, but both moves proved completely unnecessary. A rally sponsored by Black Lives Matter organizers outside the Hamilton County Courthouse, at the very site where an angry mob burned down the previous courthouse during the riot of 1884, proceeded peacefully. Several hundred attendees, a near-equal mix of black and white, old and young, stood in a driving rainstorm to vent their frustration.

DuBose's family members spoke from a megaphone atop the courthouse steps, calling for peace and godliness. Chief Blackwell, the second African-American police chief in the city's history, wended his way through the crowd, talking to protesters while his department largely kept its distance from the proceedings. Although the DuBose family set a relatively calm tone, the Black Lives Matter organizers sounded angrier calls for justice. Twenty-nine-year-old Kevin Farmer, wearing a neon baseball cap and a white T-shirt with "Black Lives Matter" written on it in black Sharpie, walked around Over-the-Rhine with a megaphone before the rally, antagonizing passersby for their complacency. He was visibly estranged from the family members and some other BLM leadership during the rally after, one in which many attendees questioned whether Deters would have indicted the officer if he was a city policeman as opposed to a university one. Tensing is the first police officer in the city's history who has been charged with murder while on the job.

The energy of the protest grew diffuse, with various points of dialogue due to the multiple megaphones being employed among different parts of the gathered crowd. A singalong of Kendrick Lamar's "Alright" broke out near the courthouse doors while another man in the crowd below repeatedly demanded that DuBose "have a street named after him." Some attendees criticized the DuBose family among themselves or to the various members of the local media making their way through the crowd. While some questioned why Mark O'Mara, who defended Trayvon Martin's killer, had been chosen as their attorney, others thought the DuBoses were being used by the media and by the local government to control black anger. "They always get the families to call for peace," the protestor Africa Benson told me. "They always send someone to shut us up." Many observed that the prayers of blacks, no matter how earnestly offered, had not stopped the killing of black men by police around the country.

A march commenced, winding through the section of Over-the-Rhine that has been transformed since Burton and Thomas died there, to the local police headquarters downtown, and back again. As the crowd passed sleek restaurants and clothing shops, mostly Caucasian onlookers offered uncomprehending stares. As the march made its way along the northern edge of Washington Park, some black onlookers offered vocal calls of support, honking car horns and high-fiving protesters. While one middle-aged white woman standing next to a brand-new wine bar held up a fist in solidarity, on the other side of the street a grizzled, middle-aged white man snapped "All lives matter" toward the crowd. It went largely ignored amid the shouts of "I am Sam DuBose," "No justice, no peace, no racist police," and "This is what democracy looks like." The cops came out in force, armed with guns and zip ties, when the crowd reached the police station. The protesters chanted

"The system is broken" for a few minutes before turning around and returning through Over-the-Rhine to the courthouse, and soon the march was over, but not without the sense that we were at the spark of a reckoning, not the embers.

THE DAY BEFORE THE HAMILTON COUNTY PROSECU-tor, Joe Deters, finally unveiled the footage of DuBose's killing, Erick Stoll's program drew crowds the Mini had never before seen. They had come because they were looking for new ways of seeing and talking about what was happening all around them. Wood denied them that privilege, introducing the screening with the same call to refrain from criticism or commentary about the organizations that were at the heart of Over-the-Rhine's recent transformation and her cinema's very existence. Stoll looked on grimly, before turning away from her, his head resting on the adjacent wall, arm wrapped around his shaggy mane as if to protect himself from the disrespect he, and his audience, were being shown. Surely Wood couldn't have thought all those people had shown up to the Mini, which routinely hosted screenings for half a dozen people or fewer much of the summer, to discuss documentary aesthetics and movies as "cultural products." Yet that's exactly what she suggested the conversation be limited to.

The movies were uniformly outstanding. The opener, Community Media Productions' *We Will Not Be Moved*, provides some context for the current situation; efforts to push black and

Appalachian residents out of Over-the-Rhine date back to the 1970s! The film consists only of stills of local residents and various Over-the-Rhine locales, overlaid with audio from remarkably candid interviews. In these testimonies, local residents don't mince their words as they speak about fixed incomes and the incoming development class that hoped to displace them; back then political correctness was a term that hadn't been dreamed of. "The key really isn't income, it isn't even white or black, because I'll tell you something, there are Appalachians in Over-the-Rhine in Cincinnati that are every bit as nasty as the blacks," the developer Phil Aleman suggests in one interview.

"He would buy houses because the people that lived in them were so wrong, so he would buy those buildings and throw them out," a young Kathy Laker Schwab says about Aleman, while driving through the neighborhood. (Nearly forty years later she now runs Local Initiatives Support Corporation, ostensibly "the nation's leading community development support organization," and consults for 3CDC.) "He didn't purposefully buy buildings to throw people out," she adds after a cool and genuine laugh. "I mean, there is something to be said for getting rid of people who just aren't good for the neighborhood."

Stoll's own films anchored the program. He and his collaborator Jarrod Welling-Cann's work-in-progress documentary *Good White People*, about the plight of a former Over-the-Rhine convenience store owner and karate dojo operator, Reginald Stroud, followed a startlingly edited short piece about the city's Lumenocity festival, a semiprivate end-of-summer light show that takes place in the same recently renovated park where police officers used to carelessly run over homeless women. In Stoll's telling, the city's new vision for the space (Private events! Corporate sponsors! Privatization of city services!) is more than troubling.

Despite this somber and somewhat incendiary program, there was some levity. The local artists Arthur Brum, Liz Cambron, and Aalap Bommaraju truly had the last laugh. Their short experimental piece *Pills* seems to say, with great, penetrating humor, much about the compromised ethical position spaces like the Mini inhabit. Although Wood painfully admitted during the truncated postscreening Q&A that the Mini "was problematic, I guess," the polite, city-planning term "gentrification" and its more sanguine cousins "urban renewal" and "revitalization" went unexamined in the galling talkback, one in which many of the filmmakers looked visibly strained. The ways in which we frame the creation and patronization of spaces such as the Mini, or the nearby Over-the-Rhine museum, a place where I can assure you *We Will Not Be Moved* will never screen, are actually what's problematic. The museum and microcinema are dedicated to a different vision of the past and a future unburdened by the sins of the present so meaningfully documented in Stoll's program. *Pills* suggests, with flourishes of hysterical candor that recall post-'68 Godard, that the changing landscape of our inner cities, from Brooklyn to Birmingham, should really be called class warfare.

THE DAY AFTER THE VIDEO OF DUBOSE'S SHOOTING emerged, Raymond Tensing, who was fired by the University of Cincinnati on the same day that the indictment was announced, requested his job back through the Fraternal Order of Police of Ohio, claiming he had not been given due process. "The *great American* Ray Tensing wants his job back," the local radio demagogue Bill Cunningham announced at the beginning of a segment on his popular 700 WLW broadcast, one in which he went on to complain about how little black activists cared about rising rates of black-on-black crime, citing the recent shooting of a four-year-old girl in the Avondale neighborhood where DuBose lived. His guest, Colerain High School's baseball manager, Kevin Coombs, had coached Tensing when he was a student. "He's a tremendous young man," Coombs said, before complaining that Deters had "way overstated the facts of the case."

Despite Coombs's disillusionment, and that of the Fraternal Order of Police, whose president Jay McDonald called Deters's comments "way out of line," a narrative spread in which the city was saved by the forthright actions of the prosecutor, capped by a glowing *Los Angeles Times* profile of the once-scandal-ridden former state treasurer. But his decision not to indict the other officers on the scene, who seem to have been involved in a conspiracy to cover up the nature of the killing, drew anger among many in the community, while his inclusion of a second charge against Tensing, for manslaughter, suggested the possibility that Deters believes he may not win his murder case in a city in which successful prosecution of police is rare.

In a phone call that afternoon, Harry Black wouldn't elaborate on what he felt would happen if a murder conviction didn't take place, saying, "It would be irresponsible to speculate." He suggested that the city would institute body cameras on all police officers in the following twelve to sixteen months. When asked how he would place these events in the city's history of racial unrest and whether they represented a perversion of the progress many say Cincinnati has made on these matters in the last decade, he reframed the events: "The way everyone conducted themselves, working together, cooperating, there's much more transparency and a lot of communications," Black said, suggesting that the events of the past week "serve as a validation to the work that many men and women have contributed to the city since the tragic event in 2001."

The outlook was less sanguine when a candlelight vigil at the same courthouse drew a crowd of a couple hundred people on Friday night. "This is all going to be peaceful today and hopefully justice will prevail, but the statistics have shown that they don't convict officers here," Kevin Farmer said through his megaphone at the beginning of a vigil that morphed into yet another protest march. Although Farmer's second assertion is demonstrably true, his first proved false. He was arrested, along with five others, at the end of the evening. The march had wound through downtown, along many of the same Over-the-Rhine streets that Wednesday's had, before culminating in the city's most prominent landmark, Fountain Square. In recent years the square has been under the purview of 3CDC.

As the protesters entered the square, an indie rock concert was under way at the Proctor & Gamble Music Stage on its western side, with several hundred enjoying alcohol and Skyline Chili while watching a set from a local band. That the band's corporately subsidized show and the murmurs of their mostly Caucasian audience drowned out the chants of the mostly black protesters as they entered the square was an irony lost on no one, especially those leading the march.

Things grew more tense as the marchers exited the square. A black woman drew the ire of a white motorist in a brown sports utility vehicle on Sycamore Street, just east of the square. After a heated exchange of words, she threw a cup at the driver's side window of his car. He leaped out of his vehicle, brandishing a large knife, and stared at her menacingly. Nearby protesters pleaded for calm or cried foul before the man got back in his car and sped away, past several police vehicles that paid him little attention.

As the march circled the block back toward the square, confusion set in; where would the protest end? Adam Clark, an associate professor of theology and African studies at Xavier University who had mentored many of the activists, complained just before the march reentered the square that among the local Black Lives Matter organizers there were "some constructive leaders and some not-so-constructive leaders," while others suggested that the police would finally pounce once the protesters camped out on 3CDC's property. The protesters entered the square for a second time, but didn't push past the crowd. They stayed, many with their hands raised in the air, chanting, "Hands up, don't shoot." The band's set was already petering out, but now it abruptly stopped. An awkwardness ensued, and for a brief time the protesters' chants were louder than any music. But then over the square's public address system, the Strokes' "Someday" rang out just as loud as the sounds of the previous band had, and the protesters were once again drowned out.

As the protesters moved toward the eastern end of the square, nearby vendors stopped selling beer and chili despite the fact that another set from that night's headliners, Buffalo Killers, was yet to come. At that point police finally mobilized a show of force, forming a phalanx along the park's southeastern front. Several protesters got very testy with nearby officers, screaming at them from point-blank range, their hands behind their heads in a show of nonviolence. "Don't shoot," one man screamed at the officer in front of him, speaking metaphorically; the cop didn't have a gun drawn. A nearby cop said, "I'll light your ass up," in response.

Farmer was among the first arrested. He was charged with two counts of menacing and one count of disturbing a lawful meeting, allegedly after threatening business owners in the square. As his arrest ensued, a middle-aged black woman nearby cried and claimed that Farmer had been the one roughly handled. Kimberly Thomas, a close friend of Sam DuBose—

who unlike his family has been supportive of the marches—came to the aid of several people being arrested and was violently thrown to the ground by one officer. She was charged with two counts of resisting arrest. Damon Lynch IV, son of the Cincinnati Black United Front leader, was charged with disorderly conduct for "refusing to leave an intersection and balling his fists" toward an arresting police officer.

As the deflated crowd cleared away, I glimpsed Damon Lynch III watching his son being loaded into a paddy wagon while his wife was being threatened with jail herself for failing to vacate the street, trying to see what was being done to her son. Nearby, I found Clark again. "They arrested who they thought was the leadership," he claimed. "Sean George put his hands on Hakiym," another nearby man suggested, referring to a Cincinnati SWAT team member and Brian Simpson, a member of the local hip-hop group Lyrical Insurrection, who performs under the name Hakiym Sha'ir and was arrested for "refusing to back up when ordered by police." Apparently Simpson asked George who his supervisor was. The cop refused to answer. "They pulled him back, he said, 'Why are you touching me?' and they suddenly jumped and attacked him, that's what happened," recalled Rev. Troy Jackson, the former pastor of University Christian Church and the last white person from the march who lingered on as the paddy wagon drove away.

Walking north on Walnut Street, back toward Over-the-Rhine, I passed an empty lot to my east. At least a dozen police vehicles were arrayed there along with several dozen officers.

They were exuberant with victory, red faces stretched in wide smiles or mid-guffaw, giving pounds and backslapping one another in a sickening display of celebration. I stifled bile in my throat and hit the bars.

It was lively on Cincinnati's gentrification frontier after the march, but no longer with talk over justice and peace. I intercepted some friends at a wine bar that had opened recently, Liberty's, and they were already a bourbon deep. I quickly caught up with them, navigating my emotional shell shock by flirting with a portly redhead at the bar with a trust-funded friend while conversation wandered back to *when to go to which bar/ club after how many drinks when later* . . . To most of these well-to-do young people, none of whom had been down to the march, or to any of the marches before, the notion that they could or should attempt to be part of a movement to address this problem seemed quaint at best. Certainly, for the children of some of the city's best-endowed families, income inequality was not their fight; most issued little enthusiasm for the cause. This set was too demure, too self-consciously aligned with the status quo, whatever their assumed liberalism (at least on social issues) would indicate, to challenge the great quandary of our times in such a personal way. The mere fact that I had mentioned DuBose was a bit of a turnoff.

In the local media that weekend, in print and on radio, it was the protesters who reports suggested had not remained peaceful. The DuBose family disavowed the march, as did Rev. Bobby Hilton, who heads the local chapter of Al Sharpton's National Action Network. Yet "the fire next time" hadn't come, and if it had, it surely wouldn't have been due to the efforts of those who took to what was once a public square to express their grievances. The streets north of Columbia Parkway, where the police quarantined a whole community of mostly poor African Americans during the unrest of 2001, and where one can now buy a ten-dollar gourmet hot dog, remain peaceful. But one wonders what will become of all the rage that could be glimpsed that Friday night, beneath black Cincinnati's fragile calm.

434 GREENE AVENUE

A few weeks after Samuel DuBose's killing, in August 2015, I temporarily moved to the 400 block of Greene Avenue, between Nostrand and Bedford. I had agreed to sublet my tiny studio in the Bronx through September and took over the first floor of a handsome whitestone number my ex-roommate Kevin and his wife, Heather, had been renting just half a block from 499, which I had been kicked out of two years previously. Kevin's chain-smoking, booze-guzzling, and, at least temporarily, babysitting days were behind him. Tempered and emboldened by marriage simultaneously, he had decamped for California for an animation track at CalArts' graduate film program.

The brownstone at 434 Greene had the type of high ceilings and German woodwork finishes that were now thought of as a steal for $1,300 a month, even if it was essentially a railroad with no backyard access. The change that was greeting the neighborhood could be surveilled easily from the bay windows that jutted out toward the street below. I'd wake that August to the sound of construction on one of the block's many brownstones—rat ta tat tat and a good morning to you, Mr. Jackhammer—only to stagger over to close the window and find men surfing the trash beneath my perch for cans. In the early August heat that kept me awake in the night I'd drowsily watch several men each morning, shopping carts at their hip, pilfer my discarded beer bottles and plastic two-liters of seltzer from above as the power saws roared, renovation and restoration continuing apace. About a block away, across the street from where I had lived at 499 Greene, I saw a Citi Bike rack had been set up, one of thirty-four new ones in the neighborhood according to a Citi-sponsored ad on Facebook that suggested I use the #BedStuy hashtag when documenting my Bed-Stuy adventures on Instagram and Twitter!

While sitting on a bench near one of the new coffeehouses that had opened on Nostrand, having a late-morning breakfast with a childhood friend in from D.C. for the weekend, I spotted Tony crossing the street from the opposite sidewalk with his dog, only blocks from the building his parents bought for him on Jefferson. Either he didn't see us or he didn't care to stop. My friend, who also grew up with Tony in Cincinnati, ran after him and took a selfie while I stayed behind and ate my grits, wondering if he had used the #BedStuy hashtag to document our not-so-private pain.

New restaurants lined the Bedford Avenue corridor, and the offices of Coldwell Banker, too, advertising freshly renovated brownstones to the well-to-do millennials who were being shepherded into the area by the beauty and relative affordability of the district. The suspicious eyes and fleet gait with which young gentrifiers moved through Bed-Stuy in my earliest days amid the concrete were gone; recent émigrés walked through the area with confidence now. The pale hordes, the light in their eyes, no longer cowed by the sense that they were trespassers, writ large, steeled themselves to the task of making the space in their own image, at a price point that would guarantee exclusivity.

Kevin and Heather hadn't left much furniture and I had little to speak of in the Bronx, so I bought a rickety wooden rocking chair from the new Salvation Army on Fulton Street. It was small enough to just barely fit into the back of a cab and was only twenty dollars. The toilet in the tiny bathroom had become a Rube Goldberg contraption in the hands of the previous subletter and the floors were remarkably dirty. I went to fetch cleaning supplies and an AC unit from the notoriously shoddy Bed-Stuy Home Depot. Coming out of the store, I acquired the services of a Puerto Rican named Victor, a wiry, openfaced man in his fifties. I paid him fifteen bucks to drive me and my newly acquired air conditioner the five or so blocks back to 434. We quickly began about Bed-Stuy.

"It used to be real bad down here, in the '80s," he started. "A lot of crime. It's better now." He does a brisk business in his purple van, hanging out in front of the Home Depot finding people, often new to the neighborhood, in need of a short haul for their new furnishings.

"It used to be all black and Latino here," Victor said as we neared the corner of Clifton Place and Nostrand, not far from where a new luxury building had just gone up and a bodega had closed. Victor told me his wife, Rose, operates the laundromat on the nearest intersection to 434, Greene and Bedford, as we circled the block to get back around to Greene. I asked him how he would describe the people moving into the neighborhood. "A lot of whites, a lot of gays." He grumbled about homosexuals "walking around the way they do," worried about the effect it would have on the children. I swallowed a shard of spit, wondering what he had thought of the tides that had finally brought the freedom to homosexuals to marry a few months before, but midwestern modesty told me not to ask.

"Not that I have anything against gay people," he said nonchalantly. "My son is gay."

Greene between Nostrand and Bedford is one of the most picturesque blocks in the neighborhood. Lined with immaculate brownstones, this stretch of Greene conjures "Brooklyn" as it appears in the contemporary American popular mythos, in summertime its well-kept trees providing a delicate shade for sidewalk commuters and long, lively block parties. Number 434 is a whitestone whose owner, Mr. Knight, has held the building for over three decades. A congenial black man in his eighties with fading health and children who, in Nick's words, can't wait to sell the place for millions once the old man passes, he is representative of a type of Bed-Stuy resident who, like me, may not be long for the neighborhood.

As a new order has emerged, the ghosts of the previous one are everywhere, but their echoes are getting smaller, snuffed out by the tides. In Sebastián Silva's Sundance shocker *Nasty Baby*, which had locally premiered in neighboring Fort Greene during BAMcinemaFEST earlier that summer, the talented Chilean director and Fort Greene transplant plays a version of himself, an avant-garde video maker who lives in a sunny stretch of the community next door with Mo, a towering black artisanal carpenter played by TV on the Radio's Tunde Adebimpe. Although Mo's father seems suspicious of their relationship, the film nodding to the general social conservatism of his generation of black men, the couple navigate the multicultural and affluent new regime of their urban bobo utopia with the carefree ease of a Levi's commercial. Their new Brooklyn seems blissful, save the constant sounds of a leaf blower powered by the Bishop, a mentally unstable black man on a fixed income who, as embodied by Reg E. Cathey, is a return of the ghetto repressed, of the unruly street Negrodom that the presence of these young gentrifiers is supposed to awaken the police and the developers into removing. The Bishop lives in a basement apartment one building over and, as this terrific, uneventfully unrelenting movie makes clear, is simply not capable of assuaging his perhaps less menacing but surely more economically and socially powerful new neighbors. Their own forms of solidarity will prove too much for him. The discord places Mo in the position of failed, unprepared mediator, as black invaders almost always are. He tries to come to his lover's defense in a street-level altercation about the leaf blower that involves a black female cop who is sympathetic to both sides, and the Bishop's rage greets this turncoat with a special ire. "Negro!" he exclaims at Mo, accusatorially.

The film, which lulls its audience asleep to its dramatic possibilities by inhabiting the rhythms, humor, and milieu of the average Sundanceable hipster comedy, makes a turn for the gallows late in its running time. Kristen Wiig's Polly, a friend of the couple, with whom Silva's Freddy is trying to have a child, is threatened by the Bishop, who follows her into the couple's apartment. To what end we never quite find out—Silva's character attacks him preemptively and, with an assist from Mo and Polly, suffocates the Bishop to death in his bathroom. In *Nasty Baby*, the rituals of gentrification, be they the assault of unreasonable rents by landlords and the evictions that follow, the exclusionary cultural dislocation of new pricy storefronts, or the mysterious increase in municipal services, are simply not enough to exorcise the ghosts of the violent past these streets contain; it takes a physical snuffing out of the menace of black disappointment and forbearance, of the way the policies of this country and the majority of its citizens have driven so many of us mad.

After moving into 434 Greene, I'd see Silva in Bed-Stuy—we had gotten to know each other a bit one night after being introduced at a screening in the city and later served on an awards committee together. He lived in the apartment where his character lives in the film and would often work out at the Bed-Stuy YMCA on Nostrand Avenue. Its men's locker room sauna rivaled the neighborhood's best barbershops for gossip and witty repartee. Surely he'd overheard the sentiments of men not too far removed from the Bishop in that locker room, amid all the heat and sweat and wooden stillness, where the mostly black patrons would carp about the invasion in ways they wouldn't out in the streets, where pink ears were listening and blue eyes watching. Not that it was safe from the ghosts, either; Tony belonged to the YMCA as well, as did his girlfriend, who would occasionally cast hard eyes at me from across the ellipticals.

I set about visiting old haunts that summer, but soon realized few were left. On the east end of the neighborhood, Goodbye Blue Monday had been shuttered the previous fall due to rising rent, and rumor among my friends held that M&M and his band of crusty layabouts were being pushed out of 551 Kosciuszko by Bo, or whoever his successor was. The way must be cleared for fancier buildings and people.

"Bed-Stuy was the last neighborhood in Brooklyn I really liked, the last one that really felt like a neighborhood," Liam told me one night when I ran into him on my end of Greene Avenue, walking home. He wasn't long for the neighborhood either. Liam was leaving 499 Greene after being kicked out by his black landlords, who planned to raise the rent from $2,700 to $4,200 on his middle-class ass. "I'm looking at other places because I don't know if I want to move farther into Brooklyn and start over again," the commercial producer and writer told me, saying that he was considering a move to cheaper, if not greener, pastures.

We had been gentrifiers, more humble and open than most, we assumed, and now our time to be called back into service had come again. There were surely other areas in premium metropolitan cultural centers out there that had lapsed to Negroes in the years after the Great War which remained affordable for the mostly white American middle class of 2015, and we'd have to go find one. He was, quite naturally, thinking about moving to LA, a cliché in the Brooklyn we were inhabiting, especially among the middle-class creatives who fashioned themselves as priced out, a sensation that inspired a cottage industry of Didion imposters writing "Goodbye to All That" imitations on the websites of once-veritable magazines. This is not, despite appearances, one of those. I remain too stubborn to read the writing on the wall.

THE END OF THE BUSH AGE HAD BEEN DISASTROUS FOR black American wealth. Forty percent of the black community, whose fortunes were tied up in their home value more than most other Americans, lost more than 60 percent of their net worth in the great recession. The majority of the people who lost their homes due to foreclosure were black women over the age of fifty who were first-time home owners. The Obama years, despite all of our hopes, had done little to alleviate this pain. The process that was swallowing up the Bed-Stuy I had come of age in, and many more like me, ones who had spent their lives building and securing the district under the torment of neglect, would not be denied. I had lived there in service to it the whole time. It had been displacing Negroes and the earliest white gentrifiers at least since before the towers fell.

We were feeling the ground cave in under us from an explosion that rang out before Craigslist even included New York, but the real effects were felt elsewhere. East New York, poorer and blacker than Bed-Stuy at the dawn of the new millennium, had grown blacker still, its Negro population increasing by 13 percent from the time George W. Bush won the Iowa caucuses to the time Barack Obama signed the Patient Protection and Affordable Care Act ten years later, as the displacement that accompanies class warfare set in. In the western part of Bed-Stuy, where I was passing away those late-summer months at 434 Greene, the black population dropped in those years by 14.6 percent. As in the Weeksville of six generations previous, the white population exploded, up 634 percent by the decade's end.

An odd assortment of folks were getting rich off the transition, cashing in on the market, many of them descendants of the very Negroes who had come here in an attempt to build a community of home owners among their own kind in the years of the Great Migration. Perhaps Bo was one of them now, I hoped. Had he paid that underwater mortgage? The agents of this change were still, by and large, acting either selfishly or nefariously, and often with clear racial bias.

"We started in East New York, but we sold everything we had. We didn't want to be there. Most of them are either Section 8, other government programs, and even the person that pays with cash is too much headaches," an anonymous twenty-six-year-old Hasidic developer and landlord told *New York* magazine early that summer when speaking of the lucrative work he's now doing making Bed-Stuy palatable to whites who will pay high rents for all those renovated brownstones. "If there's a black tenant in the house—in every building we have, I put in white tenants," he said, hoping to better serve new, ostensibly nonblack tenants who "want to know if black people are going to be living there. So sometimes we have ten apartments and everything is white, and then all of the sudden one tenant comes in with one black roommate, and they don't like it." Negroes may have given Bed-Stuy its particular character and cultural importance, but we didn't own it, not enough of us at least. It was clear, at least to "Ephraim" and whatever real man that pseudonym represents, that solidarity would not hold among the Negroes. "Every black person has a price," he went on, suggesting that it was still much more expensive to buy out a black person in Bed-Stuy than in East New York.

He in turn sounded like Robert Moses, the man whose vision still stalked these streets, and not just in the dimly lit corridors of Marcy. His vision for central Brooklyn was finally taking hold. "The first prescription for slum dwellers in the ghettos of the big cities is total, immediate, uncompromising surgical removal," the legendary urban planner wrote in his 1970 book, *Public Works: A Dangerous Trade*. It's hard to figure if Moses's thirst for womanizing or his hatred of Negroes was his more salient feature. If he had had his druthers, he would have moved the Negroes of Bed-Stuy to the Rockaway Peninsula in Queens. "I have recently seriously proposed a workable, uncompromising plan," he wrote, "involving at the start 160,000 people, to raze the central Brooklyn slums and move residents."

In late August, Highline Residential, a realty company that was spending significant amounts of money developing Bedford-Stuyvesant properties, released a promotional video called "This Is Bed-Stuy," in which smiling blond twenty-somethings give a "neighborhood tour." Many longtime residents found the video—in which the pair of pale hosts sip expensive coffee and brunch cocktails at recently opened establishments while offering testimony to the neighborhood's amenities and vibrancy—deeply offensive, seeing no mention of the institutions that they associated with Bed-Stuy. Highline Residential didn't give a shit about them, the general sentiment went, other than wondering when they'd get the fuck out.

Suddenly *New York* magazine and the *Daily News* were falling over themselves profiling entire blocks of Bedford-Stuyvesant real estate, interviewing generations of owners and tenants, publishing op-eds by black journalism professors who had long lived in the district, and interviewing women who had been pushed out to East New York, or all the way to the Rockaways. He, and the forces of history that animated his mind-set, would drive the dispossessed right out of this city if the market allowed.

I RAN ALMOST DIRECTLY INTO TONY ONE NIGHT TO-ward the end of my days at 434 Greene. I had surely spent the day packing up my few things so Tad and Brittany, the apple-cheeked twenty-somethings who were moving in after me, could begin their #BedStuy adventure. I was walking into Dynaco with a friend of mine. The candlelit, wood-paneled nouveau hipster dive with class-warfare prices and an almost exclusively white patronage was where I had begun taking Polish women I'd had affairs with in the past to ask them to give me a real shot at loving them. I couldn't bear doing the same with Tony, attempting reconciliation as I found myself suddenly standing next to him in the crowded bar, even though I missed, so badly, the camaraderie that had passed between us and had long been a boon in my life. But by that point, we had been estranged for as long as we had ever been close. Instinctually, I turned right around and ushered myself and my friend out, lacking the stomach to face the sadness of our lost solidarity, sullied as it was by these expensive Brooklyn nights.

485 LEXINGTON AVENUE

The first season of Steven Soderbergh's turn-of-the-century hospital drama *The Knick* shot its exteriors mostly in and around Bed-Stuy during the fall of 2013, right around the time I first began dating Anne with some earnestness. I was living at 730 DeKalb and recall, upon several long daytime strolls south, past Herbert Von King Park and into the heart of the neighborhood, watching large swathes of people, all decked in early-twentieth-century garb, shuffle from a nearby holding area to a stretch of Putnam Avenue that had been blocked off for filming. They walked past the production trucks, along a series of long white craft tables nearby, where underneath makeshift tents sweet and savory food items were laid out. Nearby, men and women stood snacking on Kind bars and sipping cans of San Pellegrino Limonata while wearing corsets and bowler hats, a video village for the producers set up just past them near the street corner, the towering old Bedford-Stuyvesant school building that plays the Knick on TV looming above them all. I followed along the street until I encountered a knit-cap-wearing PA, about the age of the film students I teach in Westchester County, chewing gum loudly. His walkie beeped as he gently asked me to cross the street to the other side of the intersection.

Soderbergh had the type of career I, in my magical-thinking years, had once dreamed of for myself, oscillating between studio and independent films, shooting and cutting his own work, remaining defiantly intellectual and a remarkable manager of people at once. I had met him years before, at a screening at Warner Brothers of his unfairly maligned World War II film *The Good German.* He had been a good sport when I chased after him and told him he should make good on a promise he made in an interview with *The Believer* to remake *Alphaville* for $10,000. "They'd pillory me," he said with a smile, before getting into the back of a black Lincoln. "They'd have me for lunch," he said out the window before being driven away.

The ten-hour first season of the show revolves around the brilliant, cocaine-addicted Dr. John Thackery (Clive Owen), a whirling dervish of a man who takes over as chief of surgery at a beleaguered Lower East Side hospital after his mentor shoots himself in the head following one too many childbirths gone awry. The futility of so much modern medicine, and the slow march of progress toward alleviating ailments we now routinely diagnose and cure, is a dominant theme of the hour-long episodic, but this is a sprawling ensemble drama that has more than hospital administration and doctoring on its mind.

The kaleidoscopic canvas Soderbergh and his writers paint is one teeming with latent tensions between native and foreigner, faith and reason, old traditions and new ways of seeing. It takes stock of the city's immigrant landscape of the early twentieth century, visiting Negro SROs and roach-infested convents, Irish tenements and Upper East Side country homes, as no television show has ever done. The hidden world of Manhattan municipal planning, often in cigar-smoke-filled private university clubs instead of the corridors of City Hall, is glimpsed alongside the world of banquet-sized Negro dance halls and Chinese opium dens. *The Knick* introduces us to a bygone New York that, at first glance, seems far removed from our own. But unlike *Mad Men*, which delivers us to an elegantly rendered 1960s nostalgia factory while reminding us of how far we've progressed since those bad old days of patriarchy and racism, *The Knick* reminds us that, in our own time, the latent tensions between cultures and races and classes persist. We are no better than these people.

In line with the liberal sensibilities of the Robertsons, the prominent Manhattan shipping family that dominates the Knick's board of directors, the hospital serves the city's lowliest new American families. When few other hospitals cater to them, the Knick serves the white ethnic commoners who are crowding into Lower Manhattan looking for a better way. The only people they don't serve are Negroes, of course.

The staff's sole black doctor, Algernon Edwards (André Holland), the son of the Robertsons' servants, trained in France because of America's peculiar aversion to educating Negroes. His hiring, at the behest of the Robertsons, draws the ire of some other doctors, notably Dr. Everett Gallinger (Eric Johnson), by Season Two a noted eugenics enthusiast whose trust and respect Algernon will never earn, even as he works twice as hard to gain everyone else's. Not considered for advancement despite his medical pedigree and troubled by the hospital turning away black patients, he turns to fighting in back alleys or barroom brawls as a means of releasing his anxiety, and treats black patients in the Knickerbocker Hospital's basement, where he sets up, with the help of a black nurse, a makeshift infirmary of sorts, unbeknownst to any of the other staff.

Juliet Rylance plays Cornelia Robertson, an administrator at the underfunded hospital. Beautiful and serious, she is an upper-class WASP who, as a woman taking managerial employment (or any employment at all), is violating the ethic of her tribe. The oldest of Mr. Robertson's children, she grew up with Algernon, their servants' child, and clearly has a fondness for him the rest of the staff at the Knick do not. Although she shows an acumen for the work, making the best of a difficult budget as the hospital seeks to modernize in the midst of an age of great technological advancement and boardroom handwringing over its stated mission to serve the immigrant lowly, her time as a hospital exec is seen as a temporary arrangement, something to do until she gets to the real business of being a wife to the scion of an appropriately rich WASP family that has something to offer her father and brother.

After his hiring, she protects Algernon from slander when she can, trying to assure the other doctors of his competence and somewhat forcefully suggesting to them that he is at the Knick to stay. Their interactions are cordially professional at first; the attraction is there immediately, of course, but the flirting comes only gradually and with great caution, as it must have for any black man intrigued by the body of a white woman in 1902. It is in his secret basement infirmary for Negroes that she makes the first move, after a particularly valiant display of heroism on his part following a full-scale riot by an Irish mob outside the hospital.

They begin a delicate dance of attraction, Algernon and Cornelia, one that culminates in a torrid affair, all clandestine midnight carriage rides to the wrong side of town, a corseted white woman slipping out of a Negro tenement at dawn to escape unnoticed. They take comfort in sarcasm together, making fun of all the cultural events Cornelia is allegedly attending when she's at work late, as opposed to sitting in a chair, opposite his bed, smoking a cigarette in the nude. "I'm not sure a woman like you should have any business in a place like that," a stage driver says to Cornelia when she requests a ride to Dick's Hotel at Sixth Avenue and Twenty-Sixth Street, where Algernon awaits her early in their affair. "And I'm quite sure you have no business questioning me" is her reply.

Things go awry, predictably so. They never discuss the discrimination he faces at every turn; not only is there so much else to talk about, but somehow he tricks himself into thinking she can empathize, a common delusion integrated blacks hold concerning their white friends and lovers—people want to think the best of one another, and besides, isn't it obvious, this shit we go through? Then Cornelia gets pregnant and everything changes. She demands he abort his own child.

Hunched over his lover in his makeshift basement infirmary, Algernon cannot bring himself to do it, to kill the baby he had been foolish enough to think Cornelia might bear for him in Liberia, a place "where attitudes are different." She must go to the Catholics instead! When she marries, at the end of Season One, against her desires but in line with the expectations of her family and class, it is to a boorish, wellborn San Francisco heir with a leering father. Meanwhile, filled with despair, Algernon gets himself knocked out, in self-destructive lunacy, by starting a fight with a much bigger barroom Negro he must surely know will beat his ass. Cornelia's insistence of fealty to her family's expectations leaves him on no less of a suicide mission than Dwight David Taylor may have been on during his last dance with Paul MacLeod.

A desperate reckoning with deep-seated American truths becomes unavoidable; she cannot possibly carry on with this Negro, as this country did not mean them, the daughter of a white shipping magnate and the son of a black chauffeur, to be together. The pain in Ms. Rylance's bright blue eyes at her inability, despite her intelligence and awareness, to truly say this plainly, staring into the barely contained rage and stoic sorrow writ ever so carefully on Mr. Holland's features as he casts aside their affair, is one I was familiar with—I thought I had seen something similar in Anne's eyes, too.

ANNE MOVED TO BED-STUY JUST AS MY TIME AT 434 Greene was up; she took a room in a ground-floor apartment that a production manager friend of hers was leasing. You could have cut the air with a knife when she told me, during one of our rare phone conversations just weeks before I was set to leave an apartment I had begun to dream of gentrifying with her, after we had decided to give our on-again, off-again romance another try. The place she was moving into was recently renovated and complete with garden access on the ground floor of a walk-up just west of Throop on Lexington Avenue, eight blocks from where I had first lived in Bed-Stuy and only a scant few blocks from the building that plays the Knickerbocker Hospital on television.

It was quite the departure for her. When I moved to Bed-Stuy for the first time, a girl like Anne would have never thought to live there. When we met, in 2011, she was living in the Upper East Side. Despite the tony zip code, she lived in a place her mother, whom I never met despite three years of dating her daughter, allegedly found wanting—it lacked a doorman. At the time we became acquainted, I was dating a niche film marketing specialist named Andrea with class hang-ups of her own; like me, she had grown up in proximity to the wealthy and the well-to-do, was more or less surrounded by them, but had a decidedly petit bourgeois household compared with theirs.

Andrea's mother, formerly a progressive rabbi, worked at a Home Depot in Hartford and raised a black child, the daughter of her stepsister, as her own. Her father, a professor of Middle Eastern studies, made a habit of pissing his pants when he got drunk and had a ringing desire to have his daughter tell him how large my cock was (was it true!?). He asked her to promise she'd marry a Jewish man if he voted for Barack Obama, but she opted for a Jewish woman instead; I was her last boyfriend.

Like the flag her family has long bled for in reverence, the prominent colors of Anne's body are her deep red hair, pale, freckled skin, and swimming-pool-blue eyes. She had been a movie publicist for a prominent film festival when I met her, yet I could see from the start her ambition was to make her own films. She has a reserved, almost inquisitive disposition she likes to refer to as "uptight," but eventually I got her to warm up, plying her with gregarious, encouraging e-mails about her film, sharing just the details about me I thought she'd find alluring. We had both directed small first features about grief and seemed to have, despite the obvious differences between us, something resembling a genuine connection from the start. I was with someone else, unhappily so, and couldn't stop myself from trying to woo her. The night before her predecessor broke up with me, Anne and I had our first seemingly innocent drink together, after a press screening leading up to the festival. She traveled with me to a party at the Film Society of Lincoln Center, where I was headed to meet my girlfriend, knowing somewhere that the relationship I remained in wasn't long for this world.

It took me a year and a half from the time I met her to the moment, in a Lower East Side bar, when I said, "I just don't understand why we haven't made out yet." I knew how to seduce Anne, to be palpably black in ways that were exotic and yet familiar simultaneously. She knew how to seduce me right back, admitting straightaway, but in an indirect, joking manner, to having a thing for black guys. I had been taken with redheads for as long as I could remember, but it wasn't simply fetishistic; there was a mutual respect in each other's talents, intelligence, and calm. I couldn't get enough of her. I wanted to bottle Anne and take her with me everywhere I went, but I also felt an immediate trepidation.

On Facebook I saw photos of her father and her brothers in oxfords and sweaters next to a house that looked like a southern slave plantation. She occasionally found herself at impossibly lavish weddings, the brothers in military garb, or perched next to some handsomely trimmed hedges while her siblings, sitting on either side of her, both wore white button-ups and jackets. This was a girl who knew her way around formal wear. The dogs and the hedges, all the trappings of WASP privilege, oozed off the pixels on my screen. They were almost a parody of such privilege, this family, so much so that my best friend from Cincinnati, the one who had had his own cotillion and had grown up in Hyde Park despite his father's working-class Bond Hill origins, immediately called foul when I suggested, while surveying her Facebook profile during Christmas 2011, that he pursue Anne instead of I.

"I can't marry into that," he insisted, waving his hand at the petite blonde mother and the pinstripe-wearing father, a financial industry executive and wealth-management specialist who once managed an $18 billion family fund for one of America's richest clans. He thought these people were too stodgy and conservative for him. If that was the case for my friend, who had a high-priced education and a pair of high-powered lawyer parents, then certainly to "marry into that" wasn't in the cards for me either, a black man educated among east side wealth with social-climbing "philanthropist" grandparents who nonetheless remained the son of a black janitor.

Years later, my friend admitted to me that his sister and father were likely to be unhappy if he didn't ultimately commit to an upper-middle-class blonde white woman, like the one he was currently dating. It was an act of great peril, to love people for whom America means something entirely different than yourself, but this was present-day New York, not 1902. A dashing child of miscegenation was presiding over the country, felling the myth of the tragic mulatto forever. What good did fear ever do?

Before she began dating me, Anne told me she struggled in her relationship with her parents, whom she very much reveres publicly, because they were still sore that she didn't go into finance. She drove a Mercedes her father gave her, one she was weary of, seeing how it signified her family's wealth. Anne claimed she would never receive any money from her family. Her father, who was a "self-made man," would not allow her or her brothers an inheritance. I didn't believe her, but let it slide; I lied to people I loved too, out of solidarity with whomever they wanted me to be.

I never had a problem code-switching in front of white girls until I met Anne. It never made me self-conscious, being a Negro who liked chicken wings, watermelon, and *Martin* reruns who could nonetheless talk with great affection for European slow cinema, Portishead albums, and Toms shoes. Yet, whenever I would hang out with her, something in her gaze made me feel like I had something to prove. Despite the *Do the Right Thing* poster on her wall and the ease with which I wrote long, hauntingly personal e-mails to her in which I hinted at my class incoherence and the vulnerability I felt surrounding the management of my parents' declining fortunes, I struggled to find ways to reveal myself to her without feeling judged. We always struggled to find an easy, consistent mode of communication in person beyond flirting, and never were good at speaking to each other on the phone about anything of importance, even as a profound affection flourished between us such as I had never felt before. She made me laugh, and I found her prim style to be both alluring and also a ruse; she has, despite the stereotypes, a more voracious sexual appetite than I, is a far better dancer, and, despite her coastal rearing, maintains a far more colloquial, if not down-homey, way of speaking.

We struck a balance, my abrasive, emotional, oversharing qualities and her straitlaced but quick-witted vibe, that was magical at times, fun and sexy and freewheeling; I found, as I grew closer to her, an emotional satisfaction my other relationships lacked, and when I felt distance from her, an alienation I had never previously experienced, it, oddly, made me want to solve the puzzle that was Anne even more.

In random moments, sitting on the subway or standing at a urinal, I would worry that we were simply playing characters for each other, as people do at the beginning of a relationship. Had these characters allowed us to trick ourselves into thinking we could create a solidarity that would hold? I'm still not quite sure. I'd frame my relationships with friends I knew she wouldn't approve of in the long run, like Frank White, for instance, as being paternal, spaces where I was a do-gooder shepherding a lost friend. I hid the extent of my marijuana addiction, at least at the beginning, and emphasized, in our flirtatious correspondence, my private education and bourgeois sensibility; when I was tempted, I would code-switch and slip a "mothafucka" into an exclamatory comment or refer to black people as Negroes, but I'd feel her recoil a bit. I knew to pull back around certain kinds of white people. We were entering realms of experience outside her purview.

She played a character for me, too, talking up her father's up-by-the-bootstraps, son-of-Polish-immigrants story, and her love of '90s R&B. She'd hit a blunt and play pool with you; she had a tomboy's way about her that girls with brothers almost always have, despite the girlish charm she could turn on at a moment's notice. But get her around the darker corners of black experience, the ones that keep us perpetually frustrated, the ones I have spent much of my young career discussing in film journals and fancy national magazines, and a blankness sets in just underneath those azure irises, one that never fails to chill my blood, the palpable sense of disconnection and lack of understanding that crosses her features.

In the fall of 2014 I traveled to a film festival in which Anne had taken a managerial role, one that brought many of the country's best documentaries to coastal Maine. We had only been dating for a few months, but had been fucking for the better part of a year and had known each other for three times as long. Friends from our New York circles, many of whom were at her festival that weekend, wondered aloud if I had met her parents yet.

They were in attendance that weekend, standing not far away at the opening cocktail party for the event, at an upscale seafood restaurant not far from the ocean. Later, and at the party following the opening screening, in an impossibly posh barn nearby, they were closer still.

Anne never thought to introduce them to me. I nervously looked at them over my drinks. Whenever Anne would come by and smile, I'd only ask how she was holding up, offering what support I could with a hug or a peck, as she went about her business of hosting without thinking to have me shake her father's hand or impress her mother with whatever stolid gentleness I could muster.

BY THE FALL OF 2015, ANNE HAD BROKEN UP WITH ME several times, but had always come back. Despite my personal reservations, and ongoing dalliances with other women, I refused to give up completely; I always welcomed her return, hoping we could grow into people with each other who could transcend all that stood between us. But this last time, it was me who pursued reconciliation. On the advice of a mutual friend, I went to Maine, where she lived during the summers, running the festival, to win her back, telling her I wanted her to plan a life with me. She cried, mostly in fear but also in genuine love for me, and suggested she would. I didn't know what that meant for her, or for me, exactly, but I had never felt for anyone else the way I felt about her. Any day of mine that didn't begin and end with her felt like a lost one.

We had discovered, in fits and starts of earnest reckoning and sharing, that we were an even odder couple than Andrea and I had been. Whereas I was not one to shirk a challenge, at the first hint of discord, either mine or hers, Anne would grow cold and then break up with me, giving up on the thing with little communication as to why. She had never dated anyone seriously before, so such communication was entirely new to her. In the years since we met, Anne had grown into a budding film producer and film festival organizer; she knew how to talk to people clearly, efficiently, and eloquently. But with me, she always relied on clichés and diversions. Even while I yearned to put all the cards on the table, my mouth was always full of her half-truths at the decisive moment.

An employee of Anne's at her festival, a woman at least ten years her senior, moved to Bed-Stuy shortly before Anne did. The woman showed great trepidation about it. She asked me, in person and in increasingly desperate Facebook messages, if she had done the wrong thing. People in the neighborhood had mostly been very nice to her, she wrote, but she was filled with guilt when people weren't. Anne and I made light of all this, caustically joking, but deep down, I wondered if Anne thought about such things, the displacement and price inflation our mutual presence in the area was fueling. If she did, she certainly never mentioned it. Was she capable of guilt in this way? It didn't seem so.

Sharing ourselves, however far we had come, remained difficult. It was awkward to discuss cohabitation and my parents' increasingly shaky finances with her, the daughter of a man who invests the money and files the taxes of billionaires, taking a hefty cut for his trouble, assuredly. And whenever I was in a mostly black space with her, which was more common now that she lived in Bed-Stuy, I would feel not unlike Richard Pryor, who on *That Nigger's Crazy* observed that certain "black women would look at you like you killed your mama when you out with a white woman."

Anne maintained that I was her first serious boyfriend, although I personally knew several of the men she had slept with more casually over the years. During our flight after what had been a charming, romantic getaway at a film festival in Savannah, she confided that she had brought another boy home once, a very charming East Asian guy of remarkable wealth. Then she began to cry before continuing. I knew trouble brewed. In between tears and gentle sobs, she revealed her past fears that her mother was a racist. I stiffened; surely she understood I had heard it all before? Apparently the mother had said some less-than-generous things about the young man in private, but was more than charming in person. Anne wondered whether the boy would have received the same courtesy had he not been wealthy.

She had been taught to hide her emotions, to recoil from help in moments of vulnerability. When her mother's health grew poor, on top of her grandmother's imminent death, my overtures of affection turned her cold. She struggled to tell me she loved me and often simply referred to me as her "friend." She wasn't alone in this; it was always my own family's newfound financial frailty that kept me from being direct about my own circumstances, increasingly stewarding my father's housing prospects and supporting him financially on occasion. Even though I knew she'd be empathetic and loving in the face of it, I feared her judgment of him and, by extension, of me. Her father had shown some compassion about my parents' living situation—"Is Brandon okay?" he allegedly would ask upon her visits to his home in suburban Boston, one that used to belong to Abraham Lincoln's best friend—but whereas familial frailty only made me want to build something of our own that would last, it also made me a poor communicator, turning away from connection instead of toward it. I'd walk past the Knickerbocker Hospital on my way to her place and project our entire relationship onto Algernon and Cornelia, hoping we could find some way to bridge the gaps they had been unable to, despite, as Tony had drunkenly pointed out years before, how little things had changed.

My attempt to radically alter course, after we had a miserable Thanksgiving apart from each other at our families' homes, was the beginning of the end. I asked her if I could move in with her. I imagined no better place than Bed-Stuy. I had put the sweat equity in. A pall came over her pink face, but she took some time to respond. "I don't think I'm ready for that," she told me, with maximum chilliness, while she lay in my arms. I'm sure I covered the silence with something like "that's understandable," but inside, I knew we'd never recover.

I LEARNED ONLY LATE IN OUR RELATIONSHIP THAT Anne traces her ancestry back to one of America's first settler families. Her father's surname, given his Polish immigrant ancestry, is strangely Germanized and comes equipped with a term of nobility, but her mother's lineage is where the real "America is ours" story resides. Her line began its American journey on one of the earliest boats over from England, part of an already distinguished family that had ruled over Nottingham and Yorkshire before the Magna Carta was drafted, and had been among the English nobility for over a thousand years by the time I asked her daughter for a cigarette in front of the film festival press office where she worked against her parents' wishes.

The day before Anne and I broke up for the last time, I played myself in a scene about a third of the way through my friend Russ Harbaugh's film *Love After Love*. In it, I'm a young author writing a book about Bedford-Stuyvesant. The Irish comedian Chris O'Dowd plays a character that is the likely author surrogate, while Juliet Rylance, Cornelia on *The Knick*, plays his ex-girlfriend. In the scene, the first in the second act, I pitch *Making Rent in Bed-Stuy*, going on and on about the loss of the neighborhood's black character. The ex-lovers who get most of the screen time are the focus, however; now you realize, after seeing them struggle through a terrible family illness and their own feeble understanding of themselves as a couple, that they have to bear the indignity of working together.

Anne and I just have the indignity of still being Facebook friends, of the 400-odd people we share, of our mutual thwarted ambitions to push past the bigoted expectations of both of our tribes; my mother, always respectful of the few women I have brought to Cincinnati, told me never to bring Courtney Love home. Although Anne doesn't have any tattoos and I've listened to "Doll Parts" at least two hundred times while writing this book, I have thus far heeded her call.

The last time I saw Anne in my Bronx apartment, after twelve desperate hours of crying and fucking and eating and crying and fucking and eating a few weeks after our fourth breakup, which we performed via Skype on the penultimate night of 2015, I told her, "America is not designed for us to be together." After a long pause, she told me she didn't believe that. Since the year of our birth, black households in the United States have accumulated, on average, seven times less wealth than their white counterparts, I wanted to say, showing her the evidence of the divide that had been an unspoken chasm between us, but it was time to stow away the journalist in myself. I was still trying to win her back!

To no avail. When I would press her a bit more as to why she felt we had to part, she would speak in vague ways about how we had "different ideas about what kindness was," and that perhaps I was too "edgy" and "controversial" for her. "I can't make a case for us breaking up," she said a bit later, only to suggest that one day, when she could finally articulate why she wanted to leave again, "it will be so painful to tell you."

This was code, of course—the increasingly strident tenor of black radicalism had found its way into much of my film and political writing over the ensuing years since we met, and this was something that, despite how passionate I was about it, Anne was just unable to discuss with any authority. Perhaps she was afraid of saying "the wrong thing," or felt no authority in such conversations. Perhaps the specter of beliefs so different than those she had been raised around made her nervous, or ashamed, but it also probably pushed her to ask questions about herself that she simply wasn't willing to answer in front of me.

Anne counts, among her forebears, Quaker abolitionists and Mississippi slavers, Revolutionary War heroes and New Jersey governors and the former owners of the land upon which Princeton University was built. The legacy she carries in her blood is not something she could easily acknowledge to her, depending on the hour, upper-middle- to working-class boyfriend. She casually mentioned being courted by an organization her mother belonged to, the Daughters of the Mayflower, or some such thing, as she entered my Bronx hovel one night during our last fall together. And she did discuss how her brothers, both of whom have served in the armed forces, were invited to join the elite secret society Skull and Bones, a group that includes several ex-presidents among its legion. But her family's closest link to the White House was Barack Obama, a distant cousin of Anne's. They are descended from the same man who reached these shores on one of the first English voyages to the New World, long before the prospect of a United States was a glimmer in any white man's imagination.

She didn't know this until I told her about it. This was months after we broke up, seven years into the Obama presidency. I deduced the connection following an encounter with her grandmother's obituary and ten minutes of googling. Anne was flabbergasted. "We thought you knew . . . that's why we thought you were a supporter!" her mother allegedly responded when asked if she was privy to their presidential relations.

Surely this was not the type of thing that was brought up at family dinner, being related to America's first black president, no matter how much love of country they have. It was also not the type of thing discussed at the New Hampshire Republican Party fund-raisers she and Anne's father, a man who without irony wears his collar popped on Sunday mornings and generously gives to the Republican-leaning super PAC of one of Boston's most significant financial firms, host at their home on occasion. In this family, which has sacrificed for America and to whom America has given so much, to be related to the first black president seems to be anathema, but potentially hosting a party for Jeb Bush, a man who holds a special admiration for Charles Murray's two-bit neo-eugenics tome *The Bell Curve*, is not.

Sometimes, when I think back on it and want to believe the best about her love for me, I imagine, in the worst faith, her navigating a patrician dinner scene not unlike that memorable one about a quarter of the way through Hal Ashby and Bill Gunn's *The Landlord*, the grandest filmic text of Brooklyn class warfare.

Having decamped from the opulence of his parents' leafy mansion for a Park Slope walk-up full of Negroes he hopes to displace in the years before that type of class warfare became the raison d'être of bourgeois bohemians, Beau Bridges's Elgar Enders returns for dinner at his parents' manor in a scene that betrays Gunn's screenwriting brilliance. While his sister's out-of-place suitor, a burly Jew played by a young Robert Klein, watches on, Elgar's older brother William Jr. complains about investment in "a Negro neighborhood" and William Sr. laments his younger son's racialized liberalism ("Let me tell you something, Mr. Lincoln, if you march into this house with an arm full of pickaninnies of yours . . ."). The scene reaches its apex when Elgar flees, reminding his bigoted family that "NAACP" can also stand for "Niggers Aren't Always Colored People."

SOMETIMES I WONDERED IF ANNE'S DISTANT COUSIN could relate to my consternation. Being not quite at home with whites in black spaces and feeling unmoored as The Head Negro in Charge of a country built on white supremacy are not completely unrelated I imagined. In the aftermath of our breakup, the movies began to provide a clue.

Until recently, it was rare anyone had the gumption to make a fictional film about a sitting president. *Primary Colors* was lucky enough to arrive just in time for peak Monica Lewinsky in 1998. Oliver Stone's tepid and underwhelming *W.* opened in late October 2008, weeks before Barack Obama defeated John McCain to succeed George W. Bush. But 2016 is proving to be the year that breaks all the rules, so here we are, in the final months of the Obama administration, presented with two different major motion pictures that dramatize opposite ends of the young Barack's journey through the Reagan years: Vikram Gandhi's *Barry*, which was recently released by Netflix, and Richard Tanne's *Southside with You.*

Both films revolve around romantic developments in the young Obama's life: while *Southside* meditates on a mixed-race youth's bliss with his future wife, *Barry* is about romantic failure, the inability for love to bridge racial and class differences. To ask which film veers from the historical record in its rendering of the life and loves of young Mr. Obama is beside the point. But verisimilitude remains a lingering concern: while Tanne's film presents two young people who will become the world's most recognizable couple, Gandhi's film invents a composite female foil for Obama who comes to represent the forces in American life that Obama will never quite win over, largely because of race.

Together, the two films form a bildungsroman unlike anything in American movies since John Ford's 1939 film *Young Mr. Lincoln*, an elegant and oddly terrifying presidential hagiography—*Cahiers du Cinéma* once argued that it was produced by Darryl Zanuck on behalf of "American Big Business" to mythologize the country's most famous Republican and produce an election year defeat of FDR in 1940—that premiered seventy-five years after Lincoln's death. No one has bothered to make a persuasive movie that focuses uniquely on the early life of Dwight Eisenhower or Gerald Ford, Jack Kennedy or Ronald Reagan, Jimmy Carter or George H. W. Bush. Most presidential biopics—like Spielberg's *Lincoln*, HBO's *Truman*, and Rob Reiner's *LBJ*—are firmly set during their subjects' respective presidencies, premiering long after the men in question are dead and buried. *Barry* and *Southside with You* are a curiosity in this context, positively rogue ventures with few precedents, acts of mass mythology that provide vastly different quasi-historical windows into the formation of Obama's value system, presidential persona, and basic understanding of the American promise through his attempts at coupledom.

Southside with You stakes out a charming inoffensiveness as its safe haven. Thirty-year-old Obama is working as a community organizer in Chicago in 1989. A legal intern with holes in the bottom of his car, he picks up Michelle Robinson, an associate at the firm, for a date: they go to a museum, for a walk in the park, and a screening of *Do the Right Thing*; in between he shows off his burgeoning political skills at a community event. Plenty of "wink wink, nod nod" moments unfurl. The tone is triumphant; we know the Obamas will work out, that their love will endure, and that Barack, the son of a white, single mother, who never fit in much of anywhere, will find a union with a black woman that will prove both emotionally satisfying for the characters and appropriate to his future constituents. *Southside with You* could have been written into the Democratic Party platform itself.

The more melancholic, searching, and insightful of the two films, *Barry* is the film we're more likely to remember when the afterglow of the Obama presidency has long receded. While no less predictable in its conclusion than *Southside with You*, *Barry* proves to be a far richer and sobering experience, one that paints a portrait of a young Obama who painfully learns that regardless of what he says or how he says it, he'll never truly win over the elite who run this country.

Set in 1981, it focuses on an afroed, dope-smoking, poetry-obsessed twenty-year-old Obama, who has just transferred to Columbia University. With Adam Newport-Berra's impressive lensing and Miles Michael's spot-on art direction, *Barry* inhabits a grimy, post-1970s New York City much mythologized in our more sanitized era, from HBO's *Vinyl* to Netflix's celebrated *The Get Down*. Gandhi, a correspondent for HBO's *Vice News*, is also a filmmaker of great versatility. A Columbia graduate himself—as an undergrad he lived next to the row house on 109th Street that Obama once resided in—he burst onto the scene with *Kumaré*, a fake documentary in which he tricked various expanded-consciousness-seeking whites into thinking he was an Indian guru.

Barry arrives in a grim, bottomed-out Manhattan during Reagan's first year in the White House. Cigarette in hand, he reads a letter from his estranged father as he arrives on a flight from Hawaii during the opening credits. By the end of the sequence, he's kicked off the campus for not having a student ID, locked out of his apartment, and is sleeping on the street. This is only the first of several rude awakenings for the future president. He and his roommate don't have campus housing, so he settles into a crime-infested area south of the campus. His friend Saleem (Avi Nash) is the only person he knows in New York; Saleem is a drug-addled, well-off-but-hiding-it Pakistani student who speaks directly to Barry's radicalized malaise; that is, when he's not shouting drunkenly out toward the street at Negroes who are pillaging his garbage cans.

Barry features an affecting and affected performance by Devon Terrell, and in their electric scenes together, Terrell and Nash are two men of color who are comfortable with their sardonic pose of mild disaffection from the elite pale faces. But Saleem is all ironic hard edges where Barry still has some vulnerability. Informing Barry of how nonthreatening he'll have to sound to bed the rich white girls who are his only options for love in this rarified Ivy League environment, Saleem takes on a mocking "safe white dude" tone, a voice not dissimilar to the one a generation of black comics, aping Richard Pryor, have used to describe the absurdity of being black in white America. The film almost suggests that Saleem has a more salient understanding of the crisis of the young black intellectual, but despite his brown skin, Saleem retains privileges of legacy Barry never will—his rich daddy with Wall Street connections can always bail him out. By the movie's end, Obama's father is dead.

Terrell, a young Australian actor, looks and sounds like Obama well enough, but he also shows us shades of the man we've never glimpsed in public before. He deftly introduces us to a college student who is still trying to figure out what he believes, what he wants to do, and what he'll have to compromise to get there. At twenty, Barry has yet to figure out how to navigate the country's great racial divide and—as we now know all too tragically in these stratified times—never will, despite great hope to the contrary.

Barry senses this and makes it plain. His romantic entanglement with Charlotte (Anya Taylor-Joy), a porcelain-faced Barnard brunette who comes from a well-heeled Connecticut family tied deeply to the Democratic Party, draws out Barry's budding realization that America is not designed for them to be together; no matter how hard he tries—despite a bloodline that links him to several of America's earliest WASP clans—the good-natured ignorance with which he's treated in their environs, despite their best intentions, will never result in real solidarity.

"Pretty uptight people here, huh?" a bow-tie-wearing white guy remarks to Barry at a wedding, which is held in a massive country mansion where Barry once again finds himself, other than the servants, the only black person in the room. "I'm an uptight kind of guy," he replies, half-serious, half-empty, just as I had thought to myself dozens of times over, ruminating on how to make it all work with Anne. He knows he'll never fully belong in these environs, but he finds it equally hard, no matter how "down" Charlotte is, to take her into black spaces. Buying books on the streets of Harlem, eating soul food at Sylvia's, they are hounded with looks from stoic, stately black women, giving rise to Pryor's contemporaneous observation of sistas watching you with white women. Seeing bellicose Black Hebrew Israelites in their outlandish costumes pontificate on a street corner wouldn't normally be a point of concern for Barry, but he deftly steers Charlotte away in order to avoid a verbal scolding.

The costs of assimilation are high, and Barry begins to pay. He arrives on campus wanting to be a poet, as quaint as that sounds, but soon realizes the privilege of his situation beyond the iron gates of Morningside Heights. Playing basketball in a Harlem park, he befriends PJ (Jason Mitchell), a student from the Graham Projects who is finishing a master's degree in business at Columbia. PJ has no illusions about what his degree is for: he is there to make money, to get the credentials America requires of Negroes who want to advance into the middle class. Mitchell is every bit as terrific as he was in *Straight Outta Compton*, and often steals his scenes, including one where he invites Barry to a party in the projects. In a deft single-tracking shot, we are introduced to the world of "pissy stairwells" and elevators that don't work. "Don't forget that this is how your country does your people," Mitchell tells him. Barry is as foreign in this environment as he is later in the Yale Club with Charlotte's parents. Here we see the political skills start to form as he charms them, emphasizing not his father's drunkenness but his Harvard pedigree. Barry neglects to mention that Charlotte's dad slipped him some money while in the men's room before being introduced, thinking he was the washroom attendant.

Despite his ability to code-switch, Barry is haunted by confusion and pain; unable to cope with a father who abandoned him, and an inability—despite his insidious emotional intelligence—to feel at ease in all-black or all-white milieus. This costs him more than his fair share of acquaintances, friends, and, most painfully, lovers. When Barry's mother (Ashley Judd) arrives, he is embarrassed by her rah-rah liberalism and admits, in an unvarnished way he normally keeps buttoned up, how out of place he feels. Columbia's classrooms are dominated by the kind of privileged blowhards who ask during a discussion of Plato's *Republic*, "Why does everything have to be about slavery?" It's a question the rest of the film answers by simply showing us how this black boy, no matter how yellow his skin, is treated by both working-class white cops and rich, well-meaning white ladies alike. In the end, code-switching simply gets tiresome, no matter how talented you are, when white people seem to have no idea black people have to do it at all.

ONE LONELY NIGHT EARLIER THAT FALL, JUST BEFORE Anne moved into 485, I ventured east, up Kosciuszko Street from Nostrand Avenue to Malcolm X Boulevard. Signs of the invasion were omnipresent. Construction rang out in at least one building on each block well into the evening, with the evidence of more to come, in old schoolhouses and barren tenements, everywhere you looked. A man said, "We live here too," his tone of voice piercing the night from a forlorn-looking canopied flop as I walked along Kosciuszko. Another brother standing near him, in a do-rag and white warm-ups, whispered back as I strode past, more construction quickly drowning them out, a new, hashtagable, and de-Negrofied #BedStuy being erected all around us.

I was jittery. When an SUV slow-crawled not far away

and then abruptly stopped in front of me, I crossed the street and walked a block down to DeKalb, having briefly feared a jacking. After a stroll past the Marcy Projects, I wound back over to Kosciuszko on the next block, walking where once were mere warehouses, ones now adorned with signs of the modern-looking renovations in store for them, stamped with the logos of various developers and city agencies, the true authors of this blood-sodden land's next evolution, the words "Residential" or "Commercial" emblazoned atop each sign.

M&M wasn't around when I reached 551 Kosciuszko, and neither were the photos I had taken in high school, many of them surely of Tony and me and our many shared friends, ones M&M had found cleaning up and organizing the place in preparation for the move to come. He thought it wouldn't be right to throw them out, whatever animosity still existed between us, and texted to see if he could send them to me. I told him I'd pick them up that Tuesday night, but when I arrived, a wild-haired gentleman with face tattoos showed me into my old living room.

Much of the artwork that had been in Goodbye Blue Monday had been salvaged by M&M, including a memorable Impressionist-inspired painting of a black church service in wide shot and a gorgeous photographic portrait of Billie Holiday. The place was as cluttered and dirty as ever. No sign of my photos was found. Across the street, the building where Roger and Pierre had lived with their mother was being renovated.

Haitian boys would never sit there dreaming of fathers ever again, it seemed.

Walking back down DeKalb near the intersection with Throop, I encountered a pair of obese black women in their late teens or early twenties. One had a stroller with a young child in it. The other had two children of her own, buzzing with halfhearted play at her knees. "We don't want your money," one of them said as I was on the quick draw to give her ten dollars. "We want you to buy us food," she said, pointing to the Kennedy Fried Chicken across the street. They were living in a shelter nearby after losing their apartments. As we walked into the chicken joint, a hobbled homeless man asked me for change, telling me he was a vet. I told him I'd get him on the way out. Without enough money on me to snag an eighteen-piece and a half dozen sodas for the women and children, I clumsily used the ATM, yellow Negro hands quickly passing across the three-dollar fee, fresh currency exchanged across the bulletproof glass of the ghetto chicken outlet before the long wait. Then you have to decide what to say.

"Thank you, mister," one of the children uttered, her mother too timid to chat amid my attempts to find out where they had lived ("Down on Quincy"), how long they had been homeless ("Eight months"), and how hard it was to get into Marcy (long and bureaucratized). I handed the heavyset women chicken boxes with which to feed their brood, wishing in shame that I could buy them kale, knowing that calories are all that keeps some broken hearts going. On the way out I handed the vet a ten spot, brought to him by my State of New York salary, and walked back down DeKalb, only streets from 730.

As I passed the old walk-up I was spotted by Rudy, sitting on a crate across the street, his tall cap backward and pushed low as his friend, a black, baseball-capped teen of few words, rolled a blunt. Clearly his efforts to squat at 730, which I had passively facilitated, were abandoned. "Yo, Brandon," he bellowed, my attention suddenly diverted from my old dwelling. I offered him a nip of the bourbon I had meant to bring M&M, an olive branch for a drunkard, symptom of a sanguine gloom; I suddenly didn't mind drinking on the street with a recently laid-off janitor and his blunt-rolling friend. I took a perch on one of the crates near him as we drank and smoked, staring out at 730. The rent he supplemented with his odd jobs had gone up, and with his mother struggling, Rudy needed more work. He occasionally dealt weed out of the barbershop a few storefronts away from where we sat, but not enough to get by amid the bombardment of higher rents and ever-more-expensive goods.

My paranoia grew after a half dozen sips of bourbon from the tiny plastic cups Rudy invested in for the occasion, and I took leave of them, staring out at 730 DeKalb. It, too, had undergone a rent increase, one I'd known was inevitable since Neftali and his Hasid enforcer the previous March. One night earlier that summer, after a Biz Markie concert in Herbert Von King Park, I passed 730, seeing from the street that the door leading into my former apartment was open. The gate door was closed, but peering in, it was clear someone was home. Without realizing quite what I was doing, suddenly I found myself on the landing, looking down into the long hallway. A Radiohead poster from the *Hail to the Thief* era hung, in an elegant frame, near what had been the door to my room. At the end of the long hallway a young man with Asian features and a bright purple NYU sweatshirt sat at a table. I rapped on the gate door, startling him. "Sorry to bother you, I, uh, live in the neighborhood and I was wondering if I could ask you a question."

The young man shot out of his chair and sauntered down the hallway. He was tall and young and clearly new to the area. "What do you need?" he asked, looking at me uneasily, as if I posed a threat.

I lied and told him I lived on the block. He nodded. "If it's too invasive then feel free to tell me so, but I was just wondering if you mind telling me what you're being charged in rent?"

I explained I was writing about the area and it was strictly for research purposes, in cadences that were meant to soothe; I knew how to use my black voice to make white and assimilated Asian people feel comfortable, slowing down and raising it a register. It rarely failed. He smiled a bit, hearing in my voice the rhythms of someone who did not mean him harm, who was one of his kind instead of, well, an other. As long as these streets were full of brown people, America had taught me to reckon, this would remain a common concern for those that had been taught to see them through a skewed lens of fear and ignorance.

"Yeah, no problem. We pay $4,200."

Looking past the gangly kid, my jaw melting toward the hallway floor, I regained my senses after a couple seconds of oblivion. I could see that Neftali had done hardly anything to the place. Once we left, with the market as it was, he must have realized all he had to do was raise the rent. Sure, he had taken Al's cat-infested rug from the stairwell and likely repaired the hole in my wall. I imagine he must have fixed the stairwell leading to the garden and insulated the pipes, a privilege we had requested and been denied as our $2,800 a month in rent was sabotaged in order to give this young man a home in a land he found strange and new. But by and large, the place remained more or less the same as it had been when I moved in a year before.

"Thanks," I said, standing in something resembling awe, my heart racing, summer heat beading on my face. He nodded and walked back down the hall, the gate door shutting behind him. I turned away and cowered back down the stairs, toward the orange halogen-lit summer darkness where everything I saw was slipping through my fingers.

On the phone, as I mumbled through my plans a few years before, my mother asked if Tony would cut me a deal on an apartment in his building, one that rests in what no one would now ever question was Bedford-Stuyvesant, where the forgetting was planned and the remembering never ended. I told her I didn't want him to. After all, I was finally living within my means.

ACKNOWLEDGMENTS

Although he once threatened to attack me with a hockey stick if I didn't stick with him during our time working together, Keith Gessen deserves special recognition for editing early versions of the material that inspired this book and convincing me to write about Bed-Stuy in the first place. That collaboration provided the kernel for a mode of self-exploration this work relies on. Astra Taylor, the great filmmaker, writer, and activist, first introduced me to Keith and edited my earliest work for *n+1*, which Keith helped found and where I've encountered a remarkable community of writers over the years.

I am forever indebted to teachers and mentors such as Chuck Rybak, Greg Taylor, and the late Robin O'Hara, who, respectively, exposed me to works of literature, motion pictures, and the realities of a career in independent filmmaking that bore tremendous effect on the narratives and perspectives contained herein.

Thanks to a wide array of friends, ones who are also talented magazine and Web editors, for thoughtfully editing much of this material as it appeared in other places: Scott Macaulay (long a mentor and dear friend), Dayna Tortorici, Nikil Saval, Malcolm Harris, Leo Goldsmith, Rachael Rakes, Carla Blumenkranz, David Wolf, Moira Donegan, James Yeh, and Jesse Barron.

Thanks are also due to Barry Harbaugh, who believed in this book from the start and acquired it when few others would, as well as to my editor, Tracy Sherrod, whose remarkable patience, insight, and good humor were perhaps more important than any other factor in this text's evolution over the years I worked on it. The thoughtful opinions and unyielding encouragement of early readers of this manuscript, people such as Paul Felten, Michael Barron, Michael Lipschultz, Kaleem Aftab, and my agent, Matt McGowan, were invaluable. Of course, this book would not be possible without the enduring love of my mother, for which I am so eternally grateful. And for the years I spent in the presence of the people depicted in this text, for many of whom I still hold such tremendous affection and unending love, I wish to express my appreciation. You know who you are.

Lastly, this book would simply not be possible without the music of the following acts, played loudly on a variety of sound systems in the myriad contexts in which I wrote this book: Stereolab, Portishead, Hole (especially "Doll Parts"), Flying Lotus ("Getting There" and "Phantasm" were crucial for this text), and Sonic Youth (their entire oeuvre, but especially "Massage the History") were key at various early stages, while albums as disparate as Kendrick Lamar's *Good Kid, M.A.A.D City*, Broadcast's *Tender Buttons*, Arcade Fire's *The Suburbs*, and Gil Scott-Heron's *Pieces of a Man* allowed me to get through the doldrums of the final months of this process more or less intact.

ABOUT THE AUTHOR

B randon Harris, originally from Cincinnati, Ohio, lives for the time being in Brooklyn, New York. Currently a visiting assistant professor of film at the State University of New York at Purchase, he is the director of *Redlegs* (2012) and has published reporting and criticism in *The New Yorker*, *The Guardian*, *The New Republic*, *VICE*, and *Filmmaker* magazine, where he is a contributing editor. *Making Rent in Bed-Stuy* is his first book.